AF292055

# Dick Kirby
## has also written:

### Memoirs

**Rough Justice**: Memoirs of a Flying Squad Detective
**The Real Sweeney**
**You're Nicked!**
**Killers, Kidnappers, Gangsters and Grasses**: On the frontline with the
Metropolitan Police

### Biographies

**The Guv'nors**: Ten of Scotland Yard's Greatest Detectives
**The Scourge of Soho**: The Controversial Career of SAS Hero Detective
Sergeant Harry Challenor MM
**Whitechapel's Sherlock Holmes**: The Casebook of Fred Wensley OBE,
KPM, Victorian Crime Buster
**Scotland Yard's Gangbuster**: Bert Wickstead's Most Celebrated Cases
**The Mayfair Mafia**: The Lives and Crimes of the Messina Brothers

### True Crime

**Villains**: Slashings, Fit-Ups and Dodgy Deals from the 60s and
70s Underworld
**The Sweeney**: The First Sixty Years of Scotland Yard's Crimebusting Flying
Squad 1919–1978
**Scotland Yard's Ghost Squad**: The Secret Weapon against Post-War Crime
**The Brave Blue Line**: 100 Years of Metropolitan Police Gallantry
**Death on the Beat**: Police Officers Killed in the Line of Duty
**The Wrong Man**: The Shooting of Steven Waldorf and the Hunt for
David Martin
**Laid Bare**: The Nude Murders and the Hunt for 'Jack the Stripper'
**London's Gangs at War**
**Operation Countryman**: The Flawed Enquiry into London
Police Corruption
**Scotland Yard's Murder Squad**
**The Racetrack Gangs**: Four Decades of Doping, Intimidation &
Violent Crime
**Scotland Yard's Flying Squad**: 100 Years of Crime Fighting
**IRA Terror on Britain's Streets, 1939–1940**: The Wartime Bombing
Campaign and Hitler Connection
**Scotland Yard's Casebook of Serious Crime**: Seventy-Five Years of
No-Nonsense Policing
**The Brighton Police Scandal**: A Story of Corruption, Intimidation
and Violence
**Missing, Presumed Murdered**: The McKay Case and other Convictions
without a Corpse
**Scotland Yard's Bravest and Best**: Outstanding Gallantry by Metropolitan
Police Officers

# Praise for Dick Kirby's Books

'He treats criminals the only way they understand. His language is often shocking, his methods unorthodox.' *NATIONAL ASSOCIATION OF RETIRED POLICE OFFICERS' MAGAZINE*

'The continuing increase in violent crime will make many readers yearn for yesteryear and officers of Dick Kirby's calibre.' *POLICE MAGAZINE*

'His reflections on the political aspect of law enforcement will ring true for cops, everywhere.' *AMERICAN POLICE BEAT*

'Its no-nonsense portrayal of life in the police will give readers a memorable literary experience.' *SUFFOLK JOURNAL*

'A great read with fascinating stories and amusing anecdotes from a man who experienced it all.' *SUFFOLK NORFOLK LIFE MAGAZINE*

'A gritty series of episodes from his time in the Met – laced with black humour and humanity'. *EAST ANGLIAN DAILY TIMES*

'This is magic. The artfulness of these anti-heroes has you pining for the bad old days.' *DAILY SPORT*

'Crammed with vivid descriptions of long-forgotten police operations, races along like an Invicta tourer, at full throttle'. *DAILY EXPRESS*

'Rarely, if ever, have I been so captivated and moved by a book … the way in which Mr Kirby has gone about it is exceptional.' *POLICE MEMORABILIA COLLECTORS CLUB*

'Dick Kirby has chosen his fascinating subject well.' *LAW SOCIETY GAZETTE*

'Thrilling stories of gang-busting, murder and insurrection'. *BERTRAMS BOOKS*

'A scrupulously honest and detailed account of the unfortunate events leading to police shooting an innocent man … nobody is better qualified to write an account of this story than Dick Kirby.' *THE LONDON POLICE PENSIONER MAGAZINE*

'Dick Kirby knows his stuff!' *SURREY-CONSTABULARY.COM*

'Kirby looks to untangle facts from speculation and questions everything'. *GET WEST LONDON.*

'Murder, torture and extortion all feature prominently as Mr Kirby investigates some of the most famous incidents of the post-war era.' *THE MAIL ONLINE*

'Only an insider with the engaging style of Dick Kirby could have produced this nakedly forthright page-turner.' JOSEPH WAMBAUGH, AUTHOR OF *THE CHOIRBOYS*

'Kirby's wit and extremely dry humour comes on straight away as early as the prologue which, of course, makes heavy reading subjects easier and creates a relationship between the author (narrator) and the reader.' *THE LOVE OF BOOKS*

'Dick Kirby's book gives precious insight into its exploits for over a century.' PAUL MILLEN, AUTHOR OF *CRIME SCENE INVESTIGATOR*

'Dick Kirby has written a book that all crime aficionados will want to read.' *THE WASHINGTON TIMES*

'Kirby does not hold back in detailing the grisly parts, bringing home to the reader the harsh reality that these ruthless killers had no boundaries.' *THE LONDON POLICE PENSIONER MAGAZINE*

# Scotland Yard's Supergrass Years

# SCOTLAND YARD'S SUPERGRASS YEARS

## The Flying Squad's War Against Armed Robbers

### DICK KIRBY

First published in Great Britain in 2026 by
Pen & Sword True Crime
An imprint of Pen & Sword Books Limited
Yorkshire – Philadelphia



ISBN 978 1 03619 328 7



Typeset by Mac Style
Printed in the UK by CPI Group (UK) Ltd, Croydon, CR0 4YY.

The Publisher's authorised representative in the EU for product
safety is Authorised Rep Compliance Ltd., Ground Floor,
71 Lower Baggot Street, Dublin D02 P593, Ireland.
www.arccompliance.com

For a complete list of Pen & Sword titles please contact

**PEN & SWORD BOOKS LIMITED**
47 Church Street, Barnsley, South Yorkshire, S70 2AS, England
E-mail: enquiries@pen-and-sword.co.uk
Website: www.pen-and-sword.co.uk
or
**PEN AND SWORD BOOKS**
1950 Lawrence Road, Havertown, PA 19083, USA
E-mail: uspen-and-sword@casematepublishers.com
Website: www.penandswordbooks.com

# Dedications

## To the Supergrasses

'Ihr Racker! Wollt ihr ewig leben?'
(Rascals! Would you live forever?)

*Frederick the Great, rallying his hesitating guards*
*at the Battle of Kolin, 18 June 1757*

## To those who ran the Supergrasses

'But screw your courage to the sticking place, and we'll not fail.'

*William Shakespeare, Macbeth, 1.7.*

## And to Ann

'There is a lady, sweet and kind,
Was never face so pleased my mind.
I did but see her passing by
And yet I love her till I die.'

*Found on the back of leaf 53 of 'Popish Kingdome or*
*Reigne of Antichrist', in Latin verse*
*by Thomas Naogeorgus and*
*Englished by Barnabe Googe, printed 1570*

# Contents

# About the Author

Dick Kirby was born in 1943 in the East End of London and left school at the age of fourteen without a single academic qualification to his name (and nothing has happened in the years which followed to change that situation). He joined the Metropolitan Police in 1967, and half of his twenty-six years' service was spent as a detective with the Yard's Serious Crime Squad and the Flying Squad.

Before being discharged with an injury award and pension in 1993, Kirby was commended by Commissioners, Deputy Assistant Commissioners, Chief Constables, Directors of Public Prosecutions, Judges and Magistrates for variously displaying 'courage, determination and detective ability' on forty-five occasions.

He appears on television and radio and can be relied upon to provide forthright views on spineless, supine senior police officers (and other politicians) with their insipid, uninformed, absurd and mendacious claims about how they intend to defeat serious crime and reclaim the streets.

He contributes regularly to newspapers and magazines and is employed by television and film companies as a researcher and consultant. He also writes memoirs, biographies and true crime books which are widely quoted – this is his twenty-seventh.

Married with four children and five grandchildren, Kirby lives with his wife in a Suffolk village, in semi-retirement. He parted company with the Metropolitan Police over three decades ago but, as he admits, 'I've never really left it!'

He can be contacted via his publishers at enquiries@pen-and-sword.co.uk

# Acknowledgements

irst and foremost, I have to thank my chum and commissioning editor Brigadier Henry Wilson of Pen & Sword Books for his unstinting encouragement, not only over the past fifteen years but particularly for this book.

Next, Tony Yeoman; he describes us as being 'old muckers' and he's right. A friend for over half a century, Tony was the bravest of the brave on the Flying Squad; and I'm indebted to him for his very kind foreword.

The staff at Pen & Sword Books have always provided me with their full backing, including Matt Jones for his assistance and helpful ideas, George Chamier for his lynx-eyed editing and Jon Wilkinson for his brilliant illustrations; my thanks to them all.

The editor of the *London Police Pensioner Magazine*, Susi Rogol, has always been immensely helpful, as has Bob Fenton QGM from the Ex-CID Officers' Association.

As always, there are those who might have assisted in the compilation of this book but for whatever reason, chose not to. However, I'm immensely grateful to those who did and they are: Terry Babbidge QPM; Rodney Briggs; Dave Chappell; Bernie Craven; the late Fred Cutts; Dave Driscoll; Alec Edwards; Jeff Edwards; Colin Ellis: Bob Fenton QGM; Errol Flanighan; Mick Geraghty; Ken Grange; Brian Greenan; Chris Jackson; Gordon Livingstone; Paul Lowden; John McSwan; Paul Millen, FCSFS; Alick Morrison; Peter Moyes; Michael Nesbitt; Steve Parker; Albert Patrick; Gordon Reynolds; Bob Robinson; Roy Rossiter; Kevin Shapland; Andrew Sladen; Roger Smith; the late Henry Stevens GC; Stephen Stocker; Steve Wheatley and Peter Young MBE. I apologise in advance for any inaccuracies or omissions; the faults are mine alone.

Photographs were supplied by Dave Driscoll; Paul Millen; Michael Nesbitt; Marshall Peters; Kevin Shapland and Roger Smith; others come from the author's collection. While every effort has been made to trace the copyright holders of all photographs, Pen & Sword and I apologise for any inadvertent omissions.

As always, I have received the greatest support and encouragement from my family, especially the cyber skills of my daughter Sue Cowper, her husband Steve and their children, Emma Cowper,

B. Mus; Jessica Cowper, B. Mus and Harry Cowper, M Theatre. I should also like to thank my daughter Barbara Jerreat, her husband Rich and their children Samuel and Annie Grace Jerreat, together with my sons, Mark and Robert.

More than anybody else, my dear wife Ann of sixty-plus years of marriage, who despite recent atrocious ill-health has exercised loving restraint over my enduring and often exasperating impetuosity.

Dick Kirby
Suffolk, 2025

# Foreword

## Former Detective Sergeant Tony Yeoman, Flying Squad, New Scotland Yard

Dick Kirby and I go back well over fifty years in the Metropolitan Police from the time when we were 'Scaley Aids' – this term is satisfactorily explained in the book – and we were later reunited on the Flying Squad; we were the last of those officers ever to be based at Scotland Yard, before those Squads were devolved to the other four area Flying Squad offices over the Metropolitan Police District.

It was during our service that saw the birth, then the rise of the supergrass; those dangerous armed robbers who, caught 'bang to rights', did not exactly see the error of their ways, but faced with the prospect of perhaps twenty years behind bars, decided – for a greatly reduced sentence – to confess not only to their own crimes and misdemeanours, but those of their trusted comrades; it was high-level grassing that came as a profound shock to their betrayed companions!

So Dick Kirby has decided to chronicle those times, and there are few better authors who could do so, because he was there and he did it. He commences with the exploits of 'Bertie' Smalls, the first supergrass (and the only one to walk away scot-free) and then describes the whole tsunami of supergrasses who followed.

Best of all are the exploits of the Metropolitan Police's one and only double-supergrass, Don Barrett, who supergrassed once and then upon his release committed a series of diabolical robberies. In addition to firearms being used and petrol being poured over terrified custodians in cash-in-transit vehicles, his gang used proxy bombs on their victims: explosive devices strapped to the victims' bodies with the threat that if they refused to comply with the demands that were made, these would be detonated by remote control. In the field of armed robbery never had such appalling devices been previously utilised. Caught in the act of hijacking a security van containing gold bullion, Barrett decided to supergrass once more.

Dick Kirby was not only involved in the arrest of Barrett but also debriefed and 'ran' him; and never have the curtains been opened so wide in the world of criminality to describe how the professional criminal mind ticks. It amuses, captivates and shocks the reader.

Casting his net far and wide, Kirby has obtained first-hand, authentic accounts from those officers who were there, who rolled their sleeves up and 'got cracking', and it makes for fascinating reading.

In one of his previous books Kirby describes those times with the Metropolitan Police – and in particular, the Flying Squad – as 'seat-of-your-pants' policing, and that is a particularly apt metaphor. We agree that we had the best of times that the Metropolitan Police had to offer; alas, they are no more.

But read and enjoy this meticulously researched book about policing of days gone by. You might well think that they were hair-raising times; and you'd be right!

# Introduction

Because the Flying Squad features so prominently in this book, it is essential for the reader to understand how and why it evolved and its purpose in the war against crime.

Following the end of the First World War, crime in the Metropolis had spiralled out of control. The reasons were many and varied. Disgruntled servicemen returned from the war, often bringing with them a variety of weapons; young men had grown up without parental control; then there were the various types of criminal who had always been present, plus lawless members of the immigrant communities, which then – as now – were completely out of control. Added to that, housing – despite Lloyd George's vacuous promise 'To make Britain a fit country for heroes to live in' – was poor, unemployment was high, poverty was staring people in the face and world trade had all but collapsed. The Russian Imperial family had been slaughtered by the Bolsheviks in 1918 and there was a real fear that the anarchy that followed could spread to the British Isles. With the country entering a period of austerity, crime figures went through the roof. England was plunged into a crime wave.

Cars were stolen to be used in crime, especially of the 'smash and grab' variety, banks were targeted and cashiers knocked down and robbed. Masked, armed burglars operated in the suburbs, gang warfare, which had previously been confined to the racetracks, now flooded out onto the streets, buses and trains, and pickpockets flourished everywhere.

In 1918 a third of police officers went on strike; one year later, out of the 18,200 officers to police the capital, 1,056 struck and were immediately dismissed; woefully inadequate numbers were left to protect the city's 7,200,000 inhabitants. And if that were not enough, the influenza pandemic, commonly known as 'Spanish Flu', which started in March 1918, now gathered momentum. The disease was estimated to have claimed the lives of 100 million people worldwide, and a further 500 million were infected but recovered. One and a half thousand Metropolitan Police officers went sick with the flu on the same day, and it was not until June 1920 that the pandemic was got under control.

Added to this, the Metropolitan Police still persisted in using pettifogging rules and regulations: if a thief lived in one area and committed an offence in another, permission had to be sought from the superintendent of the miscreant's home area to arrest him. It was permission that was not necessarily granted, since some of those autocratic senior officers saw the area that they controlled as their private fiefdom.

Something badly needed to be done; and lessons should have been learnt in 1877, when the commissioner appointed Sir Charles Edward Howard Vincent KCMG, CB as Director of Criminal Intelligence. This former soldier and Home Office official was tasked to create a Criminal Investigation Department (CID) for the Metropolitan Police, and to do so he went to Paris, where he studied the methods of *La Police de Sûreté*.

The Sûreté had been founded in 1812 by Eugène-François Vidocq, a forger, conman and escapee who had spent the first fifteen years of his adult life in prison. But he recruited a team of twenty-eight former convicts (some of them women), and by 1820 4,000 criminals had been arrested, bringing the crime rate in Paris down by 40 per cent; these agents received no wages but were paid a commission. A rogue Vidocq may well have been, but he established written records and a card system with details and descriptions of 30,000 criminals, as well as introducing the preservation of footprints with the use of plaster of Paris. After Vidocq resigned from his post (allegedly 500,000 francs the richer), the Sûreté was reorganised in 1832; agents now received 4.75F for an 11½-hour day, and there were several efficient departments, including what was known as the Flying Brigade. Officers from that branch mingled with crowds on the streets, at omnibus stops, in banks, churches and at racetracks, concentrating on thieves who stole from vehicles (*roulottiers*), conmen (*voleurs à l'Américaine*) and pickpockets (*à la tire*) – and they were enormously successful. This was one aspect of the Sûreté that Sir Charles should have imported into Scotland Yard, but didn't. The person who would later do so was, at the time of Sir Charles' dithering, a 12-year-old boy who had just left school in Taunton, Somerset. Fred Wensley later joined the Metropolitan Police and during a career spanning forty-two years became arguably the finest Scotland Yard detective of all time.

★　★　★

Detective Superintendent (later Chief Constable of the CID) Frederick Porter Wensley OBE, KPM was responsible in October 1919 for selecting twelve officers from all over the Metropolitan

Police area, all of them known for their knowledge of criminals, their thief-taking abilities and their use of informants. So while the Flying Brigade in Paris had hundreds of officers policing France's capital, for London, with two and a half times the population of Paris, the Met provided just twelve. Well, it was a start. Better late than never. However, there was an important innovation: the petty rulebook was consigned to the dustbin, and the detectives were told to go whenever and wherever their services were needed to smash the gangs and prosecute them to conviction. To afford them mobility, they were initially provided with a horse-drawn wagon leased from the Great Western Railway with spy holes cut in its canvas covering, and their success rate was phenomenal. Within months, the wagons were replaced with former Great War Crossley Tenders and later, following a series of sensational arrests, fast cars – Lea Francis tourers, Bentleys, Lagondas – were added to the fleet.

What had initially been dubbed the 'Mobile Patrol Experiment' was forgotten; within a year of its inception, the *Daily Mail* reported on 'Flying Squads of picked detectives with motor transport at their disposal', and the name 'Flying Squad' stuck.

The men who crewed the cars were top-notch detectives and hard as nails. There were the Dance brothers: Frank 'Squibs' Dance was an expert undercover officer, while older brother Alf was a master of disguise and a fearless fighter. Both men mingled with criminals, attended the same weddings and dances, got to know their hideouts, girlfriends and drinking dens.

Ted Greeno was the terror of the racetrack gangs; unaccompanied, and confronting forty of the gang's worst hoodlums, he told them to 'clear off'. Only one demurred, Greeno sent him flying with a single punch and, before his body hit the turf, the remainder fled.

Henry 'Chesty' Corbett – so-called because of his daily exercise with a chest expander – had both an encyclopaedic knowledge and a fanatical hatred of pickpockets. His nights were spent in a lone patrol on foot, tracking down pickpockets (or 'dips'); utterly without fear, he would arrest up to six dips at a time.

Detective Inspector Ted Ockey – he joined the CID after being shot in the hand at the Siege of Sidney Street – was awarded the King's Police Medal after being hit with an iron bar when he leapt onto the running board of a thieves' car during a high-speed chase.

This is just a selection of the type of men who were responsible for arrests totalling 515 in 1929. Later that year, when the *Daily Mail* announced, 'The Flying Squad is to be strengthened', its personnel was increased to forty.

In ten short years, the exploits of these dedicated officers were on everybody's lips. J. Ord Hume composed *The Flying Squad Quick*

*March* for both military and brass bands, the author Edgar Wallace had added a play to his already famous book, *Flying Squad,* which was turned into a film of the same name, directed by Arthur Maude, and the hero of one of Alfred Hitchcock's films was a Flying Squad detective. The Flying Squad was crowned with success.

As the years went by, one triumph followed another for detectives who were knowledgeable and hugely disinclined to take 'No' for an answer. Known as 'The Sweeney' (rhyming slang: Sweeney Todd = Flying Squad), the biggest criminals and their gangs were the Squad's prey: robbers, country house burglars and receivers. They, like their counterparts of the 1920s and 30s, were described by the head of the wartime Flying Squad, Peter Beveridge MBE, as being 'tough, clever and unorthodox with a terrier-like ability to shake a case until every prisoner was arrested'. When the Great Train Robbery was carried out in Buckinghamshire in 1963, with rich pickings of £2,631,684, it was the Squad that was responsible for making the arrests. But although coshes and axes had been used instead of firearms, the majority of the gang received 30-year sentences. It sent shockwaves through the underworld. Their self-justifying reasoning was, 'If we're going to get those sorts of sentences, let's use guns; we can always shoot our way out of trouble.' There was just one little niggle attached to that; if during the course of a robbery a bystander was killed, then through the doctrine of 'joint enterprise', the whole gang could be sentenced to hang. A bit tricky, that. But when, the following year, the death penalty was abolished, that gave the green light for the use of firearms to become much more desirable.

The Wembley Mob was getting nearer.

★   ★   ★

In 1978 the number of armed robberies in the capital had risen to 734, and it was clear it was not going to stop there; within another five years they would soar to 1,772. It was decided to devolve much of the Flying Squad (which by then numbered 173 officers at the Yard) to four area offices, situated in different areas of the Met, to investigate the proliferation of armed robberies to the exclusion of any other offence and to prosecute those responsible.

That left four squads at the Yard of which, 10 and 12 Squads continued to operate in much the same way as their predecessors; these were officers who were physically tough, absolutely committed, knew their criminals and worked with informants to get the necessary information to arrest ne'er-do-wells who had just carried out a crime or – better still – were about to commit one. Officers who joined the Squad did so only on the personal recommendation of existing

Squad officers; it was a good system and it worked. If a newcomer misbehaved, not only did he get his marching orders, but his mentor fell on his sword as well.

Two or three officers, detective constables and sergeants, were assigned to a car driven by a Class I driver, a uniform police constable in plain clothes, and we simply went out, patrolled the streets, kept observations and worked on the information fed to us by our snouts. When I was a member of 12 Squad, the rivalry was intense with other teams on that squad, all of us vying for the best results; but from 1981 to 1983 I spent two happy, productive years as a member of 12 Squad.

However, when I returned to the Squad in 1985, things had changed somewhat. There were no longer squads left at the Yard – all the officers had been sent to enlarge the four regional offices, each covering a quarter of the Metropolitan Police areas.

The abolition of the Yard squads was, in my opinion, a huge mistake. I believed then – as I do now – that it was essential to keep a reserve of officers, ready to be deployed at a moment's notice. Their worth had been demonstrated in 1983 when those two squads, 10 and 12, were called in to trace a highly dangerous armed criminal named David Ralph Martin, who had shot and wounded a police officer, then escaped from custody, after a young man named Steven Waldorf had been mistaken for Martin and had been shot and seriously wounded by police. Martin's arrest was accomplished by the Flying Squad in just eleven days, without a shot being fired.

Three months later, the assistance of those two squads was required once more in the Security Express robbery in Shoreditch, where £5,961,097 was stolen; then again, seven months later at Heathrow, when the Brink's-Mat robbery of gold valued at £26 million threatened to swamp the Flying Squad offices at Walthamstow and Barnes respectively, with their already heavy workloads.

Nevertheless, the introduction of those four area offices was a good idea; what was more, when a bunch of villains from one area strayed into another, cross-border operations were carried out between the different offices. It was all highly efficient and fruitful.

So that was what the Flying Squad was all about.

And now, as Errol Flynn once famously said, 'There is no use in telling a story arse-backwards' – so let's begin with an account of the arrest of a shoplifter, almost half a century ago, which, had the Flying Squad heard of him and his arrest at the time, would have been of no interest to them whatsoever.

Ten years later, he would be …

# Prologue

Police Constable 508 'J' Charles O'Doherty was one of the first of the police officers stationed at Ilford police station to apply, and be accepted, for the post of a home beat officer when this concept first emerged in the late 1960s. So when he should have been patrolling the pastoral streets around Loxford Lane in the eastern boundaries of Ilford's manor in 1977, it may have come as a bit of a jolt to his system to be told to arrest a shoplifter in a department store in the High Road, two miles to the west.

An observant store detective had noticed the activities of one David Terrence Croke, who had ingeniously devised what appeared to be a Gladstone bag. It was operated by a trigger in the handle which, when activated, caused the bottom of the contraption to open and close. Placed over a suitable item, the trigger was released and the purloined article was consumed into the bag's interior.

The 35-year-old miscreant was arrested, and although this was almost certainly not the first time he had offended, it was definitely the first time he had been arrested, which was confirmed when his fingerprints were taken at Ilford police station.

The following day, he arrived at Barking Magistrates' Court, pleaded guilty and, being a first offender whose inventions, he said, had got a little out of hand, was treated with a leniency he really did not deserve, left the court and went home to Enfield, North London.

Within a few days, a buff-coloured docket bearing his name and CRO No. 11991/77 arrived at Ilford police station. After the result portion of the form CRO74 was filled in, showing how the matter had been disposed of, and his not-very-interesting antecedents had been inserted on a form CRO 100A – one of five children, he had left school aged fourteen without any qualifications and had worked intermittently as a driver – the docket was returned to Scotland Yard. Once there, the dispatch service took it up to Criminal Records Office (CRO) on the third floor, Victoria Block, where it was lodged on a shelf with lots of other buff-coloured dockets, in strict chronological order. And there it remained, gathering dust. Nobody drew the docket – who was interested in a first-time loser shoplifter? – until somebody realised that the shelves at CRO were sagging under the weight of the files. Croke's file, containing just two pieces of paper, could hardly be thought to be contributing to the load on the groaning, overworked shelves, but nevertheless, like all the other files, it was microfilmed and the original docket was destroyed. Was the resultant microfiche stored in a location where it, too, could gather dust? If it was, then it did – nobody could have cared less about Dave Croke. Not then, at any rate.

⋆　⋆　⋆

An offence of much greater gravity had also been committed in Ilford High Road, seven years prior to Croke's arrest and about 100 yards away. Not that Croke had in any way been involved, when what was described as London's biggest post-war armed robbery was carried out at Barclays Bank.

Someone who was involved was a man named Derek Creighton Smalls. By 1977 he was being guarded by armed police officers on a 24-hour basis because he had grassed up twenty-six persons who had participated in that and other robberies and seen them sentenced to a total of 315 years' imprisonment. One such person was Donald Walter Barrett, a serial armed robber who, as a result, was now serving a 17-year sentence. When Barrett made Croke's acquaintance he would be living in Empress Avenue, Ilford, just two and a half miles from the scene of Croke's arrest.

Ronnie Dark was another participant in the Ilford bank robbery; but the only tenuous link with Croke was that both had appeared at Barking Magistrates' Court, in Dark's case en route to the Old Bailey, where his reward for the robbery was eighteen years' imprisonment. Their involvement would come much later, as would Croke's association with George Henry Ince, who in 1977 was serving a 15-year sentence for a silver bullion robbery.

It would not be until the early 1980s that this group and others (with the exception of Smalls) would come together to become a formidable band of armed robbers. This was not because of Croke's expertise as a shoplifter. It was because he was a brilliant technician, who not only manufactured shoplifting impedimenta but also armour-piercing bullets for armed robberies, as well as diabolical explosive belts. The latter would be strapped to custodians of cash or high value articles, whereupon the gang would demand that they hand these over, with the threat that if they did not, the belt would be detonated by remote control.

This is the story of armed robberies, supergrasses, the Metropolitan Police's one and only double supergrass and how Croke's – and others' – downfall came as a result of his own negligence and the sharp eyes of a 14-year-old boy.

So, welcome to the world of 'drinks', 'robbers' dogs', 'flops', 'tools', 'ringers', 'blaggers', 'frighteners', 'whacks' and 'grasses'; your outlook on 'Work' and 'The Chaps' will never be the same again!

# Part I

# The Wembley Mob

# Chapter One

# 'The Biggest Post-War Bank Robbery'

'Hey – you! Come 'ere!'

I had just walked out of the first-floor canteen at Dagenham police station and was heading, past the CID office, towards the stairs, when I heard that peremptory command. I turned, to see Detective Inspector Phil Thomas.

'Not doing anything are you? Good', he said, which nullified any reply I might have given.

He thrust a thick, Metropolitan Police folder (buff-coloured, as most of them were) headed '**CR201**' in thick black lettering, followed by a series of numbers, into my hands.

'Take this murder squad docket over to Mr Shimell at Romford; he needs it, quick!'

The 'Mr Shimell' referred to was the detective chief superintendent on the outer half of the Metropolitan Police's 'K' Division. He was the head of that part of the division's Criminal Investigation Department, and since I was but a humble Police Constable 767 'K', it was clear that Mr Shimell sat on the right hand of God. So I put my skates on to get over to Romford police station, pronto.

Upon arrival, I made my way up to the first floor, where the great and the good of the CID dwelt, their offices overlooking Main Road, Romford.

'Hello!' boomed a voice. 'What're you doing here?'

I looked round, then looked up. Detective Chief Inspector James Smith was rightly known as 'Big Jim'; he towered over my five feet nine inches. I'd known him at Ilford police station when I was Police Constable 757 'J' and he was a detective inspector, and I explained the reason for my visit. He nodded.

'When you've given the papers to Mr Shimell, come into my office. There's something I want to discuss with you.'

Bill Shimell accepted the file from me with a charming smile; tall, fair-haired with a small moustache, he had joined the Met following wartime service as a captain in the Royal Artillery. He had only been at Romford for the past four months; prior to that, much of his time had been spent with the Fraud Squad, and three years after our initial meeting, having served exactly thirty years, taking his war service into account, he retired.

Now I was seated in 'Big Jim's' office.

'Y'know, when I was out and about in Ilford, I'd often see you on your beat', he said. 'And whenever you reached a road junction, you weren't like the majority of coppers there. You always stopped and carefully looked left and right to see what was going on. That impressed me. I always meant to ask you if you'd like to come out as an aid to CID but then I got promoted and ended up here – and now, here you are again! So how about it? D'you fancy coming out aid? We've got a few vacancies.'

I was momentarily nonplussed. Jim had used the expression 'aid to CID', although that had now been replaced with the rank of temporary detective constable. But whatever expression was used, it still meant the same: the first step into the world of the Criminal Investigation Department.

I liked the idea of working in plain clothes; I had carried out several rowdyism patrols at Ilford (and had the bruises to show for it), as well as being the plain-clothes observer (ditto) on the area car. However, under the regulations, uniform officers were only permitted to wear plain clothes for a certain number of days per year. But the CID? Although the long hours worked by the CID didn't faze me, I hadn't been too impressed with some of the CID officers I'd had dealings with, and my wife had had her thought processes poisoned by the wife of a neighbour who emphatically stated that all CID officers were corrupt, drunks and adulterers.

Rather cravenly, I replied, 'I don't think so, sir. I don't think my wife would be too happy with the hours, for one thing …'

'That's all right', said Jim, breezily. 'I don't mind having a word with her.'

'No, don't do that!' I said, quickly, knowing of my dear one's uncertain temper. 'Let me think about it.'

We stood up, and Jim shook hands with me.

'You do that', he said, heartily, 'and then put your application in!'

I returned to Dagenham, my thoughts full of what Big Jim had said, and walked into the reserve room where the reserve officer controlled the switchboard, the personal radio centre and the teleprinter.

'Seen this?' he said, handing over a teleprinter message. 'Seems they've had a bloody great robbery on Ilford's patch.'

This was Monday, 9 February 1970. There had indeed been 'a bloody great robbery' at Ilford, the biggest since the end of the Second World War. And it had happened when my old 'D' relief had been on duty – if only I'd been there! I could have covered myself with glory, I thought at the time – although in fact I'd more likely have found myself peppered with a sawn-off shotgun. Because what I didn't know – what nobody knew at that time – was that the robbers involved were part of the feared 'Wembley Mob', none of whom would have thought twice about pulling the trigger.

But I acted on what 'Big Jim' had suggested and I did put my application in to become an aid to CID. I was accepted, later became a member of 'The Department' (as the CID was known) and later still became a detective sergeant with the Flying Squad. And as a result, sixteen years after that meeting at Romford police station, I would become acquainted with one of the members of the gang who was involved in that 'bloody great robbery' and who would go on to achieve a unique status – never attempted before and never repeated since – in the annals of the Metropolitan Police Supergrass system.

★   ★   ★

In fact, the bank robbery at Ilford might never have happened, had the intended robbery at Barclays Bank, Wanstead, planned one month previously, been successful. Six members of the gang were ready (with the connivance of a crooked cash-in-transit custodian), but the plan was aborted at the last moment; the Security Express van pulled up too close to the doors of the bank, thereby denying the robbers access. A further meeting discussed the possibility of hitting Barclays Bank at 144 High Road, Ilford.

On 9 February 1970 a Security Express van had collected £237,736 9s 10d from a chain of supermarkets and delivered the money to Barclays Bank. At 9.45am six bags containing the money were taken from the van to the bank's lift, for transfer to the vault. Eight members of the gang were waiting. As the robbers rushed in, one of the custodians, Robert Blaber, threw the sixth bag at one of the robbers who was wearing a black wig; another member of the gang pushed a shotgun into Blaber's back, telling him, 'Down on the floor or you're a dead man'.

The bank staff were told to lie down on the floor, before four members of the gang snatched the money bags and loaded them into a waiting white Ford Transit van. Even allowing for the robber who had had the cash bag thrown at him to squirt ammonia into Mr Blaber's eyes, the whole raid had taken just ninety seconds.

★   ★   ★

The officer in charge of 'J' Division's CID was Detective Chief Superintendent Bert Wickstead. He was as unlike his contemporary, five miles to the east, as it was possible to be. Both he and Bill Shimell had served in the army in the war (Wickstead in the Special Boat Service), but there the similarity ended. Whereas Bill Shimell was as smooth as silk, Wickstead, to many, resembled Ian Fleming's description of James Bond as 'a blunt instrument, wielded by a government department'. The plainer view of others was that Wickstead resembled an apoplectic bull in a china shop. Reaching Ilford from his headquarters at Leyton in record time, Wickstead swiftly assembled his team and whilst police photographers popped their flashbulbs, Scenes of Crime Officers dusted the scene plus the Transit van, abandoned a mile away for fingerprints, and officers obtained statements from the traumatised bank staff and other witnesses, Wickstead's team of detectives were dispatched to find out what their informants, plus other members of the underworld, knew.

Now, should this case have been handed over to the Flying Squad for investigation? Certainly, those officers – particularly those on 10 Squad who covered London's East End – had good sources of information and, eight years later, when the four area offices of the Robbery Squad were formed, there would have been no argument.

But not in 1970, when the man in charge was autocratic Bert Wickstead, who loathed C8 Department – the Flying Squad at the Yard – to such an extent that he marked up his Divisional Record Sheet with the words in red ink, **NOT C8** – in case by some hideous mischance he'd be posted there. No, the outrageous Barclays Bank robbery had been committed on his manor, it was his pigeon and he was going to solve it.

His team knew that; they also knew that to return to the office to report that 'Nobody knew anything, Guv'nor' would earn them a swift, one-way transfer to Waltham Abbey on the northern outskirts of 'J' Division; failure was simply not acceptable. Anybody who was suspected of knowing anything was pulled in and interrogated. It was a scattergun approach which would not – could not – be tolerated in today's Metropolitan Police climate of fairness and transparency; but then it was, and what's more, it worked.

One East End hard man unconcernedly accepted an invitation to Ilford police station for an informal chat; once it was established that his interviewer was going to be Wickstead, he burst into tears and had to be carried bodily, struggling, up the stairs to the CID office to reveal what he knew. And with that – plus other sources of information – Wickstead gathered together the guilty (and, as it transpired, the not-so-guilty) members of the gang. Some of them, at least.

Michael John Paul 'Micky' Green was certainly a guilty party and had the credentials to prove it. When he appeared at the Middlesex Sessions in January 1959, aged seventeen, for shopbreaking, stealing cigarettes and tobacco and being in possession of housebreaking implements by night, he already had one finding of guilt (approved school for stealing a motorcycle) and two previous convictions. He was sentenced to Borstal Training and, since he had breached probation orders on two occasions, he also received concurrent sentences of one month's imprisonment.

He was released from Borstal in November 1962 – he had been sent there on three occasions and collected three more convictions (one of which was for indecently assaulting a 13-year-old girl) – and at the London Sessions in February 1963, for warehousebreaking, he received an 18-month prison sentence. Green was initially charged with stealing a lorry containing wines and spirits valued at £3,049, but at the Middlesex Sessions in February 1965 he was found guilty of receiving part of that haul, valued at £1,514, and was jailed for two years.

In fact, Green had been responsible for planning the aborted Wanstead raid at his flat at Burnt Oak Broadway, Edgware, plus the actual robbery at Ilford.

Behind his mantelpiece clock was found £226, and when questioned, he said, 'If I go down for this, I'll get a lot of bird, won't I?' adding, 'I'm in the first division now.'

He certainly was; he would receive an 18-year sentence.

Wickstead believed there was an inside man – and he was one-third right, because there were actually three. Edward William McCarthy, a 53-year-old guard employed by Security Express brought in after £500 was found inside a plastic bag at his home in Wilmot Street, Bethnal Green, would be sentenced to six years' imprisonment. His 27-year-old driver, Charles Bowman, would go to prison for three years, and another guard, Albert Walker, received four years.

One name that cropped up early in the enquiry was that of Alfred Prill, better known to the authorities and to the underworld as Ronnie Dark.

Dark was on the run – nothing out of the ordinary for him. Born in 1935, he served an apprenticeship in approved school and Borstal and graduated as a violent criminal, burglar and armed robber. He had been on the run for eighteen months before pleading guilty in 1960 to stealing a safe containing £2,051 and blowing another safe containing £2,470, for which offences he had received a 5-year sentence. Released, he enjoyed eighteen months of freedom before being sentenced to four years' imprisonment for wounding with intent and causing grievous bodily harm. He remained in Wandsworth prison for just one month, before scaling the 30ft wall with the help of a grappling hook. It took three months before he was recaptured.

Now Dark was on the run once more, before – six months after the robbery – he was run to ground in a Devon hotel by Regional Crime Squad officers.

'Don't interview 'im', said Wickstead when he heard the news. 'Just bring 'im 'ere.'

He was duly brought and, like Green, received an 18-year sentence.

Others filled the dock at the Old Bailey. Lionel Thomas Herbert Jeffrey had been identified as one of those who visited Green at his flat and refused to provide an account of his movements on the day of the robbery, but he was acquitted. A James William Jeffrey was later named (and similarly acquitted) as being one of the conspirators, so perhaps there was a facial as well as a nominative similarity.

George Gladwin, a 37-year-old scrap metal dealer, who had asked his interviewers, 'Superintendent Wickstead doesn't think I did the blagging, did he?' and added, anxiously, 'Has someone's bottle gone?' was also acquitted.

Someone who wasn't was Arthur John Frederick Saunders. He had disappeared for three months after the robbery, lodging a statement with his solicitor (as many innocent people do) saying that if he were arrested he would not answer questions unless a legal representative was present. When he was arrested at his Hendon flat, the following items were found: £1,000 in a cupboard, £141 on his person, a black wig and a key that was found to fit the ignition of the getaway Ford Transit van. ('When I gave evidence of this at the Bailey, much to my surprise, it wasn't disputed', Detective Sergeant Tony 'Gary Glitter' Stevens told me, adding, 'I was sure it was going to be alleged that I planted it.')

Interviewed, Saunders said, 'There's no point in saying "no", is there?' adding, 'Whatever I was doing, I didn't have a shooter.'

Two of his alibi witnesses, called to say that on the morning of 9 February he was nowhere near 144 High Street, Ilford, were described in court as being 'highly unsatisfactory', and Saunders went down for fifteen years.

It was not really a satisfactory conclusion to the case, for three reasons. First, only £3,000 of the cash stolen had been recovered. Next, Wickstead was still seven robbers short. And third, but not least, it would later be revealed that none of the rest of the gang had even heard of Arthur John Frederick Saunders. He was completely innocent; but it would take a professional armed robber to prove his blamelessness.

## Chapter Two

# Enter the Wembley Mob

The organisation known as 'The Wembley Mob' was more like a collective than a number of individuals under one leader. There were those who stood out from the pack, but the fact remained that everybody concerned was a thoroughly professional, First Division armed robber – or 'blagger' – who sought the biggest prizes. One man would favour a particular bank, building society or cash-in-transit van and, having researched the prize, would then suggest the scheme to other members of the group. All had roles to play. Someone possessing 'the gift of the gab' might be required to secure the compliance of an inside agent – a security guard, bank teller or secretary – to advise on the size of the prize and when and how it would arrive. One would be recruited as 'a Frightener' – someone whose size and authority could be relied upon, usually with the discharge of a sawn-off shotgun, to terrify the victims into compliance. Another would procure the artillery – usually sawn-off shotguns and pistols, but sometimes clubs, pickaxe helves and ammonia in squeezy bottles – and arrange for the items to be spirited away afterwards.

Others of the gang would be responsible for obtaining hardware for the job: sledgehammers or bolt croppers, and sometimes ladders, necessary for scaling purposes should the bank have high, protective screens to protect the tellers from unwanted attention. Additionally, parcel tape would be brought to secure – and/or gag – members of staff or hostages.

Disguises – wigs, hats, spectacles, balaclavas, masks – were dealt with on a personal basis, each robber deciding what was best for him. Only the most foolish would forget to acquire gloves of some kind, usually surgical. None of the Wmbley mob did.

Vehicles for the getaway would have to be taken off the streets and hidden whilst they were 'rung' – fitted with false registration plates. Those who took the vehicles might – or might not – be the actual getaway drivers; but whoever those drivers were, they had to be top-class. The cars would be parked at various strategic points the night before the raid. The vehicles taken were usually two to three years old, the reasoning being that they were less likely to go wrong. Once, two members of the gang – never to grow old in their service – acquired a Jaguar. When it was discovered to have a defective clutch, they were sacked on the spot. The Transit van often used to get away from the scene of the raid would be abandoned near the next getaway car, frequently blocking the road to prevent pursuit by police or public-spirited citizens.

It was essential that 'flops' be found; respectable premises, preferably close to the scene of the raid, where the robbers could go directly to stash the stolen property and leave it, usually overnight. They might then disperse, using London Transport perhaps, or taxis; alternatively, they could stay at the flop. Police would set up roadblocks, unaware that the stolen property and possibly the miscreants as well, were still within the immediate catchment area. The occupiers of these 'flops' had to be utterly trustworthy, usually without a criminal record, and they were inevitably given a handsome reward– referred to as 'a drink' – for their assistance. Dividing up the spoils might take place the following day at the flop – or the cash could be transferred to another venue for distribution to the interested parties.

Whilst a cash share-out was relatively straightforward – used notes were always favoured (as being normally untraceable), as opposed to pristine currency (which could be traced). But if the booty consisted of precious metal – silver or gold bullion – it would be taken immediately to a receiver who could be relied upon to give as fair a price as possible to the blaggers and who possessed a smelter, in order to render it down and make it unidentifiable. The same applied if the prize was diamonds, rubies or emeralds. In that case it would be necessary to employ the services of a 'Coloured Man' – not someone from an ethnic minority but one who knew the value of those precious stones and who could dispose of them discreetly, at home or abroad, for hard cash. We shall shortly be hearing more of one such person.

The backgrounds and characters of those who participated in these robberies – they were known, collectively as 'The Chaps' – was fairly diverse.

Some – and it must be admitted, they were few in number – came from respectable and solid family backgrounds. They had attended good schools, perhaps served in the armed forces and later secured acceptable employment, but somewhere along the line they had gone off the rails. Due to their upbringing, they could appear to be entirely reputable, and thanks to their ill-gotten gains being shrewdly invested, they lived in respectable suburbia; they belonged to the right clubs, their children attended private schools and their wives could be counted upon to chair meetings of the Women's Institute.

But when the bubble burst, with early morning arrests and apparently respectable householders were led away in handcuffs, their upright neighbours – who until then had assumed that they were 'something in the City' – were aghast.

Others, who hailed from rougher backgrounds, often lived in council houses where, thanks to their new-found wealth, the contents were worth three or four times the value of the property. They tended to be members of large sprawling families, in which both parents and siblings were sometimes less than respectable. From an early age they would have been indoctrinated into criminal ways – through probation, approved school, Borstal, prison – and this was reflected in their environment. Their expensive, showy clothes and personal jewellery meant they were not accepted into polite society and, with their brassy wives and insolent children, that was probably just as well. Then again, they probably couldn't have cared less. One of Tommy Wisbey's daughters was taunted at school by unpleasant children asking what her father did for a living, knowing full well that the Great Train Robber was serving thirty years.

'Wot's your Dad, Lorraine?' jeered one of them and received the crushing reply, 'My Dad's fuckin' 'andsome.'

*　*　*

Many of the gang drank heavily, their behaviour was loud, they squandered their cash and they drove expensive cars; quite a few of them sported suntans acquired in lands sunnier than England.

Almost without exception, robbers of this calibre were sexually promiscuous, and those who were married often had affairs with other women. Wives, according to their disposition, either put up with this or complained bitterly. But the fact was, because of their exciting lifestyle, women were attracted to armed robbers. Wives and girlfriends (often unkindly referred to as 'Robbers' Dogs') were obviously fully aware of their partners' occupation, and some became involved in their activities, whether by transporting stolen money, hiding weapons, providing accommodation or establishing alibis. They were often treated very shabbily, which was not a professional way for an armed robber to keep his secrets safe; it sometimes backfired, with catastrophic results for the blagger who, far too late, realised that he should have treated his inamorata with far more consideration.

Does that sound as though I've painted a glamorous, romantic picture of armed robbers? If so, I apologise. Blaggers were responsible for instilling sheer terror in their victims; in fact, this was their avowed intention. There's nothing romantic about that.

Be that as it may, the way the Chaps operated was all very democratic; the gang was very cohesive and members relied upon each other. If one was caught, it was accepted that he would stay 'schtum' under police questioning. He would be remanded in custody, of course, but would leave it to his specially selected legal team to manufacture a defence for him. After that, there were endless ways of achieving an acquittal: a crooked detective could be approached to 'lose' important evidence, crucial witnesses might be sufficiently frightened to lose their memories, or jurors approached in exchange for an extravagant bursary to bring in a perverse verdict.

However, what if one of the gang was arrested and decided to tell the investigating officers everything: what they'd done, whom they'd done it with, the whereabouts of independent corroboration, the hiding places of weapons, the names of bank accounts and safety deposit boxes where, under false names, their ill-gotten gains reposed? But that was laughable. If – in the unlikely event – one of the group decided to turn Queen's Evidence, he would still be remanded in custody, and with the liberty of his peers at stake, that very foolish person would never make it to the witness box; his next journey would be to a pine box.

What a stupid notion. All the Chaps were staunch. Such a ridiculous scenario could never happen.

Until it did.

# Chapter Three

# Bertie

Derek Creighton Smalls – known as 'Bertie' – was born on 12 June 1935. One of five children, he grew up in North London. He had an undistinguished criminal career: three findings of guilt as a juvenile (which included a spell in an approved school), then a fine of £10 for possessing an offensive weapon in 1957 and three months' imprisonment the same year for being a suspected person. The following year, he had been sentenced to eighteen months' imprisonment for poncing (living off immoral earnings) – at that time, an offence regarded as just above child molestation in the criminal pecking order – and in 1962 he received another three months for, once again, being a suspected person.

It was Bertie's proud claim that he had never done an honest day's work in his life. Such a boastful assertion really requires verification, and it was provided by former police officer Chris Jackson, who spoke of a childhood friend, Brian Garratt, who lived at 84 Wightman Road, Hornsey, N4 and whose parents rented out rooms in their large house. He told me:

> Derek Smalls, at one time, lived in rooms there. I understand he was a window cleaner and had a bike with an open box sidecar on which he carried his ladders. Brian told me that while he was living at that address, Bertie broke into an electrical shop in Green Lanes, N4 and stole a television, which he carried away in his sidecar. Brian's Mum thought the world of Derek, because he was so polite!

Bertie Smalls later relinquished his semi-legitimate window-cleaning career; he had a common law wife, and Mrs Smalls (variously known as Diane or Diana) had a small child, with another on the way. She sprang to his defence at Tunbridge Wells Magistrates' Court in April 1966 when Smalls had been caught, after a rooftop chase following an attempt to break into F.W. Woolworth Ltd.

'It's me that should be in the dock, not him', cried Mrs Smalls histrionically. 'He was out of work and I was getting so mad over money because I hadn't any for the baby. He's been trying to go straight, he doesn't steal things.'

Not that that helped, because the Bench sentenced him to three months for the attempted shopbreaking, plus three months to run consecutively for possessing housebreaking implements by night.

Mrs Smalls (who would later be known, rather impolitely, as 'Slack Alice') may have been slightly disingenuous, because the previous year, her husband had been involved in a bank robbery at Woodford, where he did indeed 'steal things'.

★　★　★

Mrs Doris Roe, the wife of the licensee of The George public house, South Woodford, Essex, looked out of her kitchen window on the morning of 10 September 1965 and saw on the other side of the road two masked men tampering with the door of the National Provincial Bank. She telephoned the police, then saw four more masked men carrying coshes and a sawn-off shotgun join the other two as they burst into the bank. Before the police could arrive, one of the men coshed the cashier, 29-year-old Michael Crisp, and grabbed two boxes containing £10,193 10s 0d, before they all escaped in a blue Ford Zephyr. They tore down Waltham Cross Street, knocking middle-aged John Briggs off his bicycle and hospitalising him with serious head injuries. The robbers then crashed into a van, wrecking their car, and commandeered a Ford Anglia parked on a garage forecourt by dragging out the driver, elderly Mr C. Cook. When Reg Mathews, a petrol pump attendant, together with some other men went to Mr Cook's assistance, the robber with the sawn-off shotgun levelled it at them, shouting, 'Stand back or I'll blow your brains out!'

The robbers made their escape in Mr Cook's Anglia, but Detective Inspector Don Saunders took up the investigation and immediately made two arrests. On 14 September, he told the Magistrates at Stratford Court that the previous day, one witness had been so frightened at the thought of attending an identification parade that he had refused to do so, and that another had been approached by two men who made 'certain suggestions respecting his evidence'. The two arrested men were remanded in custody, although one week later, one of them was granted bail and the following week was discharged and granted 10 guineas costs, having presented police with an unshakeable alibi. Another suspect was roped in, but on 30 November both men were acquitted at the Old Bailey.

That robbery might have been the first of many such excursions for Bertie Smalls.

★　★　★

It is possible that while Smalls was serving his half-a-stretch following his unsuccessful Woolworth venture, he may have met up with Leonard Walter Jones who, having previously been acquitted in 1963 of robbing a Post Office van driver, was now on remand accused of robbing another Post Office van driver of £2,260; but whatever the case, Jones was cleared of that charge as well in November 1966.

Be that as it may, on 2 October 1968 Jones was one of the men later charged with a robbery at the National Provincial Bank, North Street, Brighton. Also charged was James William Jeffrey, who in December 1958 had been sentenced to nine months' imprisonment for robbery, John Alfred 'Vodka Johnny' Richards who, at the time of causing grievous bodily harm to a black youth (for which he received a conditional discharge) had possessed three previous convictions (one of which resulted in a fine of £5 for stealing a ton of lead), and Anthony Edlin. At the tender age of seventeen, Edlin had been fined £1 for stealing a lady's bicycle but he, and the other co-accused, would go on to greater heights in the criminal world.

At a later trial, all four men would have that offence left on the file, not to be proceeded with without leave of the court or the Court of Appeal (Criminal Division). In effect, this meant they would never be further prosecuted for it.

However, now back to that sunny, seaside town in east Sussex where Smalls had been invited to take part in a lucrative robbery but, as a relatively untested member of the group, had been relegated to the back-up team, to protect the first wave going into the bank for the prize. This rather inauspicious beginning was just as well, because although Smalls could summon up the aggression necessary in any armed robber – as one who would blast a sawn-off shotgun into a bank's ceiling he was, he admitted, 'A pretty good frightener' – he was far from fit. Overweight at sixteen stone, short, with a 'Viva Zapata' moustache, this promiscuous glutton with a serious alcohol and tobacco habit was in poor health and suffered from frequent boils.

Smalls had driven down to Brighton with Diana and their small son and, leaving them in a side street, had gone to meet up with the rest of the gang and don his disguise of spectacles and a blue-green trilby hat. The bank had just received cash in used notes from Securicor when, at 10.30am, four of the gang rushed into the premises. The first man, brandishing a revolver, leapt onto the counter, shouting, 'Nobody move!' Ammonia was squirted, and the manager (who had struggled unsuccessfully with one of the gang), the accountant, a senior clerk (who had been struck on the shoulder), another clerk (who had thrown a metal chair at one of the robbers, injuring his knee) and a woman clerk were all later admitted to the Royal Sussex Hospital suffering from ammonia burns. Two shots were fired, one from the revolver, the other from a sawn-off shotgun, as the raiders fled. The shotgun was discharged by Smalls into the crowd that had gathered outside the bank; fortunately no one was injured, and as Smalls got into the back of a Ford van, one of the security guards flung his truncheon at it and, like the grey Ford Escort and the BMC 1100 getaway cars, it roared away.

Seven men had been involved in the raid, which netted them £72,000; equal shares resulted in Smalls receiving £10,000.

The next robbery was also the biggest (in monetary value) that Smalls would be involved in. The target was Ralli Bros, a merchant bank situated on the ground floor of a five-storey building at 63–66 Hatton Garden, London EC1. This time, the gang would not strike when the prize was brought into the bank, because the valuables were already there; they would infiltrate the bank first, then wait for the staff to enter before they struck. To effect entry they required the assistance of someone who already had legitimate access to the premises; this they got in the form of a cleaner named Clem Eden.

In 1941, Eden, an ex-Borstal boy had been stopped with two other men; all were in possession of cut-throat razors and were overheard to say, 'I'll do some bastard tonight!' Unfortunately, the over-hearer was a certain detective sergeant, and although Eden, an army deserter, produced an identity card in the name of Edward Rice, when his fingerprints were taken, he admitted his true identity. Described in Clerkenwell court as 'Camden Town Toughs', the three were sent to hard labour for twelve months.

To return to the robbery, what happened was described in Smalls' account; but in this, it should be noted, as well as in Smalls' other accounts of robberies, identification of other parties should not necessarily imply guilt:

> I was with Vodka Johnny Richards having been working, and he told me he had some business lined up with Clem Eden, a man I already knew whose business it was to stick things up – by that, I mean sort out robbery that could be done. He had arranged to meet him in a club in Paddington Street, W.1. I was in there with Vodka Johnny, and Clem came in about half an hour later. I listened to the conversation, which was that he was a cleaner in a diamond bank in Hatton Garden and said that the bank handled thousands and thousands of pounds of stones which were kept in a vault. I arranged to go there next morning and meet him there. I dressed up very smart and got there about 6.30am when the cleaners were there. He was the only person there. He showed me the safe behind the counter in the bank. He showed me the offices upstairs and then downstairs. He took

me through downstairs and along a short corridor and showed me the alarm turnoff. I was in there for about ten minutes in all. He said there were fourteen in staff who came in and went to their separate offices because it is not like a normal bank. I arranged to meet him the following day in a West End club called the Log Cabin. Later the same day, I met the others who were going with us, that is Micky Green, Jimmy Jeffries [*sic*], Tony Edlin, Lennie Jones and Johnny Richards. I told them it looked good to me and of the arrangements for meeting him the following day.

The plan went ahead. Eden told Smalls that the postman called at about 8.30am at the bank and that it was no good tying him (Eden) up until after the postman had left, since he had a mate who waited outside in the van. There followed a meeting of the gang at Jimmy Jeffrey's house in Kenton, where the plan was fully discussed and it was decided to carry out the robbery the following day, 26 March 1969.

Edlin and Jeffrey obtained the weaponry, three shotguns and two handguns. Micky Green supplied the vehicles, a Ford Cortina and a Ford Corsair which were 'ringers', and Jeffrey and Edlin took them to the venue early the following morning to ensure they could leave them on parking meters. Eden let four of the masked gang in – Smalls, Ronnie Dark, Jeffrey and Edlin – and they secreted themselves in the ladies' toilets and waited for the postman to arrive. Matters became slightly unsettled when the postman was late; by the time he got there, at 8.45am, several of the staff had arrived. But once the postman had left, Eden was tied up by Edlin, and one by one, the sixteen members of the staff were then pounced upon and tied up with tape.

'Where's the manager?' shouted Smalls, although this was for appearances only; he knew perfectly well that Mr Edward Phillips was the manager, from Eden's description of him. He and the deputy manager were bundled downstairs, the alarm was switched off and the manager was forced to open the vault. Inside, there were two safes, each with two locks, and when they were opened, the gang grabbed diamonds, rubies and sapphires, as well as some £11,000 in currency, a total value of £296,451. This was put into grips which the gang had brought with them, as well as carrier bags handed over by the staff. Both the manager and his deputy were locked in the strongroom, and the raiders left.

A girl assistant later excitedly described the gang as being, 'All cockneys, and they were all very gentlemanly about the whole thing.'

However, it had not gone off without incident. A 67-year-old woman cook had been hit over the head and a 49-year-old staff member was injured when he had a gun rammed in his face. A male clerk told the police, 'I was frightened out of my life', and a woman clerk and three young girl assistants were taken to hospital suffering from shock.

Their balaclavas removed, the robbers strolled unconcernedly out of the bank. The chief clerk, Mr Cyril Preston, had struggled to free himself during the robbery; when he finally did so he emerged into Hatton Garden to see two of the robbers getting into a Ford Corsair. He noted the vehicle's details and went back in to raise the alarm.

It was perhaps rather foolish of Smalls to tell Traffic Warden Andrews to 'Buzz off" when she was fixing a penalty notice to his getaway car, the Cortina, in New Cross Street. Female traffic wardens do tend to memorise the faces of men who address them rudely of and those – like Micky Green – who accompany them. Fortunately for them, however, she did not. They then drove to Smalls' father-in-law's house in Kentish Town, where the robbery paraphernalia was stashed, and then to Johnny Richards' flat in Finchley, where the rest of the team were gathered.

As well as the currency, there were the precious stones, but none of the gang had any idea of their worth. Lennie Jones said that he knew someone named David who would value and buy the stones; he would arrange for the man to come up from his home at Montpelier Road, Brighton the following day.

That person was David Kozak, a 45-year-old Pole, a man with the right credentials. In February 1947 he had appeared at Marylebone Magistrates' Court accused of receiving ninety-seven watches, valued at £490. He had previously been bailed from that court and took the opportunity to flee to Brazil, leaving his woman accomplice to face the charge alone and receive two months' imprisonment. Now, he was sentenced to six months' imprisonment, plus a £100 fine for estreating (forfeiting) bail, with the option of three months consecutive if he failed to pay.

Two years later, he was fined £2,000 and sentenced to twelve months' imprisonment for harbouring uncustomed watches, and in 1956, for a similar offence, he was fined £170 8s 0d. This sentence may have been mitigated by his solicitor informing a credulous Bench that his client had once found a ring worth £1,000 in the street and had virtuously handed it in to a police station.

Kozak now inspected the stones at Richards' flat, and what happened thereafter was later described by Smalls:

He sat down and looked at it and eventually said it would take days to value and he would need the help of a coloured man (meaning a man who knew the value of coloured stones). He eventually disposed of them over a period of two weeks in various parcels of stones. We all finished up with £10,000 each. This included Clem and David. I saw Clem about six weeks later; by this time he had been paid by Johnny and he told me about being questioned by police regarding the robbery and how he was taken to Holborn for questioning. He said he had been detained a long time and when they went to release him they took him out into the yard towards a car which he thought we had used. He thought if he put his hands on the car, he would be fitted-up, so he ran back into the station.

Clem Eden never stood trial, nor was he ever charged; he simply disappeared. Nothing has ever been heard from him since.

★   ★   ★

Micky Green had an acquaintance who worked at the Skefco Ballbearing Co., Leagrave Road, Luton, Bedfordshire and provided the gang with a sketch plan of the premises. It enabled a team of six to rush in on the morning of 6 May 1969, via a wooden staff entrance a few yards from the main door, and force the employees to lie down on the floor. Three who resisted were hit with pickaxe helves and were later taken to hospital suffering from head and hand injuries, as was a girl who was pushed aside in the corridor, suffering from shock.

The sum of £57,741 was shoved into a bed sheet, and the raiders leapt into a blue Ford Transit van that was driving slowly by and which was later found abandoned in a Luton street. The Luton police immediately blocked off access roads to the M1 motorway and started searching all cars and vans leaving the town. All to no avail. The gang were safe in a secret location in Luton, and their payout amounted to £8,000 each.

Included in the team were Donald Walter Barrett and Robert Alles King; at a subsequent trial, both were told that these offences would lie on the file.

This is the first time that Mr Barrett has been mentioned: never fear, in the pages that follow we shall be hearing a great deal more of him. We also heard of 'Britain's biggest post-war bank robbery' in Chapter One – we shall now be hearing rather more about it.

# Chapter Four

# A Gathering of Blaggers

The robbery carried out at Barclays Bank, Ilford has already been mentioned in passing in Chapter One, which dealt more with Bert Wickstead's investigation than with many of the actual participants. This was because Wickstead had no idea who they were. However, now we know who the dramatis personae were.

With Ronnie Dark, Micky Green, Albert Walker, Edward McCarthy and Charles Bowman we need not concern ourselves, since they have already been mentioned in Chapter One. And Donald Barrett, James Jeffrey, Anthony Edlin and Robert Alles King were introduced to us in Chapter Three.

However, one of the newcomers was Michael Henry Salmon, who was a childhood friend of Bertie Smalls. He attended a very good school and in between jobs in a stockbroker's office he served in the Parachute Regiment.

'You have fallen a bit low in the world', commented Sir John Cameron, the Magistrate at West London Court in July 1959, when Salmon pleaded guilty to living on a prostitute's immoral earnings, and sentenced him to three months' imprisonment.

Perhaps, like his chum Smalls, sentenced the previous year for a similar offence, he was easily led.

One thing led to another and now Salmon was sentenced to two years' imprisonment for receiving, shopbreaking and larceny; in February 1961 he was one of three prisoners who scaled the wall of Wandsworth prison, raced across Wandsworth Common and leapt over the railway track, in front of the fast-moving Brighton Belle. This slowed their pursuers but not by much; the fugitives were all recaptured almost immediately. Interestingly, one of the other escapees was one Donald Walter Barrett, serving a four-year sentence for robbery with violence. Of him – as has already been mentioned – more later.

In 1967, Salmon was accused of conspiring to pervert the course of justice by paying money to kennel maids to give false evidence in a previous greyhound doping trial; but it appears they didn't, and neither did Salmon.

Two years later, both Smalls and Salmon were arrested following an altercation outside a nightclub and charged with obstructing police, assaults on two police officers and, in Smalls' case, dangerous driving. Nevertheless, Smalls was fined just £40, Salmon £20 and both were given suspended prison sentences. In the space of twenty years, Salmon had acquired nine previous convictions.

Well-mannered Bruce Brown had received a 'very good' character assessment whilst doing National Service with the Royal Air Force, and had a spotless record until July 1958, when, as a 25-year-old bricklayer earning £20 per week, he was found guilty of two post office robberies netting £2,526 as part of a gang using guns and hammers. The hard-line Lord Chief Justice sentenced him to four years' imprisonment, saying:

> Yours is a typical case of which there are unfortunately too many nowadays, of a young man who can earn perfectly good wages giving up his job because he desires to go in for easy money by resorting to crime. These assaults on post offices are serious matters, but I reduce the sentence I would otherwise have passed because the jury have not convicted you of being a party to the violence.

That was followed in 1963 by a three-year sentence for officebreaking, and it was while serving his sentence that he met Bryan Turner.

Bryan James Turner was brought up on the Greater London Council's sprawling Burnt Oak Estate, Edgware and first came to notice in February 1957 at Hertford Quarter Sessions, when he pleaded guilty to housebreaking, asked for sixty-five other offences to be taken into consideration and was sentenced to Borstal Training. Released in August 1958, in September 1959 he was found guilty of housebreaking, stealing property worth £800 and also the theft of a ballpoint pen valued at 1s 6d, the property of a young girl student, snatched from her when she had the impudence to record the registration number of Turner's getaway car; he was sentenced to eighteen months' imprisonment.

Turner's housebreaking days were now over, and he joined a five-man team who attacked wages clerks, robbing them of £12,949 18s 2d. In June 1962, at the Old Bailey, he was jailed for ten years, with Mr Justice Paull telling him:

> You have been found guilty of taking part in a deliberate and carefully planned robbery with violence in which you and those taking part were hoping for very large sums of money and obtained them. That type of crime has become far too common. Those who play for high stakes and are prepared to

use violence in order to achieve their objective must realise that, if caught they go to prison for a very long time.

Released in 1969, he continued robbing – but also acquired a small supermarket in Kilburn as a 'front', had a one-sixth share in a gambling club in Bayswater and paid £500 for his share in the Hop Garden Club in the Portobello Road. Married with three children, Turner moved out of his council house in Calshowe Road, Borehamwood – even though he had just had a luxury bathroom installed – and in 1970 purchased a house for £13,000 in Folly Close, Radlett, Hertfordshire. Four years later, the property would have doubled in value. There were two Mercedes on the driveway: a saloon for himself, a sports model for his wife. They fitted in well with their equally prosperous neighbours, professional men, including a Barclays Bank manager.

We can mention in passing John Short, before we come to Donald Walter Barrett; but his antecedents will be found in Chapter Twenty-Three.

★  ★  ★

The first Bertie Smalls knew about what turned out to be the Ilford bank robbery was when Micky Green telephoned him, telling him that he 'had a bit of work'. Stating that he met Green at his Burnt Oak flat, together with James Jeffrey and Anthony Edlin (neither of whom were charged with the robbery), Ronnie Dark, Johnny Short, Bruce Brown and the crooked security guard, Albert Walker, Green suggested that the job would be worth between half and three quarters of a million. He added that he had two more of the guards 'straightened out', and it was arranged to meet them two or three days later.

At that meeting, the guards said they were not always on this particular run and were unable to say when they might get it; but with Albert they worked out a code to show him what they were doing as they left Lombard Street. As they left the building, they would know the run, but not the route until the custodian told them. For four or five weeks the team would sit at Micky Green's flat, waiting for the phone call from Albert. On that particular morning, Smalls' car was blocked in and he was unable to move it. He rang Green's flat to inform him of his difficulties and was told to phone again just after nine o'clock. Smalls did so, to discover that the job was on, so he travelled by tube to Wanstead, where Green picked him up in a van which also contained Johnny Short, Albert and Bruce Brown. They got into position, knowing roughly the time the van would arrive, but when it pulled up on the pavement it was too close to the doors of the bank, and the attack had to be aborted.

However, the guards mentioned another Barclays bank, this time at Ilford, where they went to make a delivery every Monday. Observation was carried out on three consecutive Mondays before the team was satisfied. On the day, Smalls picked up Micky Salmon and they parked the getaway vehicles in a prearranged place and waited until everyone was there. They then got into the Ford Transit van, with Micky Green driving and Smalls, Ronnie Dark, Bobby King and Don Barrett in the back. The others were lounging about nearby. Salmon (in a false moustache), Barrett (in a crash helmet) and Smalls had sawn-off shotguns, Bruce Brown (in a ginger wig) and Bryan Turner had ammonia bottles, and Bobby King and Ronnie Dark had handguns.

As they charged into the bank, Smalls and Dark had taken a ladder from the van to scale the counter, but because the rest of the team had everybody in the bank down on the floor, it was not needed, so the ladder was dropped. They then picked up the sacks containing the money and flung them – and themselves – into the back of the van. For some unexplained reason, Don Barrett's shotgun went off near Smalls' foot, hitting one of the sacks.

Johnny Short was surplus to requirements; he was supposed to block the road in the event of a pursuit, but because the robbery had been accomplished so speedily, he was still halfway round the block when the van roared away. At the changeover point the cash was put into the boots of two cars. Barrett and Bobby King drove off, as did Smalls, Ronnie Dark and Johnny Short, who went to a mid-terrace house about a quarter of a mile from the bank. The unnamed occupier was Jewish, living there with a young woman. There they stayed until the evening, each being then driven separately to the railway station before going home.

Mid-morning the following day, Smalls telephoned Micky Green at a farm in Rayleigh, Essex and was informed that the split came to twenty grand each. When it was dark, Smalls, Micky Salmon, Don Barrett and Bobby King made their way to where Johnny Short, Ronnie Dark and a woman that Smalls referred to as 'Mrs Dark' were counting out the money. In fact, she was Barbara Mary Hepburn, who went on the run with Dark before being arrested several months later. She was later cleared of dishonestly handling the stolen money but was sentenced to two years' imprisonment for obstructing justice.

The counting continued while Smalls waited, and then the money was shared out. Jeffrey and Edlin got £20,000 to share because they were supposed to be on the job but missed out because they thought they'd been seen. It was around that time that it was said that Salmon, Brown and Turner bought their houses and Bobby King bought the Cabin Club from Smalls for £1,800.

So that was a £20,000 payout for the gang members in February; the next job was Lloyds Bank at Bournemouth in September.

★ ★ ★

The attack on Lloyds Bank in Bournemouth was said to have been Bobby King's piece of work (although he was later acquitted of it), and it started off so well. He told Smalls that he had seen what he described as 'two big bags' collected by Security Express from the bank, and that was good enough. The two of them drove down to Dorset, reconnoitred the bank, were satisfied with what they saw, returned to London and discussed their findings with Micky Salmon, Don Barrett and a man King referred to as 'Danny Teale'. He was also known as 'Peter Dean' and 'Alan Jones', but in fact his baptismal name was Daniel Alfred Allpress, a good friend of Smalls – he had been described as 'virtually Bertie's assistant' – not a big man but a comedian and an expert driver of fast cars. In the space of ten years Allpress had been convicted on eight occasions.

One week later, Smalls returned to Bournemouth, and this time, King entered the bank to see if he could determine where the moneybags were situated prior to collection by the cash-in-transit van, which usually arrived at 10 o'clock. In fact, he discovered the bags were brought up from the vault prior to the van's arrival. Just to make sure, King and Salmon revisited the bank and confirmed what King had seen previously. The job was planned for the following week, but for some reason it failed to come off.

Now, Diane Smalls rented a flat at Talbot Road, Bournemouth, ostensibly for a two-week holiday. Also present was the Smalls' daughter, their au pair, Stella Robertson, and friends of Diane with their family. Bertie Smalls and King – for reasons best known to themselves, since they had a place to stay in Talbot Road – stayed overnight in a hotel. Perhaps the flat was getting a bit crowded.

The night prior to the robbery, Micky Salmon was said to have brought the guns down on the train. Smalls and Allpress had arrived in a stolen Corsair and King in a stolen Ford Zephyr Zodiac, both of which were left in a car park; Barrett arrived on the morning of the robbery, driving a Simca, his wife's car.

On the morning of Wednesday, 2 September 1970 the gang approached the Poole Hill branch of Lloyds Bank. Both Smalls and King wore hats, glasses and roll-necked jumpers, Barrett wore a balaclava and the others had scarves to pull up and cover their faces. There had been an argument earlier because Barrett wanted

to use a sawn-off shotgun and he handed Smalls a silver-coloured
.32 automatic. Things then began to go badly wrong.

The gang rushed into the bank just a little too early. The money,
in old untraceable notes for the cash-in-transit van, had not yet come
up from the vault. Barrett let off a shot which blasted a hole in an
inside wall, just missing a customer, and the .32 which had been
handed to Smalls was cocked and fired through the bank's front
window. In the absence of the big expected prize, all they could do
was to ransack the tills, thereby acquiring £2,226, and escape in
the blue Ford Corsair. Three men were later seen running across
the Bournemouth pleasure gardens, having abandoned the car in
the town centre. Barrett got into the red Simca and drove off to
the west, two more of the gang got into a bronze Ford Cortina and
headed off in the opposite direction.

What happened after that was a little confused. Smalls went to
Boscombe pier with his daughter, Barrett and Stella Robertson,
after which they had a few drinks and Smalls went to the cinema in
the afternoon. Stella went to fetch Diane, and they, with Allpress
and Barrett, had a few more drinks, returning to the flat rather late.
Barrett left with Stella Robertson, returning the next morning, and
most of the team returned to London. Over the next few days there
was quite a bit of drinking, and Smalls and Allpress went to Barrett's
address and knocked on the door, but received no answer. More
drinking in a nearby pub followed, before they returned to knock
on Barrett's front door again. The next door neighbour came out
and told them that before they had knocked the first time, Barrett
had left the house with half a dozen of his friends.

Unhappily for him, those 'friends' were CID officers.

★   ★   ★

Barrett had been the subject of surveillance by Regional Crime Squad
officers, who had received information that Barrett had travelled to
Bournemouth on two occasions prior to the robbery before returning
home the following day. Barrett was pulled in, and since he was in
possession of the weaponry as well as other incriminating evidence, he
admitted being involved in planning, as well as carrying out the raid
at Lloyds Bank. What was more, he named names. Stella Robertson
also named names, and as a result, Diane Smalls and two others
were arrested and charged with conspiracy to rob – Bertie Smalls
was nowhere to be seen. At Winchester Assizes the following year,
Miss Robertson failed to turn up at court to give evidence, the case
against Diane Smalls and two other defendants collapsed, and they
walked free. Micky Salmon (charged and acquitted of the robbery)

and Danny Allpress would much later be charged with attempting to pervert the course of justice by interfering with a Crown witness at that trial, something they denied and of which they were acquitted.

That left Don Barrett, the possessor of ten previous convictions, who on 16 December 1970 pleaded guilty to robbery (seven years' imprisonment) and conspiracy to rob (five years' imprisonment). The sentences were consecutive; he was now serving twelve years.

# Chapter Five

# A Whole Series of Raids

Following the debacle at Bournemouth, plus the arrest of Diane, Bertie Smalls kept a pretty low profile and was not around for the next big hit (and it *was* a big one), a particularly brutal robbery at the Midland Bank, Harlesden, North-West London.

At just before 10 o'clock on the morning of 15 December 1970, the gang blocked the street outside the bank with a van, and while two of the raiders guarded the door armed with sawn-off shotguns, five more, wearing balaclavas and stocking masks, rushed into the bank. Tom Fahey, an 18-year-old customer was hit with a blast from one of the shotguns and lost the tips of the fingers of one hand, a 50-year-old customer was coshed and a bank clerk received a face-full of ammonia. Three of the team leapt over the protective screen and helped themselves from the tills. Police Constable John Pilcher was in the shop next door when he heard the commotion and rushed to the bank. No stranger to threatening situations – six years previously, he had been awarded the Queen's Commendation for Brave Conduct after arresting a deranged armed man – he pushed the watching women and children around the corner to safety, then saw there was a baby in a pushchair in the gang's exit path and pulled the pushchair and the child out of harm's way. With that, the gang – £70,000 the richer – escaped in the van and a white Ford Cortina, leaving the unfortunate young Mr Fahey to undergo a week's stay in hospital. Bryan Turner was one of the eight that Smalls later nominated for that job; but he was later acquitted, both of the robbery and of shooting Mr Fahey.

Six months went by before Smalls and his team attacked the National Westminster Bank, Woolgate House in the City of London on 10 June 1971; £8,000 was grabbed but Smalls' share was just £1,300, and two weeks later, on 23 June, the attack on the National Westminster Bank, Park Royal was hardly more profitable. Passing schoolchildren were petrified when the gang's van mounted the pavement outside the premises, the raiders leapt out and Smalls blasted open the doors of the bank with a sawn-off shotgun. But after the robbers rushed in, all they got was £1,500 – just £250 each – because the bank staff were behind schedule and the expected £60,000 payroll never materialised. As they exited the bank, a lorry driver drove his vehicle on to the pavement, blocking their van, and they made off in a car which was pursued by a police motorcyclist who chased them as far as Western Avenue before he crashed, breaking his ankle.

Now – if we compare Bertie Smalls' financial status with that of an inhabitant of a third-world country, it would be quite wrong to say impoverishment was staring him in the face, but with his expensive lifestyle (which included heavy drinking) and lack of serious income, he was nevertheless feeling the pinch.

However, one month following the explosive (but unprofitable) expedition to the Park Royal bank, a Post Office van was hit at Portsmouth Harbour. This was Micky Salmon's piece of work, and he and Danny Allpress carried out the groundwork. It was inadvisable for Smalls to take part because he was on bail. On the day before the job was to go off, Smalls discovered that he was due at the Old Bailey, so he was faced with a dilemma: attend court, where he was expecting six months' imprisonment for possessing a firearm and ammunition without a licence, or skip bail. He decided to attend his trial, where he was fined a merciful £100 – now he really *did* have to go ahead with the job, to pay the fine!

A van and two cars were taken down to Portsmouth, together with Diane and the two children and Mrs Sylvia Allpress, who went to the beach while the team waited for the ferry and put the changeover vehicles in position. Allpress drove the getaway van down to the station and the rest of the gang walked down wearing disguises, wigs and hats. What happened then is described by Smalls, who had a handgun:

> We couldn't see exactly what was going on, then we heard a shout and a bang and we knew it was off. The next thing was that Danny reversed into position and they were slinging the bags by the side of the mail van … we began to sling the mailbags into a six or eight hundredweight van. The other three jumped out of the side of the mail van. They got into the van and I was the last one in and it was all sweet. Danny drove to the changeover, which was behind a disused building or pub. We transferred the sacks into the two vehicles we had waiting there. Then we drove to the flop, which was a hotel which Micky had arranged … we opened the bags and then realised we had a prize. It was taken out and roughly counted.

An accurate count revealed that the prize was £81,966, and the share-out for the six man team came to £12,500 each, with another £7,000 for 'drinks' – rewards to others who assisted, before and after the raid. The money was stashed in one of the changeover cars, and Smalls, Allpress and the wives and children drove back to London, having been waved through the roadblock.

The following day, the two wives returned to Portsmouth, and the money was retrieved – for this they were paid £100 each – but Mrs Sylvia Allpress, in common with a Mrs Doris Breda Webster, a housewife from East Ham, was later charged with dishonestly handling the £81,996 on or about the date of the robbery. Two years later at Harrow Magistrates' Court, the charge against Mrs Webster was dismissed, and one year after that, Mrs Allpress was acquitted of the charge.

Coincidentally, it was about this time that Allpress was able to purchase a house in Barnett for just over £12,000.

However, having successfully retrieved the money, there was one aspect of the Portsmouth robbery that Smalls was decidedly unhappy about, as he later recounted:

Having fired the silvery .32, I spoke about the danger of holding on to that gun because it was evidence against us. I told Danny that police might be able to compare the bullet with the gun. Danny brought the gun over and he suggested we throw it in Hampstead ponds. We drove over there and parked near the Heath. We went to the pond where male swimming is allowed. On the path that divides the pools Danny threw the .32 into the pond. He wrapped it in a handkerchief and just swung his arm. It went close to where two men were fishing, not more than ten to fifteen feet from the bank.

★ ★ ★

On 28 July 1971, five masked raiders, some of whom wore children's 'monkey masks', burst into the Allied Irish Bank, in Kilburn, North-West London, ten minutes after a cash delivery, and used a 14ft ladder to scale the bank's counter screens. A shot was fired into the floor to encourage the staff to lie down, and members of the gang rifled the cash desks and broke open a strongbox found in an open safe; in the process, the deputy manager was struck across the forearm with a revolver, and the gang escaped with £130,000 in a Ford Escort van, later found abandoned.

Smalls was not present on this particular job but successful blaggings are inevitably discussed later, and he was able to suggest the names of the participants, of whom the only one to stand trial, Bryan Turner, was acquitted.

Similarly, Smalls was not amongst those who stormed Lloyds Bank, Wood Green in October 1971 – a pity as far as he was concerned, because the prize amounted to £28,074 – but he was involved three months later, when he was one of five balaclava-wearing raiders who fired shots as they rushed into Lloyds Bank, High Street, Stoke Newington just after 10.30am on 17 January 1972. Only two counter staff and three customers were present when the gang fired shots into the walls and woodwork of the bank's interior, clambered over the protective screen, fired two shots into the till and grabbed the money. Having escaped with just £3,084, they ran down a side passageway, knocking an elderly lady to the ground, before driving away.

It was prior to this particular robbery that the gang had the use of a 'flop', a house belonging to a lady named Susan Mattis, a 33-year-old divorced mother of three. Naming two of those said to have participated in the raid, Smalls said:

> I remember we were looking out the guns. Jimmy had one and I had another. The gun I had had a peculiar safety catch. I was holding it across my legs and loading up.
>
> Danny said, 'Don't point that fucking gun at me' and knocked it downwards.
>
> I said, 'Don't be silly, the gun's on safety.'
>
> I had it pointed to the floor and pulled the trigger. The gun fired and it went through the carpet and the floor. Someone went downstairs and told Susan, who was getting her kids ready for school, that if anyone said anything, to say that the gas had exploded.

It was corroboration of a sort, but after calling Ms Mattis as a prosecution witness, insufficient to bring about the conviction of either Jimmy Wilkinson or Danny Allpress, both of whom were acquitted.

Following his conviction at the Middlesex Sessions in May 1962 for breaking into British Home Stores at The Broadway, West Ealing and stealing 7,728 pairs of nylons, worth £2,000, James Stanley Wilkinson, who had several convictions to his name, was sentenced to Borstal Training. Thereafter, it appears he was recklessly accused of a number of serious offences.

Just before Christmas 1966, at a re-trial at the Old Bailey, Wilkinson, together with three other accused, was acquitted of conspiring to assault a professional gambler; Wilkinson had also been accused of inflicting grievous bodily harm on the same man as well as possessing a sawn-off shotgun, but he was acquitted of those offences as well.

When Wilkinson stood trial in November 1971 at Hertford Assizes for being concerned in an eight-man £29,000 raid on the Boreham Wood branch of Barclays Bank on 29 April, when a security guard was felled with a blow from the butt of a sawn-off shotgun, he indignantly told the jury, 'In the last eighteen months I have been questioned by the police concerning five different robberies', adding, 'I have never been to Boreham Wood in my life.'

Only a month before that raid, he said, he had been pulled in and questioned regarding a robbery at the BBC – and was released the same day. On a day in April when his co-accused were said to be casing the Boreham Wood job, why, he was at Southend police station being quizzed regarding a £25,000 robbery. Of course, he was released, just as he was when he had been questioned about a £7,000 robbery at Hayes and after he was pulled in off the street in Notting Hill to be questioned about yet another 'big robbery'.

At the time of the robbery at Boreham Wood, Wilkinson said that he was having a haircut and that he later saw a solicitor about money that was owed to him. It was one of his co-accused who had driven him and his family to the airport for their holiday flight, and on 13 May, when they returned, he was met by police on the aircraft after it landed at Heathrow.

A week later, cheering broke out in the public gallery when Wilkinson and his co-accused were acquitted of conspiracy. One of the co-defendants was fined £50 for assaulting a police officer, and another – David Christopher Delaney – was sentenced to eight months' imprisonment for receiving twenty pairs of stolen jeans.

It certainly appeared that the police had got it in for the unfortunate Mr Wilkinson.

★　★　★

Eleven days after the attack on Lloyds Bank in Stoke Newington, Barclays Bank in Acton was hit for £8,188. Smalls did not participate in this raid, where shots were fired and a clerk who endeavoured to sound the alarm was kicked in the head, but he nominated Danny Allpress and Lennie Jones as being two of the three raiders. At a later trial, the Judge discharged the jury from delivering a verdict as regards Allpress, but Jones pleaded guilty and was sentenced to fourteen years' imprisonment. Someone whom Smalls did not name (possibly because at that time he was unaware of his involvement or at least his identity) was Thomas Frederick French, a 29-year-old former taxi driver, who was sentenced to nine years' imprisonment after pleading guilty to being the getaway driver on three of the gang's robberies. When not driving getaway vehicles, his taxi made excellent cover for transporting both villains and their weapons across London.

On 25 February 1972, a modest £7,722 was snatched from Barclays Bank, Stoke Newington (to add insult to injury, the gang were pelted with bricks by labourers on a nearby building site), but ten days later, to make up for it, Barclays Bank, Wood Green was hit by four of the gang for £38,428. They went in just before closing time and, after using a sledgehammer to smash open the counter door, helped themselves after shooting the locks off the tills. Smalls would later suggest that Danny Allpress and Jimmy Wilkinson were involved, but at their trial the Judge discharged the jury from giving a verdict.

No one stood trial for the robbery at Lloyds Bank, North Harrow, where £20,000 was snatched in April 1972, but on 22 May 1972 a gang of four masked gunmen seized £10,729 from the National Westminster Bank, Palmers Green, where a customer was hit over the head. It was here that matters started to unravel.

⋆ ⋆ ⋆

A shop manageress had noted four men sitting in a bronze Ford Cortina in Lightcliffe Road, N13, close to the bank before the raid. She saw a man cross the road and talk to the driver of the car. Shortly afterwards, when she heard the sound of the bank's alarm, she ran back to find the same car on the pavement outside the bank. Perusing the photographs contained in the Rogues' Gallery at the Yard, she picked out Smalls as being the man talking to the driver. Just as interesting was that three days before the raid, an off-duty detective constable had been walking through Palmers Green when he saw three men in a red Jaguar outside the National Westminster Bank. One of the men pointed to the bank, the other two got out and went inside. They then returned and drove off, but the officer thought this suspicious enough to note the registration number – KUR 7G. The vehicle was later traced to a garage forecourt near Tower Bridge; it was a business in which Smalls had an interest. Smalls had a file at C11, the Yard's Criminal Intelligence Department; it was noted that although he had no convictions for robbery, he had been pulled in on several occasions for questioning following robberies, but there had never been sufficient evidence to make a charge stick. That did not necessarily mean that nothing was being done.

In late 1963 or early 1964, the detective inspector at Hornsey police station had decided to take the war into the enemy's camp. He infiltrated the plastering company in Cheshunt run by Bertie's brother Kelvin, by inserting Roy Rossiter, an aid to CID, as an employee, to see what information he could obtain. Although Rossiter visited Bertie's address off Green Lanes on several occasions, very little useful information was obtained, although one amusing anecdote emerged. Bertie and his team were set up, fully armed, to attack the cash-in-transit vehicle delivering wages to the North Middlesex Hospital, Edmonton, but as the van approached, two marked police cars, blue lights flashing and sirens wailing, suddenly appeared on the scene; Bertie and his gang hastily discarded their weaponry in the bushes at the hospital and disappeared. It was only later that it was discovered that the 'police cars' were part of a sequence being filmed for the popular television series *No Hiding Place*, which ran for 236 episodes between September 1959 and June 1967. Detective Chief Superintendent Tom Lockhart – aka the actor Raymond Francis – never knew what an interesting capture he might have made.

But now, back to 1972, when problems were starting to stack up; a woman who had been tied up during the Ralli Brothers robbery, three years previously, had also identified Smalls from a photograph as being one of the gang. The Palmers Green offence was being investigated by officers from Edmonton police station, and now the detective inspector armed with a search warrant went to Smalls' address at Selsdon in South London. Diane Smalls was there; her husband was not. After searching the address, the officer told Diane he wished to speak with her husband; but although Smalls did telephone and make an appointment to see the officer, that appointment was never kept.

An appointment that Smalls did keep, three weeks after his failed meeting with the law, was to assist in a raid on Barclays Bank, Harringay, where a modest £3,421 was handed over to the five-man gang; and although Danny Allpress, Jimmy Wilkinson and a certain William Stanley Shervill stood trial, in each case the Judge discharged the jury from giving a verdict. During the early 1960s, Mr Shervill had been fined for rowdyism offences and later he stood trial with three others, including one James Stanley Wilkinson on charges of conspiracy to assault – all were acquitted on a retrial just before Christmas 1966.

However, on 10 August 1972 there would be a highly lucrative attack on Barclays Bank, Wembley, and it was then that matters really started to come together for the police – and to fall apart for the robbers – and although Mr Shervill was supposed to take a leading part in the raid he had by then been declared persona non grata.

## Chapter Six

# The Wembley Job

Professional armed robbers seldom (if ever) carried out one robbery and then sat around, wondering, 'What shall we do next?' There were always robberies being looked at, discussed, plotted up. If one blew out (or even if it didn't), there was always another to slot in. As we have already seen, robberies often followed each other a week at a time.

So it was with Barclays Bank at Wembley. It was probably mid-May 1972 when Smalls met up with Jimmy Wilkinson and William (referred to by Smalls as 'Brian') Reynolds at The Royal public house in Ealing. Reynolds told them that he had a bank in the Wembley area lined up that could produce £150,000. According to Smalls, Wilkinson told him to 'go ahead'. It was as simple as that. In the meantime, the gang carried out raids on banks at Palmers Green and Harringay.

The bank – Barclays at Wembley – had been identified thanks to the assistance of an inside man, Anthony Edward Holt, a clerk working there. But with a total of £14,150 in their pockets from the two previous robberies, it was time for the blaggers to take a break.

* * *

Situated at Paseo de Maritimo, Torremolinos, the luxurious four-star Meliá Hotel with its 540 rooms overlooks the Mediterranean, and it was there towards the end of June that Smalls arrived, driving a red MGC sports car, with Jimmy Wilkinson as his passenger. The car belonged to David Delaney; Smalls had thoughtfully lent his red Jaguar to Delaney, aware that it had been seen on the job at Palmers Green. If anybody was going to be pulled by police in that incriminating vehicle, it was not going to be Bertie! Smalls' and Wilkinson's wives and children were already there, as were William 'Brian' Reynolds and Billy Sherville and his wife. They stayed for about a fortnight before Smalls drove back, crossing from Dieppe to Newhaven, this time with Brian Reynolds as passenger, to deal with the profitable bank awaiting them at Wembley. At least, that was the idea.

Smalls spent the night at Jimmy Wilkinson's home, and the scene was set for the raid to take place the next morning. He, Wilkinson and Allpress had acquired their cars for the robbery the previous night; Reynolds, Delaney and Sherville were to get their own changeover car, a Jaguar. Between 7.00 and 7.30am they met up in a cafe in Ealing; Philip Morris brought the guns and put them straight into the van to be used in the raid which was parked nearby. Smalls got into the van and, with Morris driving, the team travelled in convoy to where the changeover vehicles were to be put down. Allpress and Wilkinson had parked their cars and they joined Smalls in the back of the van and set off to meet up with Delaney and Sherville. This was when things began to go spectacularly wrong.

Sherville complained that the clutch had gone on the Jaguar and that it was impossible to drive. A furious row broke out, with Sherville and Delaney trying to blame Brian Reynolds, because he had driven the car the night before and should have known it was no good. Two decisions were now made. Smalls announced the raid was off; what was more, they would have to postpone the robbery until the clerk at the bank, Holt, advised them that there were sufficient used notes to make the job worthwhile.

The second decision came from Wilkinson, who told Delaney and Sherville, 'Fuck off and tell Reynolds it's off.'

Small now takes up the tale:

The rest of us went in the van to the car park of a nine-hole golf course near the bridge in Greenford Road. Philip contacted the cabbie who came and picked him up. They went off with the tools and sometime later, Philip came back with a car and picked Danny, Jimmy and me up from a café nearby where we had breakfast. He took us back to Ealing. It was said by Jimmy on several occasions that Sherville and Delaney were sacked.

But if Sherville was said to have been sacked, it was only from physically taking part in the Wembley attack; he had, of course, conspired as part of the team. He was – somewhat surprisingly – said to be included in the stop-gap raid which followed between the aborted attack at Wembley and the actual raid.

This stop-gap was a raid on Lloyds Bank, Wood Green on 10 July 1972, when six members of the gang, wearing balaclavas and armed with a sledgehammer and sawn-off shotguns – a shot was fired into the ceiling – smashed open the counter door and blew the tills open. In all, £31,894 was stolen, although a bag containing £10 notes burst open in one of the getaway cars. A taxi was seen in the vicinity following the raid, but nobody knew it was being driven by

Thomas French, who went straight to Susan Mattis's address. Once the gang had been dropped off, they were left to count out and divide the takings. Later, Tom French returned to pick up one of the gang members and the guns. For this, as in all of the robberies in which he provided invaluable assistance, he was given £100, the same amount that Diane Smalls and Mrs Allpress had received when they returned to Portsmouth to collect the takings and the guns. Of the four who would stand trial for the Wood Green robbery, William Edward Reynolds, William Shervill and Jimmy Wilkinson were all found not guilty; only French went down for nine years.

★  ★  ★

Contact was now resumed with Anthony Holt, the venal clerk at Barclays Bank, who produced a list showing three dates: 3, 10 and 18 August, when pick-ups would be made by Security Express, although he would have preferred the robbery to take place on 18 August, since he would then be on holiday. Smalls met him in the Marks & Spencer car park at Wembley and described the meeting:

> The bank clerk told me that as the guards walked in, it varied in time from a minute to five minutes before the money came up. He also said, I believe, that if we ran in we could get it at the bottom of the lift by running down some steps if we were quick. He described the layout of the bank. The door going in is at an angle turned to the left and there's a door facing you. The Foreign Exchange is to the right, and if you went to the till there you could look through and see if the money was up. About three weeks before the job, I went there and looked at the bank. Another point that Reynolds was told by the bank clerk was about the locks. I can't remember what type he said but he said they would break easily. This was a job being done by Jimmy Wilkinson and I didn't take much notice of this.

It can therefore be seen that Holt was an indispensable part of the planning, for which he would be paid £10,000; however, Smalls would later say that he was unsure whether or not Holt was paid, and former Chief Inspector Terry Babbidge QPM told me that he received information to the effect that Holt was not paid; that was later confirmed in the witness box by Holt himself. Be that as it may, many might think that he was very fortunate to later receive a modest 5-year sentence.

Danny Allpress joined the team, and when Smalls met Bryan Turner in the car park of The Thatched Barn, Borehamwood regarding the possibility of obtaining a false passport, he mentioned the forthcoming job to him. Turner expressed enthusiasm and suggested that Bruce Brown join the team; that was put to the rest of the team, who democratically agreed. Therefore, Brown and Turner filled the gaps left by Shervill and Delaney.

A few days prior to the attack, Smalls and Allpress were responsible for acquiring the cars for the getaway; a rather flamboyant red Triumph TR6, registration number DGC 990H, was taken from Jermyn Street, although – unusually – none of the stolen cars would have false number plates attached to them. There was no need to do so with the vans used in the robbery, because they were legitimately purchased by a friend of Wilkinson's, known to his contemporaries as 'Bug-Eyed Jimmy'. Paid £500 for his services, it appears he was identified as James Joseph Marsden. Turner and Brown brought a shotgun and a handgun; Philip Anthony Morris supplied two shotguns and a handgun.

Morris is a newcomer to these chapters, but not to the world of crime. In 1958, when he had five previous convictions – car stealing, housebreaking, assault on police – he was convicted of being part of a gang who smashed up a café; after being committed to the Middlesex Sessions for sentence, he was sent to a detention centre. In January 1964, he gave his name only as 'John' when he was arrested for robbing a postal worker of £34,558. Following the robbery, he had buried the three mailbags, but when he returned to dig them up he was arrested after a chase, during which he threw a garden fork at his pursuers.

He told the superintendent in charge of the case, 'I have never used violence before. I'm sorry. I'm religious, really, and went to church this morning to think about it.'

At Berkshire Assizes, he was sentenced to six years' imprisonment, and following his release in 1968 he moved from the Rocklands Caravan Site, Gloucestershire and in 1970 bought a 60-acre farm in Troon, Cornwall, on a mortgage. After his involvement with the Wembley robbery, he went on to shoot dead a milkman in February 1973 during a £148,355 robbery. He was really sorry about that, as well. It was an accident.

But back to the Wembley robbery – the night before the raid, the vehicles were put down: one behind the back of Marks & Spencer, Ealing, the Triumph by some flats off Ealing Broadway and the Cortina and van in The Green Man pub's car park, off Dagmar Avenue, about a mile and a half from the bank.

The following morning, 10 August, Tom French, the dodgy taxi driver, brought round the guns, and the various members of the gang got into the vehicles and drove over to Wembley, joining Morris in one of the vans. They parked in the road leading to the bank and at 9.40am they moved to within 300 yards of the premises. Security Express had just pulled up, and when the guards went in to the bank, taking with them £10,000 in brand new notes, it was Reynolds who went in after them, to the foreign exchange in order to determine that the money in old notes, ready for collection by Security Express, was up on the ground floor. When he saw that it was, he strolled out of the bank, gave a pre-arranged signal and left the vicinity.

One van was used to block a nearby road junction, another screamed to a halt outside the bank, then several armed, masked men got out and Morris told a custodian from the cash-in-transit van to 'hit the deck', while he and Turner guarded the doors. The masked raiders carrying sawn-off shotguns then rushed in, firing shots into the ceiling.

Smalls yelled, 'Lie down or we shoot!' and everyone, bank staff and customers, obediently lay down on the floor.

As the first shot was fired, a mother and her small daughter ran screaming from the bank; two women ambulance drivers were ordered away from the premises by Morris, and later, one of those ambulances would be used to convey a shocked baby to hospital.

Using a sledgehammer, Jimmy Wilkinson was said to have smashed in the bank's inner doors and then he, Allpress and Brown pulled out the trolley holding nine bags containing £138,111, made up of £10, £5 and £1 notes, which were grabbed after the robbers jumped over the counter.

'Move and we'll shoot!' shouted one of the raiders, and to provide encouragement, a revolver was fired into a window.

Smalls, whose role it was to keep everybody in the bank quiet, was last to leave, and with Allpress driving, the van roared away.

The gang was not interested in the pristine £10,000 that had just been delivered; similarly, they were indifferent to the contents of the cash tills. They knew exactly what they wanted: the used notes. From start to finish, the raid – just like the Barclays Bank, Ilford robbery – had taken no more than ninety seconds.

The van was spotted by a representative of the Chubb burglar alarm company in his radio-controlled van and he sent up a 'Mayday' call before giving chase. He lost the getaway van, which was later found abandoned.

The money was put into the boot and the back of the Triumph; prior to the raid, it was realised that space was at a premium, so some golf clubs and a musical instrument were moved from the Triumph into the back of the stolen white Ford Cortina, registration number SUR 492D. Wilkinson and Smalls (who collected the guns) drove off in the car and later abandoned it; Turner and Brown, with the money, left in the Triumph, with Allpress driving.

There followed a slightly confused assortment of tube train and cab journeys, before the share-out took place at a maisonette in Bluebird Walk, Chalk Hill Estate, occupied by Bryan Turner's girlfriend, Maria Mercedes Dadd. That – she would later say that Turner had given her £150 after she vacated the premises for the whole of 10 August – was a mistake. Allowing for expenses, the shares came to £17,500 each.

And now we must bid adieu to William Stanley Shervill. Banished from actual participation in the Wembley raid, he threw his lot in with others and, four months later in November 1972, he was stopped in a car which contained a firearm; he and others were charged with conspiracy to rob. The police were unaware that he was a member of the Wembley Mob at that time, and on 26 September 1973 he appeared at the Old Bailey, pleaded guilty and was sentenced to six years' imprisonment.

But for others of the Wembley Mob, there was no let-up. The week following the robbery at Wembley, on 18 August, a Security Express van was ambushed in Totty Street, Bow, East London after a stolen car pulled out and blocked its path. The driver jumped out and, at the same moment, four other masked men got out of a nearby Austin van and smashed the windscreen of the cash-in-transit vehicle with a sledgehammer and poked two sawn-off shotguns through the aperture. They ordered the two custodians into the back of the van, squirted ammonia in their eyes and escaped with £40,760. The van was later found abandoned with £200 inside it, in Bethnal Green; the robbers' share was £6,000 each.

Smalls was not one of the team but he was able to name the robbers involved – however, none of them stood trial.

By that time, he and Bobby King had gone to Spain. Eventually, most of the rest of the team, with the exception of Philip Morris and Bruce Brown, joined them.

Torremolinos was like a second home to them; it was also cheap, sunny and safe, since Spain had no extradition treaty with England. It was a prudent move.

Chapter Seven

# A Most Remarkable Document

When John Short arrived in Torremolinos in 1970 he had sufficient capital to invest in a half-share of the Duke of Wellington public house. Since that cash had possibly come out of his 'whack' from the Ilford Bank Robbery, he also had a ready-made clientele in the shape of other members of that piece of work. So, following the successful robbery at Wembley's Barclays Bank, whilst members of what had initially been known as 'The Crash-Bang Gang' (and would soon be renamed 'The Wembley Mob') sunned themselves, boasted of their good fortune and drank copiously, the police back home in Blighty had got to work.

*　*　*

At that time, serious crimes such as murder, rape or robbery were dealt with on a provincial basis. Therefore, when a high-value robbery occurred – such as the one at Ilford – it was Ilford police station that dealt with the investigation, calling in resources from within that police division. But – as we have seen from Wickstead's investigation – the successes were overshadowed by failures, i.e. the limited number of robbers who were caught and convicted and the paucity of recovered cash. Additionally, because so many police stations were involved with their individual investigations, other offences from neighbouring stations were seldom linked; investigating officers were mainly concerned with solving crimes on their own patch.

The Metropolitan Police was split into four areas, and the majority of the police stations hit by these robberies came under the umbrella of No. 2 Area; it was the officer in charge, the Deputy Assistant Commissioner, who got it in the neck from the new Commissioner, Sir Robert Mark GBE, QPM, who demanded swift, positive action. The DAC in question was Trevor Humphrey Williams, who had rejoined the Met in 1946 as Police Constable 675 'J' after completing war service and had climbed the uniform ranks, mainly dealing with administrative and disciplinary matters. No intrepid crime-buster himself, Williams called for reports on all unsolved bank robberies in No. 2 Area (of which there were many) over the previous two years and then also summoned more professional assistants. One was

DAC Bernard 'Bob' Halliday OBE, who like Williams had seen war service, Halliday having served as a member of No. 3 Commando. There the similarity ended, however. Halliday was a detective through and through, who coordinated CID operations throughout the Met. With him he brought his own adviser, Commander Roy Yorke. Like Halliday, Yorke had seen war service and was a career detective; both had served on the Flying Squad and both had been commended many times by the commissioner. A supervisory eye was kept on Detective Inspector Vic Wilding of Wembley police station, who had acquired the services of Detective Sergeant Mick McAdam, both of them Flying Squad veterans, with McAdam having an impressive record of using informants. Whilst forensic evidence and witness statements were being collected, Wilding had search warrants taken out for likely robbers. Two resulted in arrests for matters unconnected with the series of robberies. Undeterred, Wilding swore out more search warrants, and this time, he struck lucky. The suspect, alarmed at being caught for his own peccadilloes, wanted 'outers' and named names. McAdam and other officers' informants offered up the same names. It was the sort of breakthrough that the investigators had been waiting for.

★   ★   ★

Bruce Brown was found, dressed only in his underpants, hiding behind the water tank in the loft of his house in The Crossways, Heston on 30 August. This came as a tremendous shock to his neighbours who, up to then, had regarded Mr Brown as being just as respectable as they were. He ran his own property company involved in buying, renovating and selling houses, and earlier that year, he had been appointed captain of the prestigious Ashford Manor Golf Club.

There was no property in the house to connect him with the robberies, except a Chubb key No. 1703. Brown said that he had found it on his driveway, but when Wilding searched Brown's locker at the golf club he found an envelope with '1703' written on it. Brown later admitted that the key was for a safe at the London Safe Deposit Company, Regent Street, held in the name of 'D. Williams'. Photographs of Brown shown to the staff identified him as Mr Williams, who had visited the company on the day after the Wembley robbery. Procurement of a search warrant revealed that the box contained £14,940, and cashiers from Barclays Bank checked the notes and discovered their markings and initials on several of them. Fibres from a blanket found in one of the getaway cars matched those on Brown's clothing, as did minute fragments of glass and wood splinters from the debris inside Barclays Bank.

McAdam had told him he was making enquiries about the bank robbery at Wembley, and Brown, white-faced and trembling, had told him:

> I knew you were coming to arrest me; my nerve went. It was only a matter of time and I won't be any trouble. I know what you must be thinking but I didn't go into the bank. I only drove the car. I didn't know what they were going to do. I am not a violent man. I could not go into the bank with them. I cannot think straight. I want time to recover.

Later, at the police station, he withdrew his original admissions and refused to reveal the identities of any of his associates, saying:

> I didn't go on the job at all. They would kill me. I wasn't there. I was confused when you first saw me. I wasn't on the job … My life is in ruins, my business is finished, my good name at the golf club and everything.

Although Brown stated that the money in his deposit box came from the bank robbery at Wembley, he claimed another man (whom he refused to name) had handed it to him in an airline bag and he had not counted the contents.

Now the investigators knew that they were on the right track, and DAC Williams felt sufficiently emboldened to ask for more troops. He got them.

Much of Detective Chief Superintendent Jim Marshall's service had been spent on the Flying Squad and Regional Crime Squad; within a year of being commended by a judge at the Old Bailey, the Director of Public Prosecutions and the commissioner for the arrest and conviction of a gang of active armed robbers, he arrested a robber armed with a sawn-off shotgun, for which he was awarded a British Empire Medal for gallantry. A similar recipient of the BEM, for arresting a prison escapee armed with a rifle, was Detective Chief Inspector Alex Eist, plus Detective Chief Inspector Reg Dixon, a fearless veteran of the Flying Squad and Regional Crime Squad who had carried out undercover work. They, together with Detective Inspector Wilding, would form the nucleus of what would be known as the Wembley Bank Robbery Squad.

It was discovered that Bryan Turner – currently in Spain – also had a box at the London Safe Deposit Company in the name of 'Bryan James'. Like Brown, Turner had first started using the company in February 1970, following the robbery at Barclays Bank, Ilford. Once it was ascertained that Turner had last visited the company six days after the Wembley robbery, the box was found to contain £10,800 in cash, and some of the notes had the cashiers' initials on them, as well as the bank's stamp.

Door-to-door enquiries, following the discovery of the stolen red Triumph, abandoned on the Chalk Hill Estate, led detectives to the door of Maria Mercedes Dadd who, they were informed, had received a number of male visitors around the time of the Wembley robbery. Even more interesting was that a photograph of Brian Turner revealed that he had been one of the callers. A key, which Miss Dadd had tried to conceal, fitted a cupboard containing a Security Express cash bag, a GPO bag, binoculars, a jemmy, elastic bands of the sort used by bank cashiers and a radio tuned to a police frequency. She admitted that Bryan Turner had his own front door key and that she was his mistress; she also shared her favours with Tony Edlin.

'I've been used', said Miss Dadd, 'and I want to help you all I can.'

However, Turner had telephoned her, two days after the robbery, and when the £150 promised for her absence, which had been placed in a drawer, was identified as part proceeds of the robbery, she was later sentenced to twelve months' imprisonment.

Two weeks after the Wembley robbery, Alexander Weston purchased a car which cost £1,350; he told police he was unable to remember the provenance of the cash. He was acquitted of obstructing justice by going to Spain to inform Turner of the way in which the police investigation was going, but for receiving and conspiracy to receive stolen money, he would later receive a five-year sentence.

An associate of Turner's who had just returned from Spain was visited at his home in Bow Street, Islington. This was a builder named Dennis Leonard 'Fred' Haig, who denied being a go-between in a diamond deal for Turner and someone simply known as 'Miguel' in Spain. That was probably because the other party involved in the transaction with Turner was a member of the notorious Australian Shoplifting Gang, at that time taking their ease on the Costa del Sol. However, Turner was friendly with Richard and Elisa Walton ('Richard Walton' was the *nom de guerre* of John Short, Walton being his wife's maiden name), who ran the Duke of Wellington Bar in Torremolinos; indeed, he had been photographed holding the baby at the christening of the Waltons' son, and the picture was widely circulated in the press, with references to Turner as 'The Godfather'. Haig admitted that Turner had given him a cheque for £3,000 to pay into an external account which the Waltons had in the Bank of Nova Scotia in London; this was to allow money to be drawn in Spain.

However, he was also in possession of a briefcase which Turner had asked to retrieve from his father-in-law's house and mind for him, telling him it contained letters which would cause embarrassment, should his wife see them. When it was opened, the briefcase was found to contain a Colt .45 and two sawn-off shotguns. Since the approximate weight of those three items amounted to 15lbs, Mr Haig must have thought the briefcase contained a considerable amount of correspondence.

Fred Haig was accused of receiving £300 from Turner, knowing it to have been stolen; he was acquitted.

However, Turner was safe and sound in Spain, and although several of the gang members were brought in and questioned, they gave nothing away; because nothing of an incriminating nature was found, they were released. On 27 November, Brown, Dadd, Haig and Weston were committed from Harrow Magistrates' Court to the Old Bailey to stand their trial. But that was all. Another twenty villains' addresses were turned over by the investigating team, without success. It seemed the trail had gone cold. There were rumblings from the fifth floor at the Yard. Could this additional expense in manpower continue to be justified? Could those officers be profitably used elsewhere?

But then, someone remembered a name which had kept on cropping up.

Bertie Smalls.

★   ★   ★

Smalls now recounts what had happened in the interim period:

I heard from a London contact that I was wanted for the Wembley job and I didn't know how I'd gotten connected with that. But this geezer wheels off all the names so I know it's right. I knew the police had found Brucie Brown's deed box with 15 grand in it, in stolen notes, and Bryan Turner's, with 10 grand in his, and I knew the game was up. Well, we'd been doing pretty nearly a bank a week for two years and it couldn't last forever. I was living at the time in this luxury apartment block called Los Conchos in Torremolinos. But more of the firm were arriving there, all the time. I was going down to the pool at breakfast and seeing twenty faces of gangsters I knew. So I decided to blow. Even the Australian Shoplifting Mob were staying there. I took another villa and I was lying in bed one morning when the wife of one of the boys rings and says, 'The Yard are here.' I say, 'Where's the boys?' and she says, 'They've all legged it and left me', which gave me the right hump.

Smalls decided to return to Blighty but was in no hurry to do so. With a companion, he travelled to Madrid, San Sebastian, then Paris, blowing a small fortune in nightclubs, before arriving in St Malo, Jersey. They now had no need of their false passports, so they disposed of them and embarked to Weymouth. There, Smalls commenced a 166-mile journey north, where he would find sanctuary.

Or so he thought.

★ ★ ★

By 22 December 1972 the police knew that both Smalls and Turner had fled to Spain; but had Smalls returned? DI Wilding and Woman Detective Sergeant Judith Andrews paid a visit to Smalls' house at Addington Road, Selsdon. To their astonishment, the door was opened not by Diane Smalls but by Stella Robertson, the Smalls' au pair, who had mysteriously disappeared following the trial in Hampshire at which Don Barrett had received twelve years' imprisonment.

She admitted that Smalls was indeed back in England; there were two telephone callbox numbers he rang, twice a day, to keep updated about any enquiries made by the police, and he was living in a house in Northamptonshire. Although she did not know the exact address, she was willing to take them there. Late that night, the girl pointed out 49 Dingle Road, Rushden as being Smalls' bolthole; the premises belonged to his younger brother, Kelvin. At 5.30 the following morning, following a night's heavy drinking, a dazed, paunchy Bertie Smalls, clad only in his underpants, answered a knock on the door only to be swept backwards by Wilding, Detective Sergeant Michael James, Detective Constable Don Manley and a tsunami of detectives. Gasping with shock and stating that his name was Woods – the same alias he had used when staying at the hotel at Bournemouth, the night before the raid on Lloyds Bank – he suddenly came to the conclusion that he, Derek Creighton Smalls, was well and truly nicked.

Not that during the following three days of interviews he gave much away. But once he was charged and remanded, the evidence started building up, and a series of identification parades were held at Brixton Prison.

Brian Greenan – known widely as 'BGee' – a temporary detective constable working on a divisional crime squad on the day of the Wembley bank raid, was one of the first officers at the scene; he was co-opted onto the investigation squad and stayed with the enquiry for 2½ years. On the matter of the identification parades, he now takes up the tale:

Bertie had cleverly arranged for look-alike inmates to be brought in from other prisons so as to confuse any witnesses – Bertie keep changing position on the line-up and was feeling pretty confident as each witness failed to identify him – and it worked until the very last female witness was brought out into the prison yard to inspect the line of criminals. She had been a clerk working at Ralli Brothers Bank in Hatton Garden during the armed robbery some four years previously in March 1969. She was briefed by the police inspector running the ID Parade and then invited to walk along the line of thugs and if she recognised the man, to point him out.

She said, 'I don't need to walk along the line' and instead walked straight across the yard up to Bertie Smalls and pointed to him, saying, 'I would know those eyes anywhere.'

Bertie had piercing blue eyes, which the ladies loved. I watched as Bertie virtually collapsed at the lady's positive identification. He knew the game was up. He was held on remand and when he eventually agreed to turn Queen's Evidence, he said it was because none of the other blaggers had made any effort to help him while he was banged up.

Additionally, he was positively identified as the man seen talking to the robbers in a getaway car at Palmers Green. That, and other evidence, prompted his solicitors from Messrs Steggles Palmer to suggest that the police were preparing a compelling case against him.

As Smalls would later say: 'Then, they take me to Brixton nick on remand. I'm thinking now, a deal might be the best thing. I see they've got me double-strong and it might be twenty or twenty-five years and there is no way I can take that.'

If that were to be the case, Smalls, now thirty-six, could expect, even with parole, not to be released until he was in his fifties. Bold action was needed; now, with his committal to the Old Bailey looming on 3 April, matters became more urgent. Smalls stated that he would be prepared to give evidence against every criminal with whom he had worked, on condition that no action would be taken against him, his wife and brother – and that he would walk free.

It was an astonishing offer, of a kind that had never been broached before. Yes, in the past, criminals had turned Queen's Evidence, by pleading guilty and giving evidence against their co-defendants in the expectation of a shorter sentence; but nobody had ever met a criminal who would do that and expect to walk free.

Jim Marshall was initially against the plan, and so was Sir Norman Skelhorn, the Director of Public Prosecutions (DPP). But there seemed little alternative; if Smalls came up to proof, it would be an expedient way – and in the public interest – of rounding up several dozen of London's top criminals. On 2 April 1973, a contract was drawn up between Smalls' solicitors and the DPP in the following terms:

I refer to the matters discussed at two meetings at this office on 14 & 21 March 1973 in this case in which you act for the two above-named defendants, the first of whom, Derek Creighton Smalls, has expressed his wish to give evidence for the Crown, subject to certain conditions as follows:

1. The Director of Public Prosecutions will not offer, nor cause, permit or authorise the offering of any evidence upon a criminal charge in respect of any offence other than homicide which may have been committed by Smalls and which he may disclose in any future statement he makes to the police within the terms of this letter.
2. Smalls will make to Commander Roy Yorke of No. 2 District Headquarters, Portman Square, London W1 or his designated officer(s) and in the presence of representatives of Messrs Steggles Palmer a statement relating to the whole of his, Smalls, criminal activities and enterprises and those of any associates and all other information within his own knowledge relating to his own criminal activities and enterprises and those of any other person or persons.
3. On 3 April 1973 Smalls shall be remanded upon the charges already preferred against him to the police cells at Wembley police station (provided the court agrees but in this respect both parties shall use their best endeavours to persuade the court to grant bail) pending his committal for trial on 6 April 1973.
4. In that period Smalls will make the statement referred to above. This statement will not be used against Smalls or his common-law wife Diana Smalls in any proceedings that have or may be taken against them, but may be used in furtherance of any criminal proceedings against the persons whose names are revealed therein.
5. Within the period between 3 April 1973 and Smalls' committal for trial the information contained in the statement will be assessed by the police to ascertain whether it is of sufficient evidential value and Messrs Steggles Palmer will be informed at the earliest opportunity

whether or not it is intended to use the statement in proceedings against any other person or persons.

6. If the information disclosed in the statement is not considered by the police to be of sufficient evidential value to the police and it is decided not to make use of it in criminal proceedings, the same shall be kept in conditions of secrecy on Metropolitan Police files and not used for any purpose and no mention will be made of it by the Director of Public Prosecutions or the police in the proceedings against Smalls, which will continue nor shall any mention be made of any discussions between Messrs Steggles Palmer and the Director of Public Prosecutions and the police with a view to Smalls giving evidence for the Crown but this shall not relate to statements made by Smalls to the police when he was being interrogated by the police subsequent to his arrest.

7. If the statement made by Smalls discloses information of evidential value and is of genuine and substantial assistance to the police in the investigation of various crimes and if Smalls is prepared to give evidence for the Crown when so required.

(a) Both parties shall use their best endeavours to persuade the court to grant bail at the committal proceedings, or upon any subsequent application for bail.

(b) Should bail be granted, Small shall reside at such place or places as Commander Yorke shall specify.

(c) No evidence will be offered against Smalls and his brother upon the charges for which they may be committed for trial by Harrow Magistrates' Court on 6 April 1973 and at the Central Criminal Court the Judge will be invited to discharge both him and his brother Kelvin John Smalls.

(d) The police will take all necessary steps for the safety of Smalls and his wife and children and he and his wife and children will be removed to a secret place and there guarded by not less than two police officers.

(e) Upon termination of the evidence which he may be required to give (until which time the safe custody provisions referred to above will apply) Smalls and his wife and children shall be taken to a place selected by him in conditions of secrecy escorted by police officers.

8. Mrs Smalls and her children shall on 3 April 1973 be removed to a place of safety in manner to be agreed by Messrs Steggles Palmer.
9. Should Smalls abscond or refuse to give or refrain from giving evidence to the best of his ability in accordance with his statement the conditions set out in this letter shall have no effect.

The next day, at Harrow Magistrates' Court, a remand was sought and granted. Events then moved very quickly. The prison authorities were told that Smalls was to be questioned regarding further matters, and he was transferred to a nondescript van and taken to Wembley police station. At the same time, police officers supervised Diane Smalls packing her and the children's belongings, before they were taken to a secret location where, for the foreseeable future, they would be protected round the clock by armed officers.

Detective Sergeant Terry O'Regan had now served thirty-three years with the police but he had deliberately put off his retirement for the sake of this case. That afternoon, he prepared a statement the like of which he had never written before. It commenced:

I, Derek Creighton Smalls make this statement in the knowledge of the contents of a letter having been sent by the Director of Public Prosecutions to my solicitors dated 2nd April 1973. I also make this statement on the basis that it will not be used in evidence against me on any criminal trial that I may face.

And then it began. As Bertie Smalls later (slightly inaccurately) described it:

The first time we were at it from ten in the morning until nearly midnight and there's a bloke writing it all down and I can't eat nothing because my stomach is churning and all I have is cups of coffee.

The 29-page statement concluded:

I am willing to give this statement in evidence. I have read it and it is true. (Signed) D. Smalls.
    Statement taken by Det. Insp. Wilding, written by Det. Sgt. O'Regan.
    (Signed) D. Smalls. Signatures witnessed by both officers. (Signed) T. O'Regan D.S.'Q'

I have the statement in front of me as I write. It is, I assure you, a most remarkable document.

# Part II

# Supergrass

# Chapter Eight

# Round-up

In early 1973, a Swedish company had opened fifty-nine Esso Motor Hotels worldwide, eight of which were in the United Kingdom. It was in a palatial suite of the Wembley branch of this hotel chain that the Smalls family had settled, guarded by two armed (and very tough) police officers and a policewoman, but time, now, was of the essence. The prison authorities had been given a half-truth – that Smalls was being questioned regarding other robberies – but of course, they were unaware that he would no longer be remanded in prison custody. If he were not returned to Brixton Prison soon, questions would be raised by the other inmates. Before a particularly toxic cat was let out of the bag, a plan had to be made for all of the prominent players to be rounded up and their premises searched, simultaneously.

The head of the operation, Jim Marshall, had gone on holiday, and the round-up could certainly not be delayed until his return. Therefore, DAC Ernie Bond OBE, QPM, the much-admired operational head of the CID, deputed Detective Chief Superintendent Jack Slipper of the Flying Squad to head the operation. It was a monumental task, but not for someone of Slipper's calibre who had spent practically all of his CID career with the Flying Squad, where he had come to prominence investigating the murders of the crew of the 'Q' Car 'Foxtrot One-One', as well as the Great Train Robbery.

Overnight, he was seconded to the Wembley Bank Robbery enquiry and, just as quickly, he made plans. Smalls had provided a blueprint of those involved; now, on the evening of 5 April, Slipper provided pertinent segments of his statements to eleven detective inspectors, each of whom had been allocated a prisoner, and briefed them extensively. Each inspector would select his own team of seven or eight officers to accompany him; in all, 120 officers, drawn from the Flying Squad and Regional Crime Squad, would be in position at Wembley at 4.30 on the morning of 6 April. The prisoners would then be taken to eleven different police stations, in order to prevent any conversation between them.

It would not happen today. With the advent, twelve years after these events, of the Police and Criminal Evidence Act and the Crown Prosecution Service – the CPS, dubbed 'Couldn't Prosecute

Satan' – which brought a snail's pace to Criminal Justice, it *could* not happen today.

* * *

The addresses were visited at approximately 6 o'clock on the morning of 6 April, the premises were searched, and the arrested prisoners were taken to a variety of police stations. Not every one of the twenty-two people whose names Smalls had given was arrested at that time, but the detectives now had to deal with the twenty-one robberies which had been committed over a period of almost four years and netted the gang £1,288,031. But in addition, there were other offences – conspiracies, receiving stolen goods, stealing cars, possessing firearms – and the need to locate and seize stolen cash.

It is therefore slightly astonishing that four days later, on 10 April, the following persons appeared at Harrow Magistrates' Court charged with conspiracy: Philip Morris, Thomas French, James Marsden, Daniel Allpress, James Wilkinson, Jutta Wilkinson, William Reynolds, Anthony Holt, Michael Salmon and Robert King.

In addition, Morris, French, James Wilkinson, Marsden, Allpress and Holt were charged with the Wembley Bank robbery.

James Joseph Marsden had convictions for false pretences, pavilion-breaking and possessing housebreaking implements as well as an offensive weapon and cannabis. He would later be acquitted of involvement in the Barclays Bank robbery at Wembley and, although Jimmy Wilkinson was convicted of that offence and sentenced to sixteen years' imprisonment, in March 1975 the Court of Appeal quashed that conviction, mainly on the grounds of lack of corroboration to Smalls' evidence. His wife, Jutta Wilkinson, was also acquitted of receiving £12,645 after no evidence was offered against her.

Amongst those missing was Anthony Edlin; however, on 28 June he was unceremoniously dragged from his bed in a fifth-floor apartment at Whittingehame Court, Glasgow (where he was known as Mr Weaver) by Flying Squad officers, who brought him back to Wembley, where he was charged with the robberies carried out at the National Provincial Bank, Brighton, Ralli Brothers, Midland Bank, Willesden, the Allied Irish Bank, Kilburn and the Security Express robbery, Bow. He was just in time to join the others in the dock at Harrow Magistrates' Court, where there were new attendees: William Sherville, Leonard Walter Jones and David Christopher Delaney.

Delaney has been mentioned several times before; now he can be introduced more fully. Known to the police since the age of fourteen, Delaney was committed to the Old Bailey in 1968 charged with robbing a man of £70 whilst armed with an offensive weapon, and with possessing a Mauser pistol, an MAB pistol, a Lee Enfield rifle and fifteen rounds of ammunition. Three years later, together with James Wilkinson, he was acquitted of conspiracy to rob Barclays Bank at Boreham Wood of £29,000 (although he was sentenced to eight months' imprisonment for receiving stolen clothing).

As we already know, during the lead-up to the Barclays Bank robbery at Wembley, Delaney and Billy Shervill had been detailed to obtain getaway cars, one of which was the Jaguar with the badly defective clutch, and the raid had to be abandoned. They were part of Jimmy Wilkinson's team, who decided, as Smalls later said, that 'They were not the right material for the job.' They were, however, the right material for the conspiracy, and Delaney went down for twelve years and Shervill for fourteen.

Bertie Smalls' evidence had yet to be tested in court, but members of the Wembley Mob had no delusions as to how compelling it might be. Held on remand at Brixton Prison, on 30 May 1973 they decided to swing the odds in their favour. Two rented Ford Escorts were left in Clarence Crescent – within walking (or running) distance of the prison – their ignition keys in place, their tanks full of petrol. A white Ford Transit rent-a-van was left in Lytham Road, close to the rear gates of the prison, and at 10 o'clock, a Lambeth District dustcart with a hydraulic tipper trundled in through the rear gates and started collecting the prison's accumulated rubbish.

At 10.50am, a warder opened a cupboard door, to be confronted by three prisoners, and was held at what he thought to be gunpoint by Micky Salmon; in fact, the weapon was fashioned out of soap, blackened with boot polish and with silver paper added, but it was sufficiently realistic for the warder to hand over his keys to David Martin. A bisexual transvestite, Martin – he liked to be referred to as 'Davina Martyn' – was not a member of the gang but he was included in the escape because he was an expert locksmith who had memorised the warder's keys and knew exactly which key fitted which lock.

Other prisoners took advantage of this lapse of security, and seventeen of them spilled out into the compound, including Salmon, Danny Allpress, Bruce Brown, Jimmy Jeffrey and Philip Morris.

It was Allpress who dragged the driver, Mr Stokoe, out of the cab of the dustcart, and as he turned the dustcart around, other prisoners leapt aboard, using the shovels and brooms to attack the warders in the compound. Allpress put his foot down, drove the dustcart at the prison's rear gates and smashed straight through. The warders who had assembled in Lytham Road would certainly have been either killed or seriously injured, had it not been for the truck's hydraulic arms which were in the 'raised' position and jammed into the overhead frame of the gates. Eleven of the prisoners stumbled out of the truck and fought a running battle with the warders; Bruce Brown and four others got into the waiting Ford Transit, started the ignition and put it into gear but neglected to release the handbrake. This gave the warders time to smash the Transit's windscreen with their truncheons, and as the five men tumbled out of the van, Brown threatened a warder with a club. He was smartly coshed by the warder, resulting in a fractured skull, whereupon the other four lost heart and were rounded up. Meanwhile, Allpress and others got into a van; a prison officer tried to grab the ignition keys through a window, but Allpress drove at him before being pulled from the vehicle.

The fighting continued in the compound until four off-duty dog handlers and their charges, attracted by the commotion, rushed in, and within a remarkably short space of time the snapping, snarling dogs ensured that order was restored. David Martin was one of several prisoners who escaped into the street, hi-jacked a car in Lyon Road, and pulled out the driver, a Mr Talbot, but a prison officer broke the windscreen with his truncheon. After abandoning the car, Martin hailed a taxi, but he was arrested. Two other prisoners got clean away, neither of them members of the Wembley Mob.

At the Old Bailey in October 1974, the escape was dealt with by the Recorder of London, Sir Carl Aarvold, who said, 'This was a mass enterprise prepared with great skill, worthy of a better cause.'

Allpress, Salmon, Brown, Morris and James William Jeffrey were all sentenced to an additional twelve months' imprisonment, as was David Martin. There were others: Brian Anthony Richardson – nothing to do with the Wembley Mob – who was serving an eight-year sentence for robbery, received an additional nine months' imprisonment. Additionally, Lionel Thomas Herbert Jeffrey, who had been charged by Wickstead with the Ilford Bank Robbery in 1970 and had been acquitted on the directions of the judge, was sentenced to a further twelve months. Following his acquittal, he had been sentenced to ten years' imprisonment for conspiracy to rob.

Although his cell had been unlocked, there was one man who did not take advantage of the escape. He – a highly active armed robber named George Henry Ince – remained seated in his cell, awaiting trial on a £400,000 silver bullion hi-jacking. More about Mr Ince later.

★   ★   ★

The correct name for someone such as Smalls was 'Resident Informant'. Other countries had their own descriptions: the Dutch referred to them as *Kroongetuige* and the Germans as *Kronzeuge*. They were known in France was *Repenti* and initially referred to in Italy as *Collaboratore della Giustizia*, then later as *Peniti*. However, in England, they were colloquially known as Supergrasses.

There will always be officers – in common with those who say they knew the Great Train Robbery was going to occur – who will authoritatively state that they ran the first supergrass, before Bertie Smalls. They did not.

My chum, the late Leonard 'Nipper' Read QPM, who smashed the Kray empire, stated that the Krays' accountant, Leslie James Payne – 'Payne the Brain' – was the first supergrass. That statement has elements of truth in it but it is not wholly accurate.

When Payne discovered that he was on Ronnie Kray's 'Death List', he agreed to make a statement outlining all of his dodgy deals with the twins. It was 146 pages long, and in return, Nipper promised to do his best to persuade the Director of Public Prosecutions not to prosecute Payne; what is more, he succeeded.

But when evidence started trickling in regarding the murders of George Cornell, Jack 'The Hat' McVitie and Frank 'The Mad Axeman' Mitchell, it was these matters that took precedence, and after a series of trials at the Old Bailey, the twins were found guilty of murder and were sentenced to life imprisonment, with a recommendation that they each serve thirty years.

Although there were further indictments alleging fraudulent transactions, these were never pursued since, if the twins were found guilty, not one day would be added to their 30-year sentences; therefore, these charges were allowed to remain on the file.

And this is why Payne did not take the stand in the witness box at the Old Bailey to give evidence. Bertie Smalls did.

Therefore, it was arguably as the first supergrass that Smalls appeared at the Old Bailey. What happened next is described by Brian Greenan:

When Bertie was arraigned at the Old Bailey, Mick Jones and I, who were both armed, took him in, through the Judges' entrance and up in a lift to a court where the charges were read out to him. No plea was taken and it was directed that all the charges should remain 'on the file' – which meant they were not to be proceeded with without leave of the court or the Court of Appeal (Criminal Division). He was effectively a free man, albeit under 24-hour police protection, and this was the start of the witness protection system as we know it, today.

He had 24-hour protection in a safe house in Bushey, Herts and whenever he left the house it was only when his two special protection officers, both armed, were with him, Detective Sergeant Mick Jones and Detective Constable Don Manley, both Regional Crime Squad officers, both hard men, both rugby players, and Manley an ex-Para.  They worked in 12-hour shifts, 24 hours a day, 365 days a year. Whenever one of them was unavailable, then I would be asked to be the second protection officer because I was an authorised firearms man from my uniform days standing outside Downing Street.

Now, Smalls was set to give evidence against the twenty-three men and two women who crowded into the specially converted gymnasium behind Wembley police station. When the trial got underway, in July 1973, a spoof 'Press Release' was issued, which read:

Mr Bert Smalls, the famous solo singer who recently broke away from the Home Counties Choral Society, is about to give up the singing side of his career. Apparently, Mr Smalls feels that the singing may affect his throat. On Wednesday, Mr Smalls refused to comment. He said, 'My lips are sealed.'

Predictably, the defendants (with the exception of the two women) who had been charged with robberies, knowing they would never be admitted to bail, shouted obscenities at the Magistrates and threats at Smalls.

'You grass!' yelled Don Barrett, and as Smalls later said, 'This is a bloke who grassed on me a few years earlier, so I let him have a mouthful back.'

Danny Allpress derisively demanded to know 'Who was going to have Slack Alice?" while Smalls was away.

The answer was nobody, because Bertie wasn't going to go away; and what was more, his evidence was sufficient for all of them to be committed to the Old Bailey.

But before those trials got underway, there was one other matter in which Smalls had to provide evidence, although not for the prosecution but for the defence.

This was in the case of Arthur John Frederick Saunders, who had been convicted of the Barclays bank robbery at Ilford in 1970 and sentenced to fifteen years' imprisonment. Following his arrest, some pretty convincing evidence was found and some fairly incriminating statements had been recorded, as mentioned in Chapter One of this book. His appeal in December 1971 had been dismissed; however, Smalls was able to identify everyone involved in that raid and was able to say, quite definitely, that Saunders was not amongst them.

Officers from Wembley saw Detective Sergeant Henry Stevens GC of the Flying Squad, the officer responsible for recording those semi-admissions, and told him that he would have to say that they had never occurred, a statement which provoked a scoffing, 'Oh, fuck off!' Stevens was right to repudiate their suggestion, because Saunders had indeed made those statements.

The Court of Appeal, sitting on 11 October 1973, having been furnished with a sworn statement by Smalls, the previous day, quashed Saunders' conviction, with the Lord Chief Justice saying:

> We have, as I say, approached this question with caution, because the evidence of accomplices can be as dangerous when used for the defence as it can when used for the Crown and we are not unmindful of the fact that it sometimes occurs when criminals are together in prison that they put their heads together and arrange to make statements with a view to exculpating one of them. We do look at evidence of accomplices or alleged accomplices with considerable caution in this context, as in others.

The Crown prosecutor had told the court that although Saunders had not positively admitted his involvement in the robbery, 'There was a notable absence of any positive denial' and, as one of those officers mentioned to me, some forty years after the event, at the time of his arrest and interview Saunders had been drinking.

'It was not so much that the prosecution had a strong case', added the Crown prosecutor, 'but that Saunders' alibi witnesses had let him down, making the case against him stronger.'

Quashing the conviction, the Lord Chief Justice said:

> The appellant had been drinking appreciably before his arrest, and although a doctor brought in by the police to examine him described him as not in any sense incapable by drink, the court thinks that some of the slightly jocular answers which were included in that conversation do have something of the stamp of a man who had had some drink and whose responsibility for the precise language which he used might have been affected by that drink.

Saunders tottered out of the court a free man, the inference from the Court of Appeal being that his incarceration had been his own silly fault.

Although Saunders was entirely innocent of the Ilford bank robbery, fifty is not a good age to start armed robbery as a profession.

In 1986, he and other gentlemen in the autumn of their years were kept under observation by the Flying Squad, who arrested them in the act of an attempted armed robbery in London's Baker Street.

This time, the convictions stood, and Saunders, once more, was sentenced to fifteen years' imprisonment.

## Chapter Nine

# The First of the Trials

Receiving massive newspaper coverage after being photographed holding the Waltons' baby at the infant's christening, with references to 'The Godfather' and 'Mr Big', Bryan Turner kept away from Torremolinos. His wife, disenchanted with him following another adulterous affair, had returned to England and decided that she would sue the police for the return of the two Mercedes, valued at £7,000 at least, which they had snatched from the driveway of her Radlett home.

It was about this time that Richard Walton, aka Mr Frankson, aka John Short, owner of The Duke of Wellington, also decided to vacate Torremolinos, leaving a weeping 29-year-old Elisa holding the baby. More of Mr Short later – in fact, quite a bit later.

By now, Turner, using the alias 'Barry Thomas', had taken a rented villa in the town of Palo, near Malaga. It was in Malaga that he frequented the El Candado Country Club, where he partnered at bridge a very respectable middle-aged English lady, 54-year-old Mrs Jean Mathers, who soon decided that the thick gold bracelet and diamond ring that her partner was wearing did not accord with the upright persona he was attempting to portray. She identified 'Mr Thomas' from a newspaper article about 'The Wembley Mob', telephoned Scotland Yard, and Flying Squad Detective Inspector Jack Keane, who happened to be in Spain on an unrelated matter, was told to make Turner's acquaintance, which he did on the evening of 23 April 1973. As Turner entered the Country Club in company with a young lady, Jack Keane and some Spanish police officers were on hand to deprive Mrs Mathers of her bridge partner, for ever. Mrs Mathers thereafter wondered if the reward for his capture would be sufficient to provide her and her husband with a holiday back in England.

Just £3,500 was found at Turner's rented villa, as well as a forged Australian passport, and he was detained in Malaga prison. His wife arrived in Malaga on the morning of 28 April, whereupon she provided journalists from *The People* (who referred to her as 'Rose' instead of 'Eileen') with intimate details of their life together as well as her estranged husband's faithlessness:

> He can't resist a pretty girl. Never could. It's been his trouble for years. On the run? Sure he was – from me. All the time the police have been searching for him, he has been having the time of his life, right under their noses … I believe in his innocence and will help him fight to prove it … He certainly picked the right place for the birds … knowing Bryan, I would have been amazed if he hadn't been. But as for a bank robber – crazy. He is certainly a big man, but gentle with it. He wouldn't hurt a fly.

At this point, readers – already acquainted with Turner's violent, larcenous activities – might be excused if, after reading that last sentence, a look of jaw-dropping incredulity crossed their faces.

There in jail Turner stayed for three months, while extradition proceedings were underway to return him to England. In July, three judges from the Palace of Justice approved the request, and Turner was extradited the following day.

'I would give anything to be going the other way', remarked Turner as, together with Jim Marshall and Alex Eist, he ascended the steps of the London-bound aircraft, adding as he did so, 'Smalls is in the clear and he has done ten times the work I have.'

When Turner appeared at the Magistrates' Court, his solicitor Mr Anthony Blok told the court:

> It is on Smalls' evidence and his evidence alone on which you are asked to commit Mr Turner for trial on three charges of robbery. The police have made a desperate and somewhat pathetic attempt to cover up a grave error. They arrested Mr Turner and were then faced with charging him with offences which would indicate they were right in making the allegations in the first place.

It did Turner no good; he was committed for trial. And thirty-six years later, so was Mr Blok, when at Croydon Crown Court, at the age of seventy-two, he was sentenced to four years' imprisonment on three counts of money laundering, perjury and perverting the course of public justice.

★   ★   ★

The trial commenced at the Old Bailey on 11 January 1974, but the Judge, Mr Justice Eveleigh – he would later go on to preside over the trial of John Stonehouse MP – decided, quite properly, that due to the number of defendants (twenty-six) and the complexity of the charges in an indictment containing forty-nine counts, the trial should be split into three, since these charges would be disputed.

There were three exceptions to the disputation rule. Philip Morris pleaded guilty to the manslaughter of the Unigate milkman, shot dead during a robbery, and was sentenced to seventeen years' imprisonment; he also pleaded guilty to the Wembley bank robbery and received a concurrent 20-year sentence. Tom French, the taxi driver, pleaded guilty to three robberies (including Wembley) and was sentenced to concurrent terms of nine years' imprisonment. The third was Alan Jesse Davis, the former Security Express guard who was the 'inside man' on the Security Express van at Totty Street when £40,760 was stolen. He pleaded guilty to robbery and was sentenced to ten years.

The first trial got underway in No. 2 court on 5 February after fifty jurors were challenged by the defence; Bryan Turner was one of the defendants who made the maximum of seven challenges, without cause.

As the objections mounted and reached forty-six, the court administrator, Mr Leslie Boyd, worriedly told the defendants, 'I don't want to influence anyone but I have only four cards left in the box!'

With an all-male jury sworn in, it was decided to deal with the most prominent offences first. There were seven cases of robbery to consider – this included the Wembley bank robbery – as well as conspiracies to rob. The opening speech by the prosecution took six and a half days and, dealing with James Wilkinson, John Marriage QC stated that nineteen days after the Wembley bank robbery, Wilkinson had been interviewed, told police he was elsewhere on the day of the robbery and had witnesses to prove it. There the matter rested.

However, after Smalls had made statements to the police on 3, 4 and 5 April 1973, Wilkinson and his wife were arrested at their home at Brighton Court, W13, at six o'clock on the morning of 6 April.

Mrs Jutta Wilkinson had been charged with dishonestly receiving £12,645, as well as a mink coat. To these charges she had pleaded not guilty and had told the police that the money had been won by her husband on the horses.

Wilkinson, stated Mr Marriage, had denied any involvement with robberies, stolen money or firearms, and also initially denied knowing Bertie Smalls; but when he was told that Smalls had stated that Wilkinson had been implicated in four robberies, he admitted to knowing him, saying, 'I want time to think. That bastard has stitched me right up.'

Interviewed a second time, Wilkinson had asked Detective Inspector Wilding, 'Can we do a trade?'

He wanted to make a deal that he would get no more than ten years for a series of robberies and offered to provide the names of two other people who had been involved in other robberies, and the murder of a milkman at the Ewell Road milk depot. When this offer was rejected, said Mr Marriage, he offered a bribe of 'ten grand or even twenty grand'. That, too, was vetoed, and then Mr Marriage stated that Wilkinson promised that he would cause 'the biggest sensation the country had ever known'.

He stated that he had six tapes involving Wilding, his colleagues Detective Chief Superintendent Marshall and Detective Sergeant Treen, and that those tapes would show that these three police officers had 'put me up for those jobs'.

In response to this, said Mr Marriage, Wilding had told Wilkinson not to make threats and that the only deal he would make would be for Wilkinson to give a full statement of what he had done – and that the police would offer nothing in return.

With all of the defendants pleading not guilty, it appeared that this would be an acrimonious trial, especially after DI Wilding started giving evidence, which prompted Wilkinson to shout from the dock, 'I will swear to Almighty God, you're a stinking liar!'

Cross-examined, Smalls stated that the series of robberies had made him at least £100,000 richer, but now he was left with 'a couple of hundred quid'. Of his share of the Ilford bank robbery, which had 'been hidden in different places', there was nothing left, and his £17,500 'whack' from the Wembley bank robbery had been hidden in a field off the Wellingborough Road, Northamptonshire. A Lotus sports car, obtained with stolen money, had been seized by police, and he had paid for a bungalow, in his wife's name, in Lincolnshire.

Smalls' cross-examination was fiercely intensified and it was put to him, in no uncertain terms, that he had been responsible for murders – offences (together with treason and piracy) which his immunity from prosecution did not cover. One such murder related to a robbery in which Smalls admitted he had been involved, in Woodford in 1965.

'I left London and kept out of the way for a few months', Smalls replied, when this was put to him. 'When I came back, I was told that someone involved in that had been "done in".'

When it was suggested that the owner of a van used in that robbery had been strangled by Smalls, James Wilkinson was prompted to shout from the dock, 'By you, in Ireland!'

It was also put to Smalls that during a raid on a bank in Cornhill, in the City of London, a security guard had been killed by a blow to the throat and that Smalls had been responsible; he replied that he had read about it in the newspapers but had not been involved in the attack.

Giving evidence, Brown stated that on the morning of the Wembley bank robbery he was recovering from a hangover, had breakfasted on toast and Alka-Seltzer before visiting his new house and the golf club.

Turner complained that the press had engaged in 'sensational and flagrant slander' about him before coming to trial and that in any event, on the morning of the robbery, he had been paying his shop rates in Willesden.

On the morning of the Wembley robbery, Wilkinson told the jury, he was having coffee with friends, and when the robbery occurred at the National Westminster Bank in Palmer's Green in 1972, he was in a pub celebrating his wife's birthday. In his defence, he stated that he had bribed police officers and received stolen goods – this was to establish that he had, in the past, fallen by the wayside – but when it came to carrying out armed robberies, no, definitely not. It was a clever ploy that sometimes works.

William Reynolds stated that Smalls had implicated him in some of the robberies because 'Smalls has every reason to lie and I have not.'

Danny Allpress denied Smalls' testimony, saying that it was Smalls himself who was 'The Boss' and all he (Allpress) had done was to 'ring a few motors for him'. This was a rather surprising admission, since these were peccadilloes of which Smalls had also accused him. His money had come from being a mechanic and a racing driver, he said, and at the time of his arrest he admitted that he was looking to purchase a house in the £40,000 range.

The evidence lasted forty-eight days, closing speeches took ten days and the Judge's summing-up, six days, but Smalls' evidence was persuasive, and after deliberating for two and a half days, on 23 May, Brown and Turner were both convicted by the jury of the Wembley and Ilford Bank robberies. Also convicted of the Wembley bank robbery were Wilkinson and Allpress. Issuing bankruptcy orders against all four men, the Judge told them:

> This case has confirmed the existence of a large number of people known directly or indirectly to each other who are ready to be recruited in order to commit this most serious type of robbery. It has been possible to raise a team quickly when any one of them suggested a likely target. Guns have been used. Without guns, a bank robbery in daylight is virtually impossible. There was a time when a man would opt out if he knew that arms were to be carried. The fact that this seems no longer to be so, is one of the explanations for the increase in this kind of offence.

Addressing Brown, the Judge told him:

> You have been convicted in two such operations. You know I would be failing in my duty if I did not demonstrate that while robbery of any kind is serious, this kind of armed robbery is particularly so.

Telling Turner he should not be treated any differently from Brown, the Judge sentenced each of them to twenty-one years' imprisonment. Dealing next with Wilkinson, the Judge said:

> I have no doubt that you were a very dominant figure in this particular robbery. If a man enters into an armed robbery, even if he himself did not carry a gun, and if he knows that arms are to be carried he is exposing himself to a very heavy prison sentence.

Next up was Allpress, whom the Judge called 'Well to the fore in your enthusiasm in this robbery and the part you played'. Wilkinson and Allpress both received concurrent sentences of sixteen years.

William Reynolds was jailed for thirteen years for his part in the raid, the Judge telling him:

> You played two vital parts in this robbery. You showed great persistence in obtaining the necessary information and you gave the signal. You must have known that guns would be involved.

For conspiracy in respect of that offence, William Shervill was jailed for fourteen years, the Judge stating, 'I accept that you were not a leader but you knew that firearms would be used.'

Also for conspiracy, David Delaney was jailed for twelve years, the Judge telling him, 'You were prepared to take part in a highly-organised, well-planned daylight robbery in which you knew that firearms would be used.'

A social report was ordered on the bank clerk, Anthony Holt, who later received a five-year sentence. And that was the end of just the first of the trials; it had cost £300,000.

## Chapter Ten

# The Remaining Trials

The next trial commenced on 10 June and it featured two of the main players: Danny Allpress and Micky Salmon, charged with the Portsmouth robbery. Also in the dock were Mrs Sylvia Rosemary Allpress, accused of dishonestly handling the Post Office money from the Portsmouth robbery, and Joseph Beveridge, also charged with the Portsmouth robbery plus the National Westminster Bank raid at Park Royal.

Between the conclusion of the first trial and the commencement of this one, Smalls appeared in court sporting a suntan acquired on holiday. He gave compelling evidence but then was rather let down when his wife was called to provide supporting evidence to the Portsmouth offence. As she was handed the Bible in the witness box, prior to taking the oath, she exhibited her familiar courtroom histrionics.

'I cannot do it, my Lord', she cried and pointing to the accused in the dock, 'These are not bad people; they are not wicked people.'

'There is only one course of action open to me', remarked Mr Justice Eveleigh, and Diane Smalls spent the next three hours in the cells. She was then released for the weekend, with the Judge telling her, 'I will consider what to do with you later on.'

Her refusal to testify seriously weakened the case against Mrs Allpress, but her refusal may not have been to show solidarity to her former contemporaries or because of her penchant for courtroom grandstanding. The fact that Smalls had been conducting an extra-marital affair with Susan Mattis, occupier of the Wood Green 'flop' where the gun had been accidentally discharged, during the course of the trials may have been a contributory factor to Diana Smalls' reticence.

Three months later, she would tell the press, 'He denies having an affair with the girl but I don't believe him. It now looks as if we could break up.'

But a wild card was now thrown into the trial, where the evidence was nothing whatsoever to do with Smalls.

★ ★ ★

On 24 August 1972, three temporary detective constables were in London's Oxford Street following a man whom they suspected of stealing money from newsvendors' stands. They then saw two men watching them who they thought were detectives from another division; one of the men, wearing a suede jacket, was carrying a raincoat wrapped around what was thought to be a truncheon. The officers went over the two men to tell them that they, too, were police officers, and one of the temporary detective constables, Alan Baxter, showed them his warrant card and asked who they were and what they were doing. At that, one of the men produced a bottle containing ammonia and squirted it into the officers' faces, while his companion – it was now clear that the raincoat contained a sawn-off shotgun – disappeared into the crowd. Despite these debilitating injuries, the three officers hung on to the ammonia-squirter, who later whimpered that they had kicked him. Alan Baxter had to have an eye removed.

The prisoner's name was Bernard Rees, aged twenty-seven, who had impressive criminal credentials. He had served a six-year sentence for conspiracy to rob, and the previous December, following a £62,000 raid on a security van, was one of four men committed to the Old Bailey on charges of receiving the cash from that robbery, for which he received a suspended sentence. On 29 November 1972, Rees was convicted of the attack on the three officers as well as conspiracy to rob and was sentenced to a total of six and a half years' imprisonment. The identity of Rees's shotgun-carrying associate was not known until Alan Baxter, now retired from the police on ill-health grounds, stepped into the witness box at the Old Bailey and was able to say, without the shadow of a doubt, that the wearer of the suede jacket carrying the sawn-off that day in Oxford Street, almost two years previously, was none other than Michael Salmon. This, predictably, was denied.

Nevertheless, Salmon was found guilty of conspiracy to commit robbery in London and possessing a shotgun with intent to resist arrest, as well as the Barclays Bank robbery at Ilford, and both Salmon and Allpress were found guilty of the £81,966 Portsmouth robbery; Allpress was also found guilty of the £2,226 Bournemouth robbery, and both men were acquitted of other robberies. On 5 July, both Mrs Allpress and Joe Beveridge – who, at the time of his trial was serving an eight-year sentence for his part in an £81,000 bank robbery at Erith, Kent – were acquitted of all charges.

Jailing Salmon for twenty-two years and imposing a bankruptcy order, the judge told him, 'You knew when you engaged in these activities you were facing a very substantial period of imprisonment'; and imposing a 21-year sentence on Allpress, concurrent to his existing 16-year sentence, the Judge told him, 'You don't want a lecture from me. You know what to expect for offences of this nature.'

The last trial commenced on 3 September dealing with the robberies at Ralli Brothers, the Ilford bank and Skefco Ballbearing. Regarding the latter raid, Smalls told the court that the idea had come from Micky Green's brother-in-law, who worked there and had provided them with a key to a side door. He went on to say:

As I got in the door, a chap came out and I pushed him back in. All the money was on the table. We started pulling it into pillow cases and sheets and I found some more money in the vault, which was open. We scooped it all up and left.

On 27 September, after taking nine hours, the jury delivered guilty verdicts on the seven defendants. Passing sentence, Mr Justice Eveleigh said:

There are some offences of such gravity that no matter what the character and record of the accused might be, a severe sentence must inevitably follow and armed robbery is one such offence.

Regarding the Skefco Ballbearing robbery, the Judge discharged the jury from giving a verdict in respect of Robert King and Don Barrett. For the Ralli Brothers robbery, Leonard Walter Jones was sentenced to nineteen years' imprisonment and John Alfred Richards, Anthony Edlin and James William Jeffrey to sixteen years each; David Kozak received six years' imprisonment for handling the precious stones from that robbery.

For their part in the Ilford bank robbery, Micky Salmon was sentenced to twenty-two years' imprisonment, and Bruce Brown and Bryan Turner to twenty-one years each. Robert King received a 16-year sentence and Donald Barrett got seventeen years, this to run concurrently to the 12-year sentence imposed for the robbery at Bournemouth.

# Chapter Eleven

# Serious Allegations

The defence tactics had taken the form of the predictable mud-slinging against Smalls – he was accused of shooting one man ('up the arse') and, as already mentioned, of killing a security guard with a blow to the throat and strangling another person – and of course, the police came in for a hammering with allegations of 'verbalings' (attributing incriminating oral statements to the prisoners), bribery, fabricating and planting evidence, threatening witnesses, assault and drunkenness. This was par for the course.

But probably the most serious allegation was that Bruce Brown's security box, when opened, had not contained £14,940 – as the police had said – but considerably more. When the box was opened, those present were the head of 'Q' Division's CID, Detective Chief Superintendent Cecil 'Dick' Saxby, DI Wilding, the custodian of the safe deposit company and other officers. The cash was put into a sack, taken back to Wembley police station and counted.

However, what would be alleged was that there was at least £50,000 in the box, that the police had creamed off £35,000 to split amongst themselves and that the ringleader was none other than DCS Saxby, not only a golfing partner of Bruce Brown (both men being members of the Ashford Manor Golf Club) but a close friend; together with their wives they had been on a skiing holiday to Germany. Furthermore, Saxby, who was aware of Brown's previous convictions, had extended a personal invitation to him to attend his promotion party in 1972, and the two men had discussed buying a club in Hounslow. Incidentally, they had also lunched together one week before Brown's arrest. Mrs Brown had claimed that Mrs Saxby had told her on the telephone that, following the opening of Brown's safe deposit box, her husband had arrived home clutching two briefcases bulging with banknotes. There followed incriminating recorded telephone calls between the two wives (which were ruled inadmissible by the judge), and William Bowler, the Assistant Chief Constable of Sheffield and Rotherham Constabulary, was called into the witness box to say that during a six-week enquiry, requested by the Commissioner, he had found no evidence to support criminal proceedings in the matter. He had interviewed Brown, who told him that he had not been involved in any robberies and if police had said that he had admitted it, they were lying. Additionally (and rather more tellingly), the prosecuting counsel put £15,000 into the security box and then invited Brown to try to put any more than an additional £7,000 into it; it was an impossibility. The allegations droned on and eventually petered out. Saxby went sick, was required to resign and then retired from the police; he took his pension with him to Florida, but not his wife.

DI Wilding was also accused of receiving money to show favour to a defendant in a previous case which featured Wilkinson, and Wilkinson stated that he possessed tape recordings which would 'expose' the police, although they never materialised.

But far more damaging was an allegation which was not referred to in court. After Turner had been charged, Flying Squad officer Woman Detective Constable Joan Angell submitted an informant's report in respect of her snout, who used the pseudonym 'Mary Frazer' and who had identified Brown and Turner as being two of the robbers. But the report disappeared, and one senior Squad officer said the form had been returned to WDC Angell, something she denied. The entry in the Flying Squad's correspondence book had been crossed out, although the officer responsible could not recall who told him to do so, nor the reason why. Furious, WDC Angell submitted a formal complaint to the commissioner, and an enquiry was launched.

But other rewards *had* been paid out, to an informant known as 'William Wise'. These sums, both from the Informants' Fund and various banks, amounted to £2,175. The reports had been submitted by DI Wilding and in each case had been supported by DCS Saxby.

However, WDC Angell's information had been received by her on 13 August, three days after the Wembley raid and, of course, prior to any arrests being carried out. DI Wilding's first report claimed that 'William Wise' had provided highly specific information regarding the activities of Bruce Brown and Bryan Turner, plus the information regarding their safe deposit boxes. But this report was submitted on 4 September 1972, two days after Brown had been charged and after the discovery of the safe deposit boxes and their contents. When 'William Wise' first provided his information seemed to be shrouded in mystery. What is not in dispute is that at the time of submitting that report, Wilding was fully aware of the contents of those boxes and that a number of the notes, in both boxes, bore markings by cashiers from Barclays Bank, Wembley.

Wilding was later cleared of any impropriety by A10, the Police Complaints Department. Joan Angell resigned in disgust after fourteen years' service, and four years later, she appeared on a London Weekend Television programme. Wilding refused the invitation to appear, but 'Mary Frazer' (suitably disguised) did take part. She was later given £1,000 from Barclays Bank; and still continued her quest for the rest of the reward money which, she said, was rightfully hers.

In 1975 'Mary Frazer' contacted Robin Corbett MP regarding her plight, who called for an enquiry into the matter. John Hunsworth, Director of the Bank Information Service stated:

> We paid out £6,500 to three people on the recommendation of the police. If someone can prove that they assisted in the matter, even at this late stage, we will still pay an appropriate reward.

Vic Wilding retired from the police and went to work as a security manager for Barclays Bank. But in April 1980, he and another former police officer stood trial at the Old Bailey charged with stealing travellers' cheques belonging to Lloyds Bank to the value of £2,700 during the time that they worked at Heathrow airport in 1971. It was suggested that the travellers' cheques were handed to 'a well-known' Soho pornographer who – ahem! – was indeed visiting foreign climes at that time, including escorting the head of the Flying Squad, and the wives of both men, on an all-expenses paid holiday to Cyprus; that the cheques were cashed in Brussels and that, furthermore, they had sought bribes and helped criminals to escape capture. Both former detectives were acquitted.

Allegations are easily made, and some can be taken with a pinch of salt. Other claims of corruption may, of course, be felt to be more compelling.

Bertie Smalls, then ...

... and Bertie Smalls, later.

# Members of The Wembley Mob

Bruce Brown.

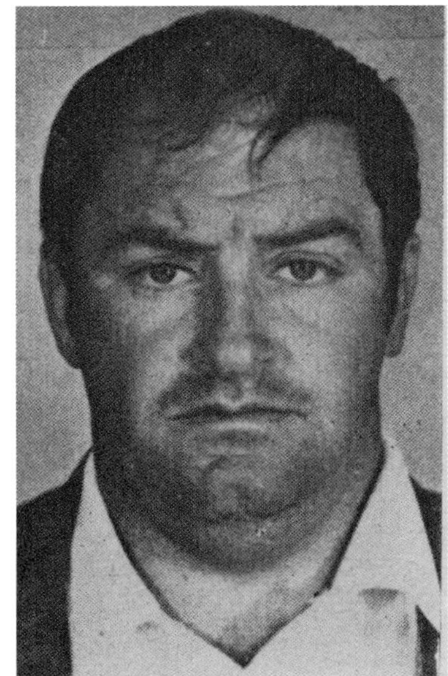

Bryan Turner.

Ronnie Dark.

Danny Allpress.

Micky Salmon.

Bryan Turner (left) being returned to the UK by DCI Alec Eist (centre) and DCS Jim Marshall (right).

Criminal mastermind Micky Green.

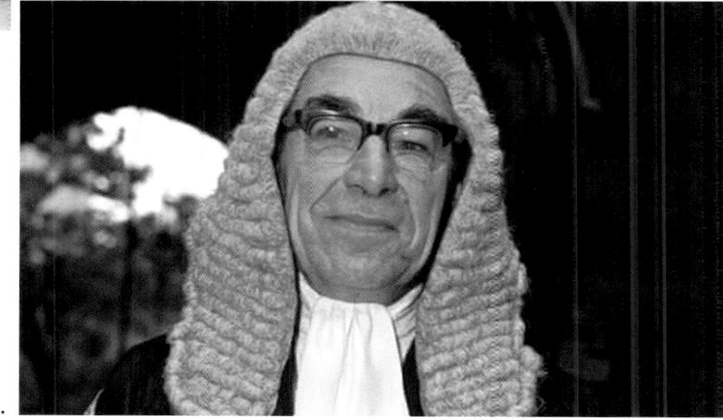

Mr Justice Eveleigh.

Flying Squad officers, from the Finchley office.

# Operation Ohio

Westcombe Park police station: Command centre for Operation Ohio.

Tie with motif for Operation Ohio.

Painting of a goshawk by supergrass John Segars.

Operation Ohio robber, Jimmy Moody.

# Members of Barrett's Gang

Don Barrett.

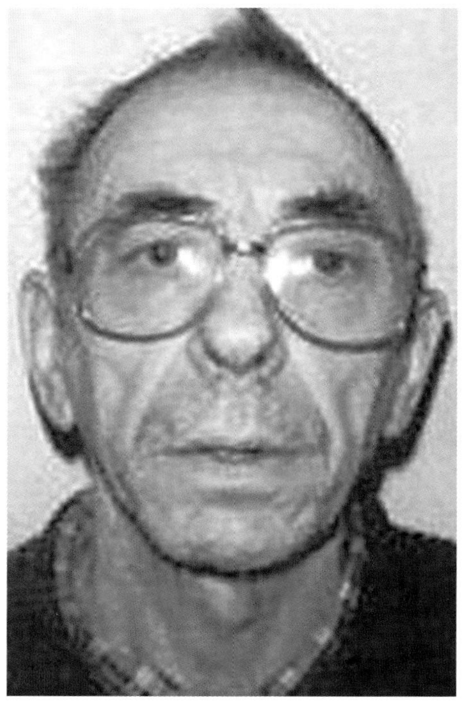

Dave Croke.

George Ince.

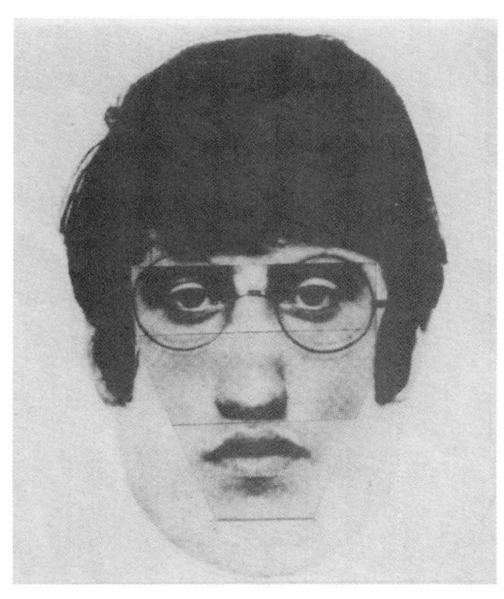

A photofit of an Armaguard robber.

A device for monitoring a victim's movements.

Interior of the explosive device at Cross & Herbert's.

Attacked security van at Mauritius Road, Greenwich.

Security van's window, fractured by a Hilti gun.

The Hilti gun responsible.

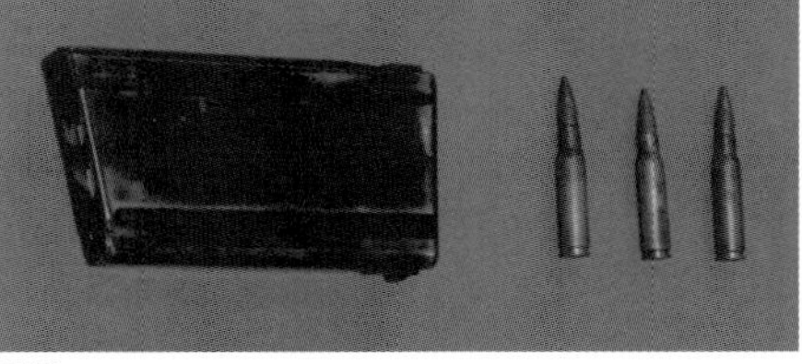

Armour-piercing bullets, used at Greenwich.

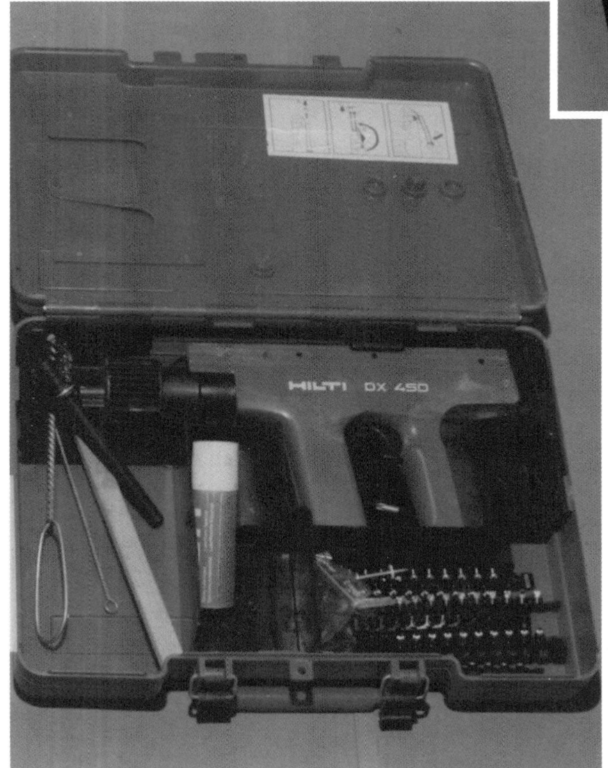

## Chapter Twelve

# The Appeals

Now back, in December 1974, to the staid world of the Court of Appeal (Criminal Division) which dealt with sixteen appeals against sentence and convictions arising from these trials. The appeals were heard before Lord Justice Lawton, Lord Justice James and Mr Justice Milmo, and judgement was delivered on 24 March 1975.

In eleven cases, the sentences were cut. Micky Salmon's 22-year sentence was reduced to eighteen; the same reduction applied to the 21-year sentences imposed upon Bryan Turner, Bruce Brown and Danny Allpress. John Richards, Anthony Edlin, James Jeffrey and Robert King had their 16-year sentences cut to fifteen, and Don Barrett's 17-year sentence was dramatically reduced to twelve. Stanley Shervill's 14-year sentence was reduced to ten, and the 9-year sentence of Tom French, the errant taxi driver, was reduced by two years.

In three cases, the convictions were quashed. Jimmy Wilkinson walked free from his 16-year sentence, as did David Kozak ('The Coloured Man') from his sentence of six years. This was because of insufficient corroboration from Smalls' evidence, and the same applied to Leonard Jones' 19-year sentence, although he remained incarcerated in respect of another conviction.

However, that was not the end of the story regarding Messrs Marsden (who had been found not guilty of the Wembley Bank robbery) and Wilkinson. Both were found guilty at Middlesex Crown Court in June 1976 of receiving a quantity of stolen coffee and other items. Wilkinson was sentenced to two years' imprisonment, and Marsden who, in the intervening period had acquired a 9-month suspended sentence, had that added on to his 18-month prison sentence, making twenty-seven months' imprisonment in all.

But Lord Justice Lawton was unimpressed with the way in which Bertie Smalls had been recruited to give evidence. He read out the original contract drawn up between the Director of Public Prosecutions and Smalls' solicitors (it had been described as 'an unholy bargain'), before saying:

The spectacle of the Director of Public Prosecutions recording in writing, at the behest of a criminal like Smalls, his undertaking to give immunity from further prosecution is one which we find distasteful. Nothing of a similar kind must ever happen again. Undertakings of immunity from prosecution may have to be given in the public interest. They should never be given by the police. The Director should give them most sparingly and, in cases involving grave crimes, it would be prudent of him to consult the law officers before making any promises.

The appellants then took their cases to the House of Lords, not that that did them any good. As Lord of Appeal in Ordinary, Lord Diplock upbraided Lord Justice Lawton, saying:

I am wondering to what extent it is right for any court to give directions to the Director as to how he should conduct his business. The Director of Public Prosecutions works under the Attorney General. He does not work under any judges at all and any directions he receives as to the way in which he does his work surely must come from the Attorney General. I would have thought it quite wrong for it to come from any judicial authority at all. He may be condemned for what he has done, but he must not be told what he has to do in the future.

★　★　★

Opinions were mixed, although on balance, most were in favour of the deal. The *Evening News* stated:

A storm has rightly arisen over Lord Justice Lawton's ruling yesterday that police must never again do deals with villains like Bertie Smalls.

No-one can relish the idea of Smalls being at large. But his evidence led to 12 others being jailed and a 60 per cent drop in armed bank raids.

On balance, society benefitted from the deal.

A senior Regional Crime Squad officer said:

I would have thought that 12 to 1 was pretty good odds. If Smalls had not helped us the way he did, then it is fair to say these villains would still be walking around, committing large crimes and possibly even shooting people.

I would have expected the Judge to have balanced his remarks with that kind of observation. As it is, we are not sure how far we can go to induce an informant to help us.

It is, in fact, reasonably rare for written undertakings to be given, but there are times when such a move is an enormous help to us. And it is the sort of thing the police in America, for instance, use widely and with public approval.

What the Judge ought to have remembered was that Bertie Smalls – admittedly a criminal himself – was not sending down people of previous good character who just happened to have strayed off the path for once. He was helping us to lock up the most diabolical villains you could ever wish to meet.

So that was the overriding opinion of all working detectives. In the meantime, that left Bertie Smalls …

# Chapter Thirteen

# Bertie – The Final Years

Smalls and his family continued to be guarded. Brian Greenan takes up the tale once more:

When I was covering for either Mick Jones or Don Manley we would drive up to the Bushey safe house to pick Bertie up and take him out for the day. He always wanted to go to The Fishery Public House, overlooking the Aldenham reservoir, which in the 1970s was a favourite of North-west blaggers for meets. The first time I went with him and Mick Jones, Bertie asked me if I was right-handed and if so, was I carrying my gun in its holster under my left arm? What was this about? When we entered the pub we would go round to the left side of the lounge, into the corner, and we'd sit on three stools at the end of the bar. Bertie was very precise about where I would sit; I would be on the first stool in the corner, Bertie would sit on my right with Mick Jones on his right. From our corner positions we had a clear view of the main entrance and out of the windows into the car park. Bertie said that if anyone came in through the door after him, then if I was slow to react he would reach across me and grab my gun from my holster. I found that really amusing, but Bertie was deadly serious, and although we had a sociable drink with him drinking large vodkas he was nevertheless fixed on who was coming through the main door. Another favourite haunt of Bertie's was the Thatched Barn Hotel on the A1 at Elstree, and he told me that several of his jobs were planned there.

One of his house protection team leaders was Detective Sergeant Bill Patten, a brilliant detective and a good friend of mine, who told me that Bertie would drink a bottle of vodka, sometimes more, each day, but he never appeared drunk. Bill did tell me that Bertie and Diana were often arguing, and the drinking didn't help. She knew he was seeing other women and that was often the cause of the rows, but Bill was so tactful, he was able to diffuse the arguments.

Bertie would talk about the jobs he planned, and his planning was meticulous. I always felt that if he had applied himself to a lawful business he would have been very successful.

He pulled jobs together and he was very good at it. There was a young lad who wanted to be a getaway driver, so Bertie put him to the test when they went out to do a blagging in a Ford Transit van. A screen was put up behind the driver, and there was a hole in it so Bertie could see what was going on. The young driver was really nervous, and as they approached the target bank, Bertie shouted, 'Stop!' The driver slammed on the brakes and the team of blaggers in the back all crashed forwards. Then they dashed out of the back doors, raced into the bank and put a shot in the ceiling. Bertie was the last out and he realised they'd gone to the wrong bank! Bertie shouted at them, 'You're in the wrong fucking bank!' so they came out of that bank, ran across the road to the target bank and successfully carried out the blagging!

Back in the mid-1980s, Diana Smalls was working in a newsagent's in Northwood, NW London and she immediately recognised me when I went in to get my kids some sweets, saying, 'Hallo BeeG, didn't know you lived round here.' She said that Bertie was using the Reindeer Public House in Northwood (no longer there), but at the time the Public Bar was used by all the local hounds, including a couple of local armed blaggers.

I thought at the time that he was taking a chance but then in the early 1980s I believe he had been nicked for cheque frauds and I believe he was banged up again but he came to no harm, which surprised me. I did hear that Micky Salmon had arranged a £10,000 bounty on him.

Alick Morrison had been subjected to Robert Mark's interchanges – from being a detective constable, he had been posted to Enfield police station as a uniform sergeant – before reverting as a detective sergeant at Holloway. One night in 1985, at 11.30pm, a prisoner stinking of booze was brought in, having been seen driving erratically, who had refused to provide a specimen of breath.

Asking to speak to Morrison alone, the man said, 'Do you know the name Alec Eist?'

Morrison had never met Eist but certainly knew of him, as did many other officers. Alec Eist divided opinion; he was acknowledged as a brilliant thief-taker, but he had acquired a reputation for striking breathtaking deals with criminals, splitting rewards between informants and himself, setting up the theft of high-value consignments and acting as a middleman in highly illegal transactions. He had also been a member of the Wembley Robbery Squad who had overseen the first supergrass. Eist appeared at Middlesex Crown

Court in June 1978 on charges of arranging an alibi for two London thieves. Not only was he acquitted, he was also awarded costs.

The prisoner – who had obviously slipped away from his guardians – went on to say, 'I'm Bertie Smalls. I'm going to give you a phone number to call. Nobody must know who I am, except you. I need to get out of here.'

In the event, Smalls was charged with failing to comply with the breathalyser procedure and bailed. Was that phone call made? Not by Morrison, but matters went awry thereafter; the prosecution solicitor failed to turn up at Smalls' first and second appearance; the court date had been altered on the file; and eventually, Smalls' charge was dismissed on a technicality.

Whoever received Smalls' urgent telephone call, it was not Alec Eist, since he had died some three years previously. I mentioned his demise to a colleague.

'Alec?' he replied. 'Nah, he ain't dead – he's middling in limbo!'

★   ★   ★

Bertie Smalls would later reflect on his past, present and future:

> I now live in a detached five-bedroom house in one of London's better groomed outer suburbs. I prune the roses and I say 'Good morning' to my neighbours and that's it; nobody knows who I am … I don't really regret what I have done. For me, life has changed 100 per cent. It's a hell of a strain wondering whether you're going to be shot, strangled or blown up. Checking the car every time you go near it in case someone has tried to plant something on you. But I am a naturally optimistic character. I reckon I'll survive. I am on my own now and the wraps are off and I don't know where I can turn. I know there is a contract out on me, and I have even heard names mentioned. I don't know what I am going to do in the long run. For a start I am laying low and I'm writing a book which will tell all about it. With any luck, that will make a few quid, and maybe I'll be able to get out of the country and make a fresh start somewhere else. That's if they don't get me first.

Brian Greenan now concludes his memories of minding the first supergrass:

> Bertie used to tell me about the jobs he'd been involved in and laughed when he mentioned the Portsmouth job, when Diane went back, after the robbery, to collect the cash that had been

hidden the day before. He said she put the money under the back seat and put the kids on top, and drove back. Although she and Bertie did have their differences, she was with him when he died.

Yes, Bertie Smalls passed away on 31 January 2008, aged seventy-two, the book unwritten, devoid of gunshot wounds or any other form of skulduggery. He died of natural causes. Yet he left a legacy.

# Part III

# Supergrasses United

## Chapter Fourteen

# 'Mo' Steps in

Bertie had certainly left a legacy all right, but like many inheritances, it was not cut and dried; there would be codicils attached.

Nervous politicians – always fearful of losing votes – realised that public opinion meant robbers who confessed all and informed against their brethren should not be given complete immunity for their sins. Yes, they would be kept in (hopefully) safe conditions, but after confessing to all the crimes in which they'd been involved, they would receive a substantial discount when it came to sentencing and be provided with a new identity following their release. When the next supergrasses appeared, having often committed an appalling litany of crimes (as well as possessing serious previous convictions), the unofficial tariff would be just five years' imprisonment.

Nevertheless, the police were delighted with the results. No longer could gangs of armed robbers rely on their colleagues to be 'staunch'. No longer could they rely upon each other – and it mattered not if they were best mates, best men at each other's weddings or godfathers to best mates' children. It went far deeper than that. Brothers informed against brothers, sons against fathers, even against mothers. One not only informed against his mistress, but put his wife in the frame as well.

But the police were not the only people to be pleased with supergrasses. Thanks to superior intelligence – both human and electronic – it was becoming more and more common for the Flying Squad to catch armed robbers 'bang to rights' in police parlance – 'going across the pavement'; in the blaggers' vernacular – 'on a ready-eye'.

So when armed robbers were caught in circumstances that gave them very little chance of an acquittal, it would be an exaggeration to suggest that they formed an orderly queue to line up and request supergrass status – but not by much. Faced with the prospect of twenty or more years inside a maximum security prison, the strong possibility of a five-year sentence – minus time spent in custody beforehand – seemed ever so much more attractive.

It was an anomalous situation. Some had to be turned away ('Sorry, pal, you were too slow!'), and others who had been supergrassed became supergrasses themselves.

But before a supergrass could be accepted as such, it was necessary that several important conditions should be met. First, the Director of Public Prosecutions had to be convinced that the evidence the applicant had to give was worthwhile, not only in terms of the number of robbers to be arrested, or the number of robberies to be cleared up, but in the recovery of weapons and stolen property.

Next, it was utterly essential that the proposed supergrass should truthfully admit to every single offence that he had committed; if he omitted even one offence, and it was discovered by the lawyers representing those he was accusing, his credibility could well be destroyed. If the offence involved was stealing a pedal cycle when he was fourteen, the excuse of forgetfulness might be accepted (Jimmy Gallant, who appears later in this book, asked for it to be taken into consideration when he was sentenced that he had stolen a bottle of milk from a doorstep in Cricklewood); but if it was a high-value armed robbery, during which members of the public had been injured, that would be a completely different matter and could inevitably lead to the whole of the prosecution case collapsing.

Lastly, the offences had to be supported by independent corroboration. If the person accused by the supergrass told the police, 'Yes, I did it', that was corroboration, as it would have been if the supergrass said that the accused person's share of a robbery was £20,000, and the following day, that sum had been deposited in his bank account. It simply was not enough for the supergrass to point the finger at an accused person and say, 'He robbed that bank with me', no matter how compelling it might sound. In fact, if two supergrasses both gave evidence against the same robber in the same trial, that was not regarded as corroboration. Therefore, it was crucial that these points were observed; and when they were not, it led to a number of very guilty people walking free.

★　★　★

One of the first of the supergrasses to be recruited was Maurice Lanca O'Mahoney, known to his fast diminishing circle of friends as 'Mo'. In June 1969, with one finding of guilt and three previous convictions, although he denied saying to police, 'It comes in handy for protection' after they found a jemmy in his car, he had been fined £25 at Marylebone Magistrates' Court for possessing an offensive weapon. However, criminal charges against him were set to become rather more serious.

He had been part of a team who attacked the crew of a Securicor van on 1 June 1974 at Heston, Middlesex. A stolen low-loader rammed the van, the windows were smashed in using an axe and a sledgehammer, shots were fired from two sawn-off shotguns, a Beretta and a 9mm Luger, and a custodian was struck over the head with a hammer. The gang were hoping that the prize would amount to £150,000; in fact, they stole just £13,152.43p.

George du Buriatte had been described by the gang as being 'as sound as a bell'; he had the right credentials. In 1960, du Buriatte, with fourteen previous convictions, had served just one month of a 5½-year sentence for robbery and possessing explosives, when he limped into hospital, whereupon he made a miraculous recovery. Discarding his crutches, he dived through a window but was later recaptured and jailed for ten years for attempted armed robbery. He was later acquitted of a series of Post Office robberies but may have had a 'Road to Damascus' moment. O'Mahoney believed that it was du Buriatte who grassed up him and the others, and he may have had a point. Du Buriatte went on to grass up a considerable number of felons as a supergrass, but in January 1978 he was jailed for four years for robbery. Unsurprisingly, he was thoroughly disliked inside; on the outside, his wife slept with a hammer beside her bed.

Ten days after the Heston robbery, the gang were rounded up, with the exception of O'Mahoney; he was arrested the following day at the home of his girlfriend. She was arrested, as were her parents, since following the raid, O'Mahoney had left his share of the proceeds – £1,200 – one of the shotguns, a pistol and some of his clothing at their address. His girlfriend made a full, frank and accurate admission about the preparation of the robbery, since she had been present at the time of its planning.

O'Mahoney said nothing to the police; he was charged and remanded to Brixton prison, and what might have happened next is pure conjecture, had it not been for other members of the team stating that O'Mahoney's girlfriend had grassed them up (true) as had O'Mahoney (untrue); and when he was threatened with having his eyes gouged out with a toothbrush (always a possibility), O'Mahoney decided to roll over and 'do a Bertie'.

At Hounslow police station on 22 June 1974, his initial statement kicked off with the usual robber's self-justification:

The reason why I didn't make a statement before is because I was in fear of my life and the lives of my wife and children, together with a number of other people. But now the police have insured [*sic*] me of protection, my mind is more at ease because they are looking after my family. There are a number of very dangerous and violent men who I know will kill them and myself at the first opportunity. I intend to make a statement later dealing with these men in more detail. I now want to tell you about this robbery in Phoenix Way, Heston on 1 June 1974 and how it all started ...

On 19 September 1974, at the Old Bailey, O'Mahoney pleaded guilty to one charge of robbery, one of attempted robbery and a burglary and asked for ninety-nine other offences to be taken into consideration. His Honour Judge Aarvold OBE, TD sentenced him to five years' imprisonment.

When he was not housed in Brixton (twice), Oxford, Winchester or Wormwood Scrubs prisons, much of his time was spent at Chiswick police station, where he made an additional seventy-two statements, comprising 249 pages. As a result, 277 people were detained, not only for armed robberies and burglaries but also murder, attempted murder and conspiracy to murder. Of these, 159 were charged with offences involving theft of property to the value of £2 million, and weapons and the proceeds of crime were recovered.

Detective Sergeant (later Detective Superintendent) Steve Parker was one of those involved with O'Mahoney at that time. Clearly, O'Mahoney was still in fear of his life because Parker told me:

> Just thinking about those days, at one point Mo was banged up at night in the Scrubs, then to Chiswick for the day. On one occasion, he was picked up in a Squad car with Geoff Brown as the armed escort. As they were driving along Chiswick High Road, Geoff's Webley went off and the round started whizzing around the car, landing at the feet of Mo, who was screaming out with horror that this was an assassination attempt. Geoff was just pissed off that it had blown a hole in his new leather jacket. I don't think that it was reported!

There were a number of trials at which O'Mahoney gave evidence, with some defendants being convicted, others not; the last trial came in March 1976, when five men received sentences of between seven and fourteen years, although His Honour Judge Griffith Jones commented that if Judge Aarvold had known more about the robberies when handing O'Mahoney his five-year sentence, he would probably have imposed a longer term, accepting as he did, that O'Mahoney's behaviour was worse than that of the defendants.

There were still three trials yet to be heard in which O'Mahoney could give evidence; he declined to do so, and no evidence was offered against those defendants.

The lesson that was learnt (or should have been) was this: don't let your supergrass be sentenced until he finishes giving his evidence.

# Chapter Fifteen

# The Chiswick Connection

Chiswick was a popular place for housing supergrasses; Billy Williams was another. He came to notice following a robbery with violence at Barclays Bank, Willington Road, St John's Wood on 22 July 1974. He was in company with others, including two brothers, James and Philip Trusty, when they forced the security screens on the bank's counter, rifled three of the tills and escaped with £11,425. But their escape did not go unnoticed; when 21-year-old Police Constable David Clements drove his panda car at the bandits, Philip Trusty fired two shots from a revolver at the car, and when the officer got out he was struck in the face, before Trusty and the other raiders drove away in a Jaguar. Undeterred, PC Clements chased the Jaguar at speeds of up to 60mph, with the raiders twice driving the wrong way down one-way streets. As the officer moved to stop the car, Philip Trusty fired again, from a distance of just ten yards, splintering the car's windscreen and hitting PC Clements in the shoulder, while his panda car crashed into a kerbside rubbish skip. Nevertheless, Clements pursued the Jaguar for another mile before he lost it.

James Trusty was arrested on 5 August, having disposed of his brother's gun in Teddington Lock on the River Thames. Philip Trusty had convictions going back to when he was nineteen and escaped from Aylesbury prison whilst serving a 4-year sentence for housebreaking and possessing firearms – and he had had a few more convictions since then. Brother James, however, had no convictions, and Philip had the bright idea of suggesting that James should admit responsibility for the shooting of the police officer, so that he, Philip, would receive a lighter sentence.

Billy Williams stated that he had been revolted by the way that Philip Trusty had callously shot the young policeman, and the upshot of this was that Williams rolled right over, made sixty-four statements in respect of forty-eight offences committed since 1965, naming forty suspects, and on 9 December 1974 at the Old Bailey, pleaded guilty to three robberies in which £37,563 was stolen and asked for thirty-three more to be taken into consideration.

'My life of crime is over', he virtuously told the Recorder of London, Sir Carl Aarvold, 'and there is no way I can turn to it again.'

He then received five years' imprisonment from the Judge – and had boiling water chucked over him by disillusioned prison inmates.

Two weeks prior to sentencing, Williams married his pregnant fiancée, 18-year-old Barbara Stanikowski. Steve Parker recalls:

> At the same time Mo was banged up at Chiswick in the supergrass unit, we had another lesser one, called Billy Williams. I can't remember much of what he did, other than he was a robber and I was at his wedding in Chiswick nick when Jack Slipper was the best man. After his speech, Jack gave Billy a large knife to cut the cake and we all took a deep breath ...

Someone who might have wished for a different use for that knife was Williams' former wife – they had divorced four years' previously.

Upon hearing of his prison sentence, she commented, 'I expect he'll finish up with a knife in his back.'

James Trusty, meanwhile, appeared at the Old Bailey on 17 March 1975, admitted three robberies and a conspiracy to rob and was sentenced to two years and nine months. He, like Williams, was going to give evidence against his brother, as well as others, including one Alan John Chard, and on 21 November 1975, Philip Trusty was sentenced to life imprisonment for attempting to murder PC Clements. He also received concurrent 20-year sentences for three robberies and 15-year sentences for five conspiracies to rob. Passing sentence, Mr Justice Nield told him:

> One of the darkest features of your case is that one gained the impression that you attempted to continue a life of violent crime while you were at liberty. It may well be that those who are authorised to recommend your release may feel that they have difficulty in making such a recommendation.

The Judge then passed sentences of five, ten, twelve and eighteen years on four other men convicted of robberies, and two other men received suspended sentences for receiving stolen money. Additionally, Alan Chard was sentenced to fifteen years, having been found guilty of three cases of conspiracy to rob.

As Chard was led away to the cells he shouted to the Judge, 'You have just sentenced an innocent man!'

His case was later taken up by Stephen Ross, Liberal MP for the Isle of Wight, who wanted an interview with the Home Secretary to discuss the matter.

Billy Williams was released on 5 April 1976 and lost no time in accepting fees amounting to £10,000 from the media for lurid and rather embellished accounts of his time in police custody.

It appears that those stories did not stop there; nine years later, in March 1985, Williams told *The People* newspaper that it was not Philip Trusty who shot PC Clements at all; it was him. This happened at a time when Trusty was wondering if he would get parole; probably not, he thought, so he decided to saw through the bars of his cell at Lewes prison, and almost succeeded. Williams told the newspaper:

> He got convicted but he never done it. I shot the copper. Philip smashed the back window out but the copper was never shot from the back window. He was shot from the side of the car, out the front seat where I was. I obviously panicked at the thought of getting done for shooting a policeman.

So that was the admission of the man who had once claimed that he was 'sickened' after witnessing Philip Trusty shooting the constable. This rather muddied the waters, because now a different member of the gang was claiming that *he* had shot the officer. Be that as it may, the following month, having dropped this legal bombshell – picked up once more by the intrepid Liberal MP, Stephen Ross – Williams absconded to South Africa, where he was arrested in May, hiding in a small township near the Botswana border.

The police in London now wanted a conversation with Mr Williams, with regard to talking bollocks to the police at Chiswick, when on oath at the Old Bailey, or to the press thereafter.

At least Police Constable Clements was awarded a well deserved George Medal for his gallantry.

And all the while, the supergrasses were pouring in.

# Chapter Sixteen

# The Finchley Connection

The biggest exponent of supergrasses was Flying Squad officer Detective Chief Inspector Tony Lundy, and he kicked off his series of successes on 8 November 1977, when he arrested Dave Smith, a serial armed robber whose latest conviction had resulted in a 15-year sentence, reduced on appeal to ten. Detective Sergeant John McSwan had arrived from the Yard to help set up the new Robbery Squad office at Finchley. It took time, but Smith was 'turned' and for fifteen months he was on bail, with a condition of residence at Finchley police station. He eventually pleaded guilty to eight robberies – including a plea to manslaughter during one of the forays – five conspiracies and a burglary, as well as asking for eighty cases to be taken into consideration. His grassing resulted in sixty-nine criminals being charged, and his evidence was so compelling that 90 per cent of them pleaded guilty. There were those who did not and, following 20-year sentences being imposed at the Old Bailey on a particularly vicious gang (of which Smith, of course had been a member), Judge Michael Argyle MC, QC said:

> Nobody, I think, listening to these supergrasses giving evidence could doubt the truth of what they had said. In any event, their evidence was corroborated, but it was nauseating to hear these hypocrites and reflect, as a matter of policy, that they have each been sentenced to five years, only.

Smith's debriefing was still ongoing when Roger Smith returned to the Flying Squad on promotion to detective sergeant in July 1978. Previously, his Squad service had been spent from the 4th floor of the Yard; now he was sent to the Finchley office where, under Tony Lundy, robbery investigations were going flat-out. Smith was assigned to Detective Inspector Pat Fleming's team, and one month after his arrival, James George Gallant was arrested on the day following an armed robbery at Sainsbury's, Burnt Oak Broadway, where £4,600 was stolen. Gallant's share – £1,900 – was found in a cornflake box at home.

After a little prevarication, Gallant 'turned' – and he had much to tell. He was an utterly professional armed robber; when he wasn't actually carrying out an armed raid, he was planning others.

Roger Smith was appointed office manager for Gallant and he now takes up the tale:

I moved into the small office already occupied by Detective Sergeant John McSwan, Smith's office manager, and we somehow managed to share the rather inadequate space available and he was more than helpful in getting me started in a capacity that was brand new to me.

As was usual with the debriefing of a new RI, Gallant was interviewed at length and his potential evidential statements taken and disseminated for immediate action, it being essential that those he named were arrested before it became general knowledge that he had 'turned' and before they could flee. And so it was that the paper mountain that I was now in charge of was beginning to grow.

What was relatively unique about this RI job was that the majority of those named by Gallant were not known as criminals previously involved in or suspected of armed robbery offences; in fact many of them were connected to the West Ham FC football hooligans, the Inter City Firm. Clearly capable of violence and with little regard for the well-being of the public, they easily adapted to serious armed crime. Gallant's main accomplice was a very violent man known as Sammy Samuels, who had on several occasions fired his handgun in the process of robbing premises.

Smith's assessment of Sammy – or rather William Frederick Samuels – was correct. There was an initiation test when Gallant introduced Samuels into their first armed robbery together; that was at the Mecca Bookmakers betting shop in Victoria Dock Road, East London in February 1977. It was an assessment passed by Samuels with flying colours; another raid at a nursery necessitated the armed Samuels threatening a mother and her seven-year-old child while the house was ransacked. At the East Lane Post Office, North Wembley in April, Gallant and Samuels threatened the Asian postmaster with a shotgun; it appears that he did not comply sufficiently quickly, and Samuels shot him in the legs. One hundred pellets went into him, penetrating an artery in his left leg; apparently, Samuels later told Gallant that he had done it because 'he hated Pakistanis'.

Samuels was present, once again, when a guard he confronted was delivering cash to Wembley Underground Station in March

1978. The guard ran to the cashier's office to take refuge, and the booking clerk tried to shut the door behind the guard, but Samuels fired a shot through the door into the ceiling. With considerable courage, the guard grabbed the muzzle of the sawn-off and tried to push Samuels out of the office, but he fired a second shot and the guard's hand was blown away.

Gallant had told the police about Samuels, 'He always wanted to shoot people and I used to have to talk him out of firing the gun. He just wanted to fire it anyway even if it was only into the ceiling or an office window.'

At the Old Bailey on 24 September 1979, Gallant pleaded guilty to ten armed robberies and one attempt and asked for sixty-two other offences to be taken into consideration. The court was told he had provided information in respect of over a hundred offences, including seventy-five armed robberies and conspiracies to rob, plus an attempted prison break, and that twenty-one criminals were consequently now awaiting trial. Passing sentence, Judge Jack Abdela said:

> It took a great deal of courage for a man who had helped the police in the way you did and you must be given substantial credit for doing it. Normally, extremely long prison sentences would have been imposed, but I will impose one of five years' concurrent, on each charge.

The following day, Samuels and others appeared before the same Judge, with Gallant's words about Samuels' misdeeds, echoed by the prosecutor, still ringing in his ears. They all pleaded guilty to a series of serious offences and, describing Samuels as 'vicious, callous and reckless', Judge Abdela sentenced him to fifteen years' imprisonment. In a vain attempt at mitigation, Samuels' counsel stated that Gallant was 'the real villain of the piece' and that his client had been 'inveigled, cajoled and wooed' into committing these offences – all without success; the uncompromising Judge Abdela told him that but for his client's pleas of guilty, he would have jailed him for twenty years.

The other defendants were far more fortunate: Stephen Evans, Joseph James Cahill and Robert Lou Farina were each jailed for four years, and Colin Stuart Bushaway was given a suspended sentence for possessing a .410 shotgun without a licence.

Roger Smith's account concludes this investigation, but then, no one is better placed than him to describe what happened next:

To sum up Gallant's RI contribution it's fair to say that he identified and helped convict a very active group of villains, who otherwise might very well have continued to rob and terrorise the good people of London for a long time.

I spent many days, weeks, and even months in total at the Old Bailey, as officer in the case throughout the whole series of trials, and it was only just after the end of that that a new RI enquiry began at Finchley. Perhaps it had something to do with the success of my first major office manager appointment that I was immediately given the job again with the next one.

A team of robbers had been identified, and the Finchley Flying Squad and C11 were actively working on establishing their whereabouts and their likely targets in the hope of planning a pavement ambush and their arrests. A connection had been verified to a block of council flats, and C11 had 'eyeball' on the entrance and exit to the estate when a cash-in-transit van was robbed at gunpoint and money stolen outside a supermarket in High Road, East Finchley. The robbers made their getaway and, from what we immediately learned of the offence, it seemed likely that it was our gang, but they had left the scene and their whereabouts were not known – until, that is, a convoy of vehicles drove into the estate that was under observation and their occupants were seen to be our villains.

I was at the Finchley office and once the update was received I, together with John McSwan, who was armed, jumped into a squad car driven by Gordon Reynolds, and we sped to the estate. There was a longish approach road to the flats that ended in the car parking spaces for the estate. As we drove into the entrance of the road a car was coming towards us. It was a 'bandit car' that upon seeing us reversed at speed back into the complex, pursued by us. There was a mini chase around the car parking area until the bandit car smashed into high metal railings at the back of the estate and the passenger decamped over the railings towards the railway lines beyond. Seeing the car come to a halt, John McSwan and I ran over towards it, John with his firearm ready if needed and me armed with a 9-iron from Gordon's golf bag that always resided in the car boot. Whilst jumping over the railings the villain had caught his coat on the top spikes and had run off without it – his handgun was still in the pocket. Other Finchley officers had rushed to a nearby rail station and had commandeered a train to get them to the place the escaping villain had last been seen. What they forgot in their haste and eagerness was that when you board a train at a station the doors are at the same level as the platform, but failed to realise that when you leave the train elsewhere it's about a 6ft drop to the ground – slight injuries ensued! However, John Kennedy was arrested.

That was my involvement, but other villains were nicked that day and one of them was Christopher Wren who became the next RI, and I managed that office too. Wren, unlike Gallant, had 'worked' with the top echelon of London robbers and the names he disclosed were a Who's Who of villainy.

It was Christopher Wren who had been driving the stolen Mercedes that crashed into the railings and John Kennedy who ran on to the railway lines; he had just been released from prison.

Squad driver Gordon Reynolds was no stranger to hostile situations; he had previously been awarded a certificate from the Society for the Protection of Life from Fire after he had repeatedly entered a burning house to rescue two children, aged three and four, who had been trapped with their father on the first floor. Now, on this occasion, although Roger Smith had been obliged to arm himself with one of Reynolds' golf clubs, Reynolds, who was an authorised shot, was fortuitously armed and, catching up with Kennedy ('He was a big bastard!' he told me, and at 25 stone, that was a fair description), drew his Model 36 Smith and Wesson.

'Move, and I'll blow your fucking head off!' he told Kennedy, and it's a matter of record that Kennedy rapidly became stationary and survived with his head intact.

John Hammond, who surrendered at the scene, had shot the security guard in the stomach during this raid; fortunately, the guard survived.

John McSwan adds his own memories of the events that day:

Kennedy was aiming a firearm at us before Wren drove into a wall. I went through the standard procedure, 'Armed police' etc., but he had none of it. He put the car into reverse and drove over my left foot, fracturing my ankle. Kennedy legged it over the fence with the 'Happy Bag'. The story goes, I challenged him after he got free from the coat he was wearing, to the point that I thought I had shot him, he let out a scream and disappeared down an embankment onto the railway line. Myself, Gordon Reynolds and Roger didn't take long to convince him to stop or be shot. With Kennedy detained, the train which had been commandeered by DS George Mason and DS Doug Milburn pulled up alongside us. I saw George Mason leaning out and wearing the driver's hat: 'Did you order a train, sir?' That was followed by a loud yell; Doug in the excitement of the event had forgotten that he was not at the station and stepped out of the cab, 12ft above the ground!

Wren mentioned Ronald Johnson, who was known as 'Brains Johnson' because of his organisational skills, and once more, Roger Smith takes up the tale:

> Wren told us about him, that he'd just come out after a term of imprisonment when the gang went to see him and told him they had a brilliant plot for a robbery but didn't know how to actually manage to do the blag – they wanted Ronnie to work out the finer details. He told them to 'fuck off', he was going to spend time with his girl and wasn't interested. But they persisted, and finally his greed overtook his reservations and he did plan the job and participated in a successful robbery. Wren had implicated him in many robberies, and Johnson saw that he was 'in the shit'. He offered himself as an RI and, indeed, could have been a very valuable one, but we already had Wren and couldn't use him too.

Johnson's prediction of his fate was a correct one; he appeared at the Old Bailey in March 1981, pleading guilty to six robberies and asking for another 119 robberies and burglaries which involved almost £2 million in cash and property to be considered. He was jailed for fifteen years, as was John Hammond, who described himself as 'a dog kennel owner'. He admitted eight robberies and a wounding and asked for twelve other offences to be taken into consideration. Penitent at last, Hammond was described as 'a right nasty bastard' who regularly misbehaved at the regular remand hearings at Highgate Magistrates' Court.

John Kennedy was also wanted for a daring armed snatch of £500,000 worth of gems from the International Diamond Sales display in Savoy Hotel's shopping arcade in June 1978, and now he pleaded guilty to that, plus six other robberies and asked for thirty-three other offences to be taken into consideration: fifteen years' imprisonment.

George Jones was sent to jail for seven years after pleading guilty to two robberies and asking for four other offences to be considered.

Wren's supergrassing had been impressive: in all, seventeen men were convicted of armed robberies, and eighty-three robberies and conspiracies to rob were cleared up, as were 105 burglaries and attempted burglaries; the total value of these raids amounted to over £3 million. But when his information was added to the material provided by Jimmy Gallant, fifty-three more people were charged and 190 more offences were cleared up, which brought the total amount of property stolen to £10 million.

* * *

However, there were those who should not have been trusted with supergrass status in the first place. One was Micky 'Skinny' Gervaise, who believed in the old adage of 'running with the hare and hunting with the hounds'.

He was arrested, having been named by Christopher Wren for a series of burglaries, and turned supergrass, and naming names and offences – but not all, especially his role in a £3,397,000 silver bullion hold-up on 24 March 1980 when, wearing a police officer's uniform, he flagged down a truck containing the bullion on the A13 trunk road and his associates kidnapped the lorry's occupants at gunpoint and relieved them of their load.

Gervaise later confessed his role, agreeing to give evidence against the rest of his team. Were alarm bells ringing? Well, be that as it may, the four other robbers admitted their part and were sentenced to between seven and ten years' imprisonment. On 8 April 1981, Gervaise admitted the robbery and asked for forty-five other offences to be taken into consideration.

Jailing him for six years and imposing a bankruptcy order, Mr Justice Pain said, 'Your case is made the more serious because you took part in the bullion robbery in which it was envisaged that violence would be used.'

In January 1982, a man accused of providing details to the gang of how the bullion would be transported stood trial at the Old Bailey.

Having heard Gervaise give his evidence, His Honour Judge Slot turned to the jury and said, 'You would not honestly hang a dog on his evidence, would you? You would not dream of finding a man guilty on his evidence alone, would you?' In the event that any doubt lingered in the jurors' minds, the Judge emphatically added, 'Well, *I* would not!'

This was obviously a view shared by the jury, who hurriedly acquitted the man in the dock.

Next, in April 1982, came the first of a series of trials in which Gervaise was to give evidence against two men accused of burglaries amounting to a total of £1,250,000. But he didn't. Now treated as a hostile witness, he maintained that he had only made untruthful statements, incriminating the men at the suggestion of police officers. In a further trial, the following month, he stated that he had been involved in ten criminal offences with three police officers, and that documentation in possession of the Metropolitan Police would prove that involvement.

Asked what those documents were, Gervaise replied, 'I am not going to leave myself open to criminal prosecution. I prefer not to answer that question.' He later added, 'I don't wish to participate because it is going to involve me having to tell lies and admit to tell the truth.'

The case collapsed, and one of the defendants was accused of jury-nobbling but was cleared on appeal. It was all very unsatisfactory.

★   ★   ★

Another suspect named by Christopher Wren was Tony Fiori. At his appearance at the London Sessions in April 1958, aged twenty-one, for a £400 shopbreaking, since he had just one previous conviction (for which he was placed on probation), it did seem a little steep to denounce him as 'a hardened and dangerous criminal'. It was perhaps unwise to pretend his name was Peter Anthony Jones, but he asked for ten other offences to be taken into consideration and was sentenced to two years' imprisonment. Two more convictions followed, and then in 1965 for receiving National Insurance stamps valued at £5,000 – they were part-proceeds of Post Office robberies at Bruce Grove, Tottenham, Highbury Corner and Piccadilly, Manchester – he received a 3-year sentence.

Now, fifteen years later, Fiori was turned and named names, and Albert Patrick, a detective sergeant, working on the Dips' Squad – No. 8 Squad – at the Yard was tasked to look after him. He recalled how matters went:

> We were briefed up in Whetstone and I was tasked to look after Tony Fiori after he had been debriefed by other officers and made a long and detailed confession of how he with others had burgled and robbed, mainly jewellers' shops in the UK. The one I remember the most was the Hoffix watch company in Birmingham. Fiori was an excellent safe-breaker. They had keys cut and used cutting gear to get into the safes.
>
> Looking after Tony Fiori, one of the three Supergrasses at the time, was an absolute pleasure. He was a very pleasant burglar, and we had respect for each other. We would take him out of the police station to eat, and to stop him getting bored would play golf and cards with him. In the '80s if you were a Supergrass you had to face at the charging stage your co-accused and say yes or no to the question by the custody officer, normally 'Is

this the Joe Bloggs you named in your witness statement to the police?' or words to that effect.

I was also tasked to execute a search warrant for Brian Reader in South-East London who was part of the Fiori team. He was duly arrested, and I eventually got a confession from him on what was a statement under caution. He admitted his part and was duly charged. He jumped bail and was on the run from me when the Brink's-Mat robbery at Heathrow took place, and he was caught in a country lane in Kent trying to escape from West Kingsdown.

Looking in on this investigation as an independent, I should not have been tasked to look after Fiori and at the same time be tasked to arrest and interview one of his co-defendants, Brian Reader. The witness protection unit was born and the rules in the Met changed, but it was a great case to be involved in. I say today, 'Never trust a grass', but as far as Fiori was concerned, he was one of the better ones.

Fiori proved his worth and was sentenced at the same time as Gervaise. He admitted 125 burglary or attempted burglary charges and was sentenced to five years' imprisonment.

★ ★ ★

It was round about that time that another supergrass, Ron Simpson, was admitting seven cases of robbery and burglary at the Old Bailey and asking for fifty other offences, which covered a period of ten years and had netted him £150,000, to be taken into consideration. Having been told that Simpson had made ninety statements naming forty criminals, the Recorder of London, James Miskin QC, weighed him off with five years' imprisonment, saying:

> Credit must be given to a man who has confessed and who has had the courage in giving evidence against those involved in serious crime, so that they can be brought to book and properly punished.

Dave Smith was released from HMP Reading in 1980, Ron Simpson a little later, in 1982, but being, as it were, birds of a feather, it wasn't too long before they flocked together and formed a very dangerous team indeed. Simpson had a luxury home in Perranporth, Cornwall, which contained not only sawn-off shotguns, revolvers and bottles of ammonia, but also a trunk full of disguises. There were clothes, wigs and props which enabled him to masquerade as a hunchbacked old lady, a city businessman, a milkman, a road sweeper, a tramp and finally as 'an elderly Jew', which was a suitable disguise for Golders Green when, on 29 September 1986, he and Smith attacked a Securicor van there. Unfortunately for them, Detective Inspector Bob Fenton QGM and his Flying Squad team were waiting to thwart them, which they did, successfully.

'They couldn't be supergrasses again', Fenton told me, 'and anyway, they only worked with each other.'

That wasn't quite accurate; Smith's 37-year-old nephew Paul had been conscripted into the team, as had 27-year-old Leslie Day. Referring to Simpson and Dave Smith, Bob Fenton continued:

> They had both been remanded into police custody as they were clearing up a number of offences since their release. Smith was in Golders Green police station and on his last night before going to court – and then to prison, pending his trial – he cut his wrists with the blade from a disposable razor.

Roger Smith also had an input on Dave Smith's second time around, as he told me:

> When Dave Smith admitted all his offences since his release from prison and implicated his nephew Paul, it was established that P. Smith and his family were on holiday in Cyprus. As a result of that, DS John Dixon and myself flew to Cyprus where we liaised with the local police and found the Smith family in Ayia Napa. We approached them and, quite informally, attempted to effect their return to the UK. Paul clearly realised the implications of that and was not 'playing ball'. However, we then received the news that Dave Smith had committed suicide, and when Paul was told that he immediately agreed to bring himself and his family back home and they then voluntarily flew back to the UK on the same plane as ourselves.

That left Simpson, Paul Smith and Day to appear at the Old Bailey on 26 June 1987, when Simpson admitted fifteen robberies, asked for nineteen other cases to be considered and received a 21-year sentence; Paul Smith pleaded guilty to ten charges and was jailed for fifteen years, while Day admitted seven charges and received thirteen years' imprisonment.

Roger Smith was able to add a matter of interest regarding Simpson. He told me:

Simpson was fully cooperative and admitted his offences in remarkable detail. He was giving such a huge quantity of information that the interviewing officers were struggling to record it all manually, so it was decided to tape-record his confessions. This was before tape-recording of interviews was in use, and permission was sought and granted for a reel-to-reel tape recorder to be used. Not only that, but Simpson made a detailed series of drawings, using 'matchstick men' to illustrate how he and Smith planned and carried out their robberies – a bit like a strip cartoon showing the stages of the crimes as they happened. It all truly was an instruction manual for how to commit armed robbery.

★　★　★

When Ray Fowles, Norman Jones and Peter Rose were arrested and turned supergrass, they were unable to be housed at Finchley police station, which was full to overflowing with its own supergrasses. They were moved to Whetstone police station, where they confessed to a total of 315 offences, named 198 criminals who had committed 640 major offences and uncovered an arms cache for the use of professional criminals.

Jones' crimes dated from 1965, they had netted him £242,000, and when he appeared at the Old Bailey in July 1979, the court was told that all those whom Jones had named had pleaded guilty and he would not, therefore, be required as a prosecution witness. Jailing him for five years, His Honour Judge Edward Clarke QC said:

> In normal circumstances the sort of tariff for the offences you have admitted is something approaching life imprisonment; certainly it would be in double figures in terms of years.
>
> There are special circumstances in your case for leniency in circumstances which are to be encouraged.
>
> In the war against crime, the principle of honour among thieves or robbers is one not to be encouraged by the forces of law or by Judges.
>
> If robbers and thieves can be persuaded to tell the truth not only about their own villainy but give evidence about the villainy of others it will help. That is why credit must be given when this occurs.

On 21 January 1980, Fowles (who asked for 116 offences to be considered) was sentenced to five years' imprisonment; one of those whom he had accused was his brother Herbert, who was jailed for three years after admitting four burglaries, involving £169,000. Rose, released only a year previously from a 14-year sentence for attempting to murder a police officer and who asked for sixty-two offences to be taken into consideration, received seven years.

Two days later, both Fowles and Rose gave evidence of a conspiracy to commit an armed robbery at Lambeth Town Hall in August 1978; the accused, a 35-year-old street trader, Peter Daley, informed the Old Bailey that his accusers were 'sharks setting out to catch innocent minnows'. Daley's picturesque language was followed by a barrage of accusations regarding the allegedly slipshod and cavalier way that supergrasses were treated at Whetstone police station. Daley's wife, in protest against her husband's 17-month incarceration while awaiting trial, had recently cut her wrists in the House of Lords. She could have saved herself the trauma; Daley was acquitted, and four other alleged co-conspirators similarly walked free.

# Chapter Seventeen

# An Unhappy Incident

A deeply unpleasant series of robberies occurred in England and Scotland between September 1976 and May 1977, which – through no fault of his own – resulted in equally unpleasant consequences for one of the detectives involved.

In April 1977, a house in Hoylake, Merseyside was broken into by a four-man gang, the 62-year-old occupier was hit over the head with a sawn-off shotgun and was tied up, as were his wife and brother-in-law, and property worth £23,426 was stolen.

There was a further raid at a home at Walmer Bridge, near Longdon, Preston, where a woman opened her door to a man in police uniform, accompanied by two men who, he said, were CID officers. A gun was then produced, the woman's son was seized and bound, and the gang took the mother's three-stone diamond ring, worth £5,000, and left with £300 in cash and other property, collectively valued at £16,500.

Another victim was a palmist and fortune-teller, who lived in a caravan in Airdrie. She was punched, dragged along by her hair, had a knife held to her throat, and tied up; the five raiders who had posed as police officers made off with £7,400 in cash and jewellery worth £550.

The final attack was at a house in Arbroath, where two men in police uniforms pushed their way in, while a third man carrying a sawn-off shotgun entered through the back door. The occupants, a garage owner and his 16-year-old son, were tied up and indecently assaulted, the gang demanding to know the whereabouts of £25,000. Their intelligence was good; the householder had been negotiating the sale of his garage for £25,000, but the deal had not gone through, and the robbers left with less than £300.

The gang had been arrested in Liverpool and one of them, William James Amies, was a very unpleasant, aggressive homosexual, understandably known as 'Billy the Queer' and later as 'The Snake'. The supergrass, Dave Smith, mentioned to DCI Lundy that Amies could become a valuable asset, not only because of the number of crimes he had committed but because there was a corrupt Liverpudlian detective who was in fief with one of the gang members in custody, John Tremarco, who was doing his best to get Amies to shoulder the blame for the robberies to lighten his (Tremarco's) load.

Officers went to Walton Prison, Liverpool to see Amies, without letting the police at Liverpool know; the visit was carried out through prison security. Amies agreed to confess all, and Lundy arranged for him to be transferred to Brixton Prison and from there, in December 1977, to Acton police station. There, Amies admitted twenty-seven robberies, four conspiracies to rob and eight burglaries, and named fifty-eight other criminals, although only five of these were convicted.

When it came to Amies' appearance at Liverpool Crown Court in respect of the robberies, there was considerable trouble in housing him there in police cells the night before.

On 12 January 1978, three of the defendants pleaded not guilty to conspiracy to rob; Amies pleaded guilty, and the prosecutor stated that he would be called as a prosecution witness The trial commenced with Mrs Betty Lee, the fortune-teller, informing the court in explicit detail of how she was maltreated during the robbery at her caravan ('We've got a knife and we'll do it!' … 'If you don't tell us, you bitch, you're dead!') and the following day, seeing the way the wind was blowing, with about twenty years' imprisonment heading in their direction, John Tremarco and Ronald Dainton changed their pleas to guilty and each was sentenced to fifteen years' imprisonment; no evidence was offered on a third defendant, who was acquitted. Amies was remanded until the following Monday for sentence.

Naturally, Lundy was unhappy at the thought of leaving Amies in Liverpool over the weekend, so he was taken back down to Finchley, to be returned on the Sunday night prior to his appearance at Liverpool Crown Court the following day.

To mind a volatile character such as Amies, the detectives concerned had to be just as tough, and they were: four years previously, Detective Sergeant Brian O'Rourke had been awarded the Queen's Commendation for Brave Conduct having arrested an extremely dangerous and violent man armed with a pistol. His companion was Detective Sergeant Bernie Craven who, almost exactly two years previously, had been highly commended by the commissioner after single-handedly tackling a man armed with a rifle; he was also awarded £20 from the Bow Street Reward Fund.

Now we come to the events of the night of Sunday, 15 January. There have been several accounts of what happened which, until now, have all been much of a muchness. What was said was that O'Rourke and Craven drove with Amies up to Liverpool, where it was anticipated that they would lodge their charge in a police station overnight. DCI Lundy, anticipating the type of problems that he had already experienced, also went to Liverpool, taking with him the deputy head of the Flying Squad, Detective Chief Superintendent Jim Sewell, to counter any difficulties or remove any obstructions which might arise. Upon arrival, the officers booked into the 13-storey four-star Atlantic Towers Hotel in Chapel Street. The two sergeants did indeed experience difficulty in getting their charge accommodated in a police station overnight, and when these problems could not be overcome, it was decided to book Amies into the same hotel. Therefore, one sergeant would have to share a double room with Amies, while the other slept next door. A coin was tossed, Craven lost, so it was he who would be spending the night with the prisoner. Lundy and O'Rourke went off to have a drink, Sewell went to bed and Craven and Amies went to their room.

What was said to have happened next was this: somehow Amies persuaded Craven to accompany him for an out-of-hours drink, and they went to a pub named the Crow's Nest, a venue frequented by friends of Tremarco's, where both Craven and Amies were set upon. Amies received several injuries and escaped, but Craven sustained severe concussion, a broken nose and cheekbone and was taken to hospital, where he was later seen by Lundy. One account stated that during the assault, Craven had 'lost his gun', whereas in fact, neither he nor O'Rourke had been armed.

The following day, the Judge at Liverpool Crown Court remitted Amies' case to the Old Bailey, where he later received his 5-year sentence. In a report in the *Liverpool Daily Post*, nine months later, it was stated that Craven had 'suffered severe brain damage and will almost certainly be invalided out of the force', while DCS Sewell said:

> The police still do not know why Sergeant Craven went into the pub with Amies and it is still being investigated. Obviously, Sergeant Craven was doing something with the informant.

Although Craven later made a statement to Liverpool Police about the matter he states that he was never asked any questions by any Metropolitan senior officers about the incident. He added that he received no recriminations from either Sewell or Lundy, and certainly no backing.

Additionally, two men who had been charged with inflicting grievous bodily harm on both Craven and Amies had their case thrown out by Magistrates after it was revealed that Craven would be unable to give evidence.

Mention was previously made of the activities of a corrupt Merseyside detective. On 15 March 1979, former Detective Sergeant John Francis Keating was sentenced to two and a half years' imprisonment for keeping hold of a reward of £150 which he should have passed on to an informant.

Bernie Craven received an ill-health pension, and eighteen months after that unhappy incident, he was commended by Judge Argyle for the way in which he had interviewed two of the supergrasses who had received their 5-year sentences.

So that was the account of what happened on the night of Sunday, 15 January 1978, as related, with suitable embellishments, in several books.

★   ★   ★

But was it an accurate version? It didn't seem right to me. I'd known Bernie Craven, years before, when he was a detective constable at Barking; he seemed a pretty level-headed type, so why on earth would he want to go out unaccompanied with a dangerous armed robber in the middle of the night for a drink – when the hotel bar was available to them – in a city where the criminal elements knew Amies to be a grass?

I contacted Bernie Craven, told him of my concerns, and he told me:

> I've been trying to think things through regarding the Billy Amies saga and next week I will be making notes of what I remember … amongst broken facial bones, I was told that I had a brain injury, as a result of which, I was barred from giving evidence at the CCC [Old Bailey] in other trials. I ended up leaving the Job after a professor of neurology at St Thomas' Hospital diagnosed me as having severe PTSD as a result of my injuries. I had never heard of PTSD back then. I think you need to know this because my memory is not perfect and I do not want to say anything that is wrong. I would like to set the record straight, as in a book entitled 'Scotland Yard's Cocaine Trail' (I think) what was written about what happened to me was totally untrue.

But later, Bernie Craven had indeed 'made a few notes'. and this is what he had to say:

> I have been thinking long and hard about the Amies saga and it has at times led me to a 'dark place'.
>
> I can say with certainty the following.
>
> There was a problem with 'housing' Amies in a Liverpool police station some time during the week ending Friday, 13 January

1978, and Brian O'Rourke and I were told to bring him back to Finchley, which we did. On Sunday, 15 January I drove Amies back to Liverpool with Brian O'Rourke to the Atlantic Towers Hotel, where it had, through Commander Sewell, been arranged for us all to stay that Sunday night. Commander Sewell travelled up with his driver as he was there to pull rank should there be any problems with the Liverpool police. I can't remember who DCI Lundy travelled up with, it was either me or Mr Sewell.

I recall we all had an evening meal, then at some stage Mr Lundy said he had two tickets to a boxing dinner and Brian or myself could go with him. He tossed a coin and declared Brian the winner. They disappeared, as did Mr Sewell and his driver, and I was left with Amies.

I took him to the bar, where we sat and had a few drinks. We had no need to go out to get a few drinks. It must have been about 9.30 pm that Amies told me that he had just remembered where there was an arms cache and, bearing in mind that he was to be sentenced to five years' imprisonment the next morning, I was more than keen to identify the address of this cache. I had no idea where the others were and had no way of contacting them.

I drove Amies and with his directions we entered an area known as Toxteth, where Amies directed me into a very poorly lit side street and told me to pull over and park, which I did. As soon as I had stopped the car, Amies got out and walked back the way we'd just driven, and I was out after him. I saw him walk into a pub on the corner, which I later learnt was the Crow's Nest which featured in his statements. I had no idea he had walked into the Crow's Nest and there had been no mention of it on our journey to Toxteth. I had been expecting him to point out a house where the cache was stored.

As I walked in I was immediately struck by the fact there was a horseshoe-shaped bar and that the side of the bar where we had entered was unlit, but the other side of the bar was fully lit with people drinking there.

I had just caught up with Amies at the dark bar when a curtain on my left opened and six heavies appeared and surrounded us. I immediately received a heavy blow to the back of my head and I fell to the ground. I curled up into a ball to try and protect myself as I knew what was about to come my way. I had my arms pulled from my face and I was held down whilst many punches and kicks rained down on my head. I was stamped on as well. I thought to myself, 'Is this ever going to stop?' then felt a blissful blackness envelop me; it was lovely.

I came to and found myself dangling over metal railings at the side of a main road. There were flats behind me and I managed to get myself there and I knocked on the first door through the main entrance. Someone shouted what did I want, so I took a chance and posted my warrant card through the letter box, then the door was opened and I was taken inside. The last I remember was towels being put over my head.

It must have been days later that I began to be aware of being in hospital.

My injuries were a badly broken nose, broken cheekbone, broken ribs and more importantly frontal lobe brain damage, which directly resulted in my being pensioned off. I was in hospital in Liverpool for six weeks and after returning to London I had further surgery on my nose at St Thomas' Hospital. I was also seen by a Professor of Neurology who told me I was suffering from severe PTSD, of which I'd never heard.

A few months after I was retired injured I was called to the CCC to give evidence against a number of armed robbers. I was just about to enter the witness box when a panic suddenly ensued and I was taken to the prosecuting solicitor's office, where I was told I was not allowed to give evidence because of the brain injury. I returned home and had to attend the CCC again at the trial's conclusion, when the Judge called me to the witness box and commended me and ordered that I should receive a small amount of money which would be presented later. I returned home again and after a while I was asked to attend the Tower of London at 7.00 pm on a specific date to receive a certificate. My wife and I attended the ceremony, as did Sewell and Lundy. Neither made an effort to speak, and I avoided them. I was presented with a certificate and a cheque for the small amount. My wife and I then left and Sewell's driver, Bob, took us back to the train station from where he had collected us earlier. How this had been arranged I have no idea.

I have found this very difficult to put down on paper, Dick, but I do hope this will help you.

There have been suggestions that some officers running supergrasses can 'get too close' or become involved in a sort of reverse 'Stockholm Syndrome' with their charges; and given the cunning exhibited by supergrasses, this is no doubt true – with some officers. Not, however, with Bernie Craven, who told me, 'I got on well enough with Amies when taking statements from him, both in HMP Walton and later at

Finchley. When I met him on the first couple of occasions I made it clear to him that should he not cooperate, he would be "gate-arrested" upon his release, which was imminent.'

Craven took the only possible course of action open to him; unable to contact his fellow Met officers, he certainly could not call upon the services of the Liverpool police. Supergrass Jimmy Gallant pointed out the whereabouts of an arms cache in another case, and for the police to be able to seize weapons and get them off the streets was absolutely paramount. As Craven told me:

> Sewell was correct when he spoke to the *Liverpool Daily Post* in saying that I was doing something with the informant. We went out solely for Aimes to point out the location of an arms cache, bearing in mind he was to receive five years imprisonment a few hours later.

There was a quote from that well-respected detective Ian 'Jock' Forbes which my Squad driver thought so cogent that he pinned it up on a notice board. It read:

> The CID has no place for cowards or look-before-you-leap types. They must be resolute and determined men who are ready to act upon information, no matter where it comes from.

Bernie Craven was one such detective.

What happened thereafter was as troubling as what had happened previously. In 1986, South Yorkshire Police were investigating allegations of corruption against Tony Lundy and after a year's investigations found no evidence to prefer criminal or disciplinary charges against him. However, they did ask Bernie Craven if Lundy had been present when he had been attacked; Craven replied truthfully that he had not.

But oddly, those investigating officers seemed somehow to have links with Bernie Craven's attempts to secure compensation from the Criminal Injuries Compensation Board (CICB) for the injuries he had received, as he told me:

> I tried for CICB compensation but was blocked in every possible way by a civil servant named Bilborough. I eventually threw in the towel. However, after being interviewed by the two South Yorkshire detectives in about 1986, I was told that my CICB application was still open and I was to re-apply, which I did. Eventually I attended the hearing and was awarded an acceptable sum. The Chairman of the hearing

apologised for the actions of Bilborough when he was dealing with my application.

The curtain can now be drawn across that section of the Flying Squad's Finchley and Whetstone offices which had consistently produced a stable of first-rate supergrass winners – plus one or two also-rans.

John McSwan provides a fitting epitaph for that time:

Roger Smith was office manager at Finchley ... and his contribution to the Squad over several postings was outstanding. The supergrass era was very special for C8 and the Met. Tony Lundy was the catalyst for an unprecedented period of success against armed robbers and that era of supergrasses. Our work effectively consigned armed robbery and pavement jobs to history. It was an extreme privilege to have served at Finchley with some many highly professional and brave detectives. Time and politics will sadly erase those halcyon days.

# Chapter Eighteen

# Operation Ohio

There are some police officers who are so charismatic that they become legends in their own lifetime. Such a person was Charlie Snape, who during his twenty-five years had served on the Flying Squad in several ranks, had acquired a small army of informants, was respected by the villains and hero-worshipped by the rank and file. In 1982, he was the detective chief superintendent of 'R' Division. I was in the Yard's Flying Squad office when a telephone caller asked for me by name. It was Charlie, who invited me to attend his retirement function; I was so surprised that I stammered that we'd never met.

'I know', he replied, 'but I've been told you're a good bloke.'

With man-management skills like that, it's hardly surprising that Operation Ohio was a resounding success.

A gang – nicknamed by the press 'The Thursday Gang' (because that was the day of the week when they inevitably carried out their robberies) and also 'The Chainsaw Gang' (the tool they used to cut open cash-in-transit vehicles) – had enjoyed a good run of successes, hitting cash-in-transit vehicles since 1970 and stealing something in the region of £3 million. They had struck at Lloyds Bank, Coventry, where staff members taking £5,700 to the Walsgrave Hospital were attacked by two men dressed as doctors; the wages office at Ductile Steels, Wednesfield, where a staff member was struck with the butt of a sawn-off shotgun and the raiders escaped with £8,700; four men armed with sawn-off shotguns and bolt-croppers attacked and injured guards when they stole £14,000 from Security Express on an industrial estate at Willenhall; in a similar attack, a Securicor guard was injured and £16,000 stolen at Tipton; six men armed with handguns and iron bars threw smoke canisters and squirted ammonia, hospitalising four security guards and stealing £78,000 at the Midland Bank, Darlaston; two Securicor guards were coshed with iron bars when they collected £11,400 from the National Westminster Bank, Smethwick; in the Blackwall Tunnel, southbound, £96,000 was stolen, as was £79,000 from Rochester Post Office; there were further robberies at Barclays Bank, Bracknell, Morrison's Supermarket, Bradford, London Transport garages at Plaistow and Walthamstow, and Dartmouth Auto Castings, Smethwick, where two security guards were clubbed to the ground and £76,000 was stolen; more robberies took place at Spillers & French Ltd, The Royal Docks and Heston Service Station on the M4 Motorway; a gang of six armed with shotguns and a sledgehammer attacked the wages office at Aeroplane and Motor Aluminium Castings and stole £52,000; at British Steel Ltd., Bilston, they stole £70,000, and two female employees were injured by shotgun blasts – and that was just a cross-section of the seventy-four robberies they'd carried out.

They went to great lengths to plan and carry out the raids, staying in local hotels for days, sometimes weeks, before striking. They would use taxis and public transport to leave the scenes of their robberies, or even walk away. Sometimes, getaway cars were put down as a blind to fool the police, while the gang escaped on mainline trains.

Charlie got a whisper from one of his informants – as was the case in those days, one's informants would talk to nobody else – who named those responsible. Charles Roland Knight, nicknamed 'Chopper' and 'Top Cat', was labelled as the gang's leader; Samuel Thomas Benefield was his second-in-command, and there was John Henry Segars, as well as the fearsome James Alfred Moody, who had been a member of Charlie Richardson's 'Torture Gang'. During the 1967 trial, Moody had inexplicably been acquitted and with no Charlie Richardson to guide him, he became a rudderless ship. Within a year, Moody and his brother had gatecrashed a party and, got into a fight; both brothers were jailed for six years for manslaughter, with Jimmy having another twelve months tagged on to his sentence for attacking paedophile prisoners. But following his release, he found his true metier as an armed robber.

Charlie started to piece together all that the informant had told him and realised that to catch the gang who had committed offences all over the country would be a massive undertaking. He put his plans forcefully to the Yard's senior management, who gave him the go-ahead; and now, in May 1978, Charlie recruited sixty officers from constabularies that included Thames Valley, Kent, West Midlands, Essex and Cleveland. As the intelligence poured in, an office was set up as a command centre in Westcombe Park police station at Coombedale Road, SE10, with a nucleus of Metropolitan officers (which included the expertise of C11), to form Operation Ohio, and physical and electronic surveillance was carried out in an effort to house those named by the informant.

It was while these enquiries were being conducted that the gang struck again, on 16 August 1978. Approximately nine men ambushed a Security Express van in Banstead, Surrey, blocking its passage with a stolen car in front and another behind, the latter containing Moody in a police uniform with a sawn-off and wearing a crash helmet.

Benefield blasted the tyres of the security van with a sawn-off, before the others got out of a van and cut open the cash-in-transit vehicles with chainsaws. Also involved were Charlie Knight, Brian Sims and Anthony Knightly. They helped themselves to several dozen bags containing £25,000 – a total of £788,000. Immediately afterwards, the gang went to Moody's flop in Hackney, where the spoils were divided. However, they had to send out to a shop in Mare Street, Hackney to buy seven holdalls, because the kitbags they had prepared were not big enough to contain all the banknotes.

But now, although the officers were unaware of Benefield's whereabouts, they did know that his girlfriend lived in Putney, and when she used her Barclaycard a short time after the robbery, at the Burford Bridge Hotel, Boxhill, Surrey, surveillance was taken up and she was followed to the Roof of the World Caravan Park, where the door of Benefield's caravan was bashed in and, despite his spirited attempt to escape, he – and his £82,994 proceeds from the Banstead robbery, which had been skilfully secreted behind the caravan's wall panels – were seized.

At Greenwich police station, it took no time at all for Benefield to volunteer his services to Charlie Snape as a supergrass. Detective Constable Dave Driscoll, who since February 1978 had been a member of No. 9 Regional Crime Squad, told me what happened next:

> The late DS Jim Davies and I then embarked upon taking statements from him and escorting him around the country, where he would show us where the armed robberies had taken place. Dick, his memory was unbelievable and the detail he was able to provide proved of tremendous corroborative value. He was housed in a modified cell at Eltham police station and we took the majority of statements from him at Shooters Hill police station. We lived and breathed with him for almost two years. Jim and I visited every one of those robbery sites with Sammy.

As well as admitting being involved in the robberies at Banwell, the Blackwell Tunnel and Rochester Post Office, he named names involved in those offences, as well as forty-one others. Benefield also named two security guards who had been inside-men, and one of them, Brian Upton admitted being paid £3,100 after being involved in the Rochester offence; he asked for four other offences to be taken into consideration and was later jailed for two and a half years.

John Segars was the next to be arrested – he had been spending freely, but £34,000 was recovered – and he, too, rolled over. He admitted being involved in the same robberies as Benefield as well as thirty-five others; Segars had come a long way from being fined £11 in 1967 for shooting birds out of season on Sheerness Marshes.

The net was now cast to bring in all the others named by the supergrasses; but all the time, other investigations were ongoing. When the gang had carried out the raid at Rochester Post Office – Terrence Read, David Bale, Alexander Sears, John Woodruff and Charlie Knight had also been involved – they had stolen a Post Office van in East London and fitted it with registration plates which had been issued to a van in the Medway area. The false plates had been pop-riveted on; police found the pop-rivet gun responsible in a lock-up garage beneath a railway arch, almost opposite Bow police station. Also found in the garage was an axe, and tests proved that it had been involved in the robbery at the Blackwall Tunnel; so had the five men concerned in the Rochester robbery.

There were more arrests: Anthony Knightley was captured after a car chase in Southampton; £79,000 from the Banstead robbery was found in his car boot. Charlie Knight – 'Top Cat' – was trapped in his car in a cul-de-sac in Mile End, despite having tried to escape by reversing his car with a police officer clinging to the bonnet.

There was a series of trials at Maidstone Crown Court – plans made to escape, to compromise jury members and to torch investigating police vehicles were discovered and foiled – and the trials kicked off with the Rochester robbery.

With Terrence Read howling from the dock, 'For God's sake, tell the truth!' Benefield told the court the robbery had been suggested by a crooked security guard and then went on to say:

> Knight approached me and I agreed to take part. I believe he also did the recruiting because some of them are his friends. We met in Read's sister's flat and I went to Rochester to check the escape routes.
>
> Various vehicles, including a Post Office van, had to be stolen for the robbery and Bale and I went after the van. It was taken back to a garage we had hired and false number plates fitted.
>
> Two sawn-off shotguns and two pistols were brought to the flat by Knight. On the day, we drove almost in convoy to Rochester. Another van, driven by Read, was to block the road to traffic giving us a quick getaway. Some of us were in overalls and some in jeans and we were all wearing gloves. I also had a balaclava helmet which masked my face.
>
> The plan was that we would wait in the Post van until the security van arrived, then we would drive in and wait for the money to be unloaded. What actually happened was that Bale who was in the front seat was supposed to let us know when to

attack, but Knight shouted out and we all jumped out and began attacking the guards. I had a loaded shotgun and when someone came out I told them to get back inside. I was protecting the robbers who were actually getting the money.

The money was loaded and we drove off, abandoning the van in a dead-end street before transferring to other cars. Bale and I made our way through the back streets. Back at the flat, the money was shared out and I got about £10,000. Ten per cent was taken out for the security guard and another man who made the introductions. The actual robbery only took about ten minutes and afterwards, all the clothing was burnt to remove forensic evidence.

When John Woodruff gave evidence he stated that although he had signed incriminating statements at the police station, they had already been written by the police; denying that he had participated in the Rochester robbery, he also denied knowing Benefield. Shown photographs which included one of him with Benefield, he denied it was him in the photograph.

Eventually, the gang were found guilty, and in October 1979 Knight was jailed for twenty-one years for the Blackwall Tunnel attack; he had already been found guilty of the Banstead raid – eighteen years – as he had of the Rochester robbery, for which he received fifteen years.

Stating that the gang were 'vicious, ruthless professional criminals', Mr Justice Stocker told Knight, 'You saw fit to make war on your fellow citizens and you must accept the fact that the public has to be protected against you.'

Convicted with him were Brian Sims and Anthony Knightley, each sentenced to sixteen years' imprisonment, as they were for their part in the Banstead robbery, plus Terrence Read, John Bale and Alexander Sears, who all received fifteen years; and all three received 18-year sentences for the Blackwall Tunnel robbery. John Woodruff (eighteen years), who admitted his part in the Banstead robbery, also received a 15-year sentence for his part in the Rochester raid.

On 5 November 1979, both Benefield and Segars received 5-year sentences, having asked the court to take into consideration forty-one and thirty-five other offences, respectively.

Addressing Charlie Snape, Mr Justice Stocker said:

You have had to be subjected, not only you but most of the other officers, to a great deal of suggestions of improper conduct and worse, for which I am satisfied there is no substantiation whatsoever.

I can only say once again that the thanks of the community
are due to you and your officers for the way Operation Ohio
has been conducted and the success it has brought forth.

The amount of cash recovered was £345,000; the value of property,
£50,650. But just as Bertie Smalls had given Arthur Saunders a leg-
up when he accurately stated that Saunders, who had been sentenced
to fifteen years' imprisonment, had not been part of the gang who
robbed Barclays Bank in Ilford in 1970, Samuel Benefield provided
the same service to Anthony Stock. Also in 1970, Stock had been
convicted of an armed robbery at Tesco's Supermarket, Leeds and
had been sentenced to ten years' imprisonment. He went on hunger
strike, took his case to the Appeal Court and to Strasbourg's Court
of Human Rights, all to no avail. He was released after spending
six years in Gartree top security prison. However, Benefield was
now able to say that whilst he (Benefield) had participated on the
Tesco raid, Stock had not – and a report was sent to the Director of
Public Prosecutions. It looked very much as though Mr Stock, who
had since remarried and now had two children – his first wife had
divorced him while he was in prison – was in line for an *ex gratia*
payment from the Home Office.

But there was another member of the gang who had evaded arrest
and was still missing, and Charlie Snape informed the Judge of the
dangers facing the two supergrasses, since several of the gang were
still at large, saying, 'I would not dispute that one of them is capable
of killing to protect himself.' The gang member he was referring to
was the highly dangerous Jimmy Moody.

But just six weeks later, the Ohio team received a reliable tip
that Moody was holed up in a flat in Coldharbour Lane, Brixton.
The area was surrounded by armed police, and Moody was told on
the telephone to come out. He replied that he had his 15-year-old
son with him and wanted ten minutes to get ready, stressing that
his son's safety was paramount. This, of course, was bollocks. The
reason for the ten-minute delay was so that he could stuff as much
of the stolen money in his possession as possible down the toilet; a
plumber had to be called to clear the drain.

Taken to Brixton police station, Moody admitted the three
offences of which Knight had been convicted, but no more. He
was then charged and remanded to Brixton prison to await trial.
Dave Driscoll recollects:

I was regularly handcuffed to him during his remand hearings
and on one occasion, to break the ice as it were, I asked if there

was anything (magazine, paper, etc.) I could bring him. He replied, 'A minute with Benefield'. He was a presence!

But Moody would never stand trial. One year later, on 16 December 1980, he and two others escaped from Brixton Prison's Maximum Security 'D' Block by digging through the walls of their cells, right through to an outside wall, then got down a scaffolding board, equipped with a hook and a rope. Moody's brother Richard later received an 18-month sentence for assisting in the escape, and following an enquiry, the prison's governor was transferred to another prison.

As to where Moody went then, there is only speculation; a popular theory is that he accompanied fellow escaper Gerard Tuite to Ireland, where he carried out murders on behalf of the IRA.

However, Moody was suspected of several mainland contract murders, including that of David Brindle, one of the South London family, and Moody himself was next heard of on 1 June 1993 having a drink in the Royal Hotel, Hackney. A man walked in, shot Moody four times, fatally, and walked out. No one has ever been charged with the murder.

And that was the end of Operation Ohio, which had been brilliantly carried out. It should have resulted in a Queen's Police Medal for Charlie Snape's distinguished service – but it didn't. Those types of honours go to other senior officers – and they're usually undeserved.

# Chapter Nineteen

# A Snitching of Supergrasses

Amost unusual supergrass was slim, unassuming Stuart Buckley, who was released from a prison sentence in January 1974. After he secured employment at the Bank of America, Davies Street, Mayfair as an electrician, he was approached by super-criminal Frank Maple, who suggested his connivance at breaking into the bank and relieving the safe deposit boxes of their contents. Buckley agreed and, having access to all parts of the bank (with the exception of the vault), made impressions of the bank's keys, thus giving the gang access during out-of-work hours. Their members included Micky 'Skinny' Gervaise, an expert in evaluating alarm systems. The problem was access to the vaults, but Buckley solved this by climbing into the false ceiling which housed the bank's ventilation system, poking a tiny hole through one of the polystyrene tiles with a screwdriver and inserting a monocular. When the manager and his assistant came to open the vaults, Buckley was in a position to see and memorise the combination numbers, which he duly passed on to the gang.

On the night of 24 April 1975, the gang got in, then held up the staff who had been working late and stole gold bars, gems, krugerrands and wads of currency, to a total value of somewhere between £8 and £12 million.

Thanks to some excellent work between the Yard's C11 intelligence branch and the Flying Squad, some of the gang were rounded up; Buckley admitted his role, named the rest of the gang and was treated as a supergrass. These were the early days of supergrassing, and senior uniform officers at West End Central police station, where Buckley had been housed, were outraged when, returning after an outing, his breath smelt strongly of alcohol. Flying Squad Detective Superintendent Bob Robinson defused the situation by issuing a written order saying that henceforth, whenever Buckley was taken from the police station, he had to be handcuffed to his escorts.

A little later, the same outraged officer noticed that Buckley's hair (plus that of his escorts) was damp, and Buckley admitted that they had been swimming in the Serpentine. The officer shrilly demanded to know if Detective Sergeant Fred Cutts, one of the accompanying officers, had read Superintendent Robinson's imperative. Cutts admitted he had.

'How, then', expostulated the furious officer, 'did you manage to swim whilst wearing handcuffs?'

Ever laconic, Cutts replied, 'Backstroke'.

Buckley received a 7-year sentence and duly gave evidence against the gang, who were jailed for terms of between twenty-three years for the robbery and three years for handling stolen goods. Micky Gervaise was arrested and denied everything; it was only when an incriminating diagram of a circuit was found in his wife's handbag that he admitted conspiracy and was later jailed for eighteen months.

★   ★   ★

There was a nasty blip when Charlie Lowe, who had grassed up his associates to perfection, received an 11½-year sentence. He appealed on the grounds that his assistance to law and order had been insufficiently recognised, and on 28 July 1977, Lord Justice Roskill in the Court of Appeal (Criminal Division) agreed with him. Reducing his sentence to one of five years, he said:

> It must therefore be in the public interest that the persons who have become involved in gang activities of this kind should be encouraged to give information to the police in order that others may be brought to justice and that when such information is given and acted upon, substantial credit should be given upon pleas of guilty, especially in cases where there is no other evidence against the accused than his own confession. Unless credit is given in such cases there is no encouragement for others to come forward and give information of invaluable assistance to society and the police which enables these criminals to be brought to book.

Roger Dennhardt gave evidence which resulted in 329 crimes being cleared up and twenty-nine people being sent to prison. After being released from an 8-year sentence in 1981, he appeared to have been a malign influence on one of his police minders, Detective Sergeant Graham Sayer, who in 1986 was convicted of conspiracy to rob a Post Office at Mansfield. He was sentenced to nine years' imprisonment; Dennhardt, who was never charged, denied any involvement.

Another very odd case was when the former supergrass Maurice O'Mahoney appeared at the Old Bailey in the summer of 1993 accused of robbery. He claimed that he had been approached by police to carry out a robbery in order to plant incriminating evidence on another man, and that when the robbery at a sub-Post Office at Shepherd's Bush went down, police officers incorrectly opened fire on him. The reason for this shoot-out, said O'Mahoney, was because the police wanted to kill him, since they believed he was about to incriminate corrupt officers involved with the disposal of the proceeds of the Brink's-Mat gold robbery. The prosecution regarded these assertions as nonsense, but the jury disagreed and acquitted him. Eighteen months later, O'Mahoney served a writ on the commissioner for aggravated and exemplary damages, alleging that the murder plot had been conceived to protect corrupt officers from exposure. Apparently, this claim was settled four years later without admission of liability, allegedly to the tune of £100,000. Well, well.

Another supergrass who, like O'Mahoney, was thought to have re-offended was Leroy Davies. In May 1978, Davies – a serial armed robber – was arrested for raids which had netted £317,000, rolled over and named over forty criminals involved in more than thirty armed robberies which had netted somewhere in the region of £1,500,000. He had been helped to come to his decision whilst in custody, when he married Elizabeth, a 17-year-old divorced mother of two. Admitting six charges of robbery, conspiracies and possessing firearms at St Albans Crown Court on 24 July 1978, Davies asked for thirty-three other offences to be taken into consideration, including fifteen robberies, three attempted robberies and twelve conspiracies to rob.

Mr Justice Stocker told him. 'The Court of Appeal has given directions to the effect that very substantial credit should be given to men who assist the police as much as you have – and I do.'

Davies was probably aware that three weeks previously, one Edward Martin had appeared before the same Judge and had pleaded guilty to eleven charges of handling stolen goods. The Judge had been told that, as a supergrass, Martin had provided evidence against seventy armed robbers and forgers, thereby breaking up a £1,500,000 racket, and had then been sentenced to eighteen months' imprisonment, suspended for two years. Seeing that Davies' testimony had uncovered offences totalling the same, he obviously had high hopes when it came to his own case. Therefore, receiving a 10-year sentence obviously knocked him off his feet, but an appeal brought his jail time down to seven years.

While serving his sentence, Davies was approached by officers from 'Operation Countryman' and he provided them with details about allegedly corrupt police officers that were so ridiculous that no one was ever charged – reasons for this will be found later in Chapter Twenty-Two.

Davies had only served two years, plus a few months, when he was released in 1980. Now under the name of Leslie Newton, he was arrested the following year for a robbery at the French Revolution public house, Putney Common, with his older brother Glanford, when a shot was fired. The prosecution's case was that Glanford had been arrested after a violent struggle, during which most of the stolen £2,600 had been recovered, and Leroy had escaped but was arrested five weeks later.

It seemed that grassing was in the Davies family's genes, because it was Glanford who pointed the finger at his brother; at the Old Bailey in April 1982, Glanford pleaded guilty and Leroy was acquitted, having told the jury that he would never have risked his new identity by going back to crime. Judge Lawson was not of the same persuasion as the jury; he invited them to listen to Glanford's confession, which had been excluded from the trial proceedings.

Glanford, who was on licence from a 14-year sentence for armed robbery, received a 5-year sentence from the Judge, who commented, 'I have no doubt as to the true identity of that gunman.'

Leroy, sporting a brand-new identity, walked free.

# Chapter Twenty

# Unusual Supergrasses

A most unusual supergrass was a 34-year-old lady by the name of Zenith (yes, really) 'Tina' Meer, who had not worked since she was twenty but had accepted presents of cash, jewellery, cars and clothes from men, although, as she told a jury at the Old Bailey, 'only by one boyfriend at a time'.

It appeared that she had found stability in her life with one Billy Gentry, a career criminal with fifteen previous convictions, who in 1967 had been jailed for shooting at police officers. The two officers in question were awarded, respectively, a George Cross and a George Medal, and Gentry received seventeen years' imprisonment.

Despite spending £25,000 furnishing Ms Meer's Holloway council flat and giving her a gold-coloured Mercedes for her birthday, as well as a Cartier watch and £15,000 in cash, Mr Gentry overstepped the mark when he beat her up outside a club. This led to his inamorata grassing him up to the police, not only in respect of the assault but also for large-scale thefts on the railways of travellers' cheques, cash and jewellery totalling £250,000. Ms Meer was well able to do this, because it had been her flat that had been used as a distribution centre for the stolen goods; and as a result, Gentry, Tommy Wisbey, who had been paroled in 1976 after serving twelve years of a 30-year sentence for the Great Train Robbery, and seventeen others arrived in the dock at the Old Bailey.

Having been given immunity from prosecution, Tina Meer utterly denied acting out of revenge or that she had spoken to the police for money, although she admitted asking about reward money and selling her story. In March 1982, Gentry went down for nine years, with sixteen other members of the gang receiving sentences of between six years and nine months; Wisbey escaped with a £500 fine.

Tina Meer stated that she was 'in fear of her life' and spoke of having plastic surgery, so she was guarded by armed police, after an £80,000 contract was taken out on her. However, she was unable to prevent herself being photographed in a number of sexy poses, nor was she able to resist giving a series of rather nauseating interviews regarding intimate details of her life.

*　*　*

When John Moriarty, aged eighteen, appeared at North London Magistrates' Court on 16 August 1963 and told the Bench that he was unaware that the vehicle in which he was a passenger had been taken without the owner's consent – and they believed him – it might have occurred to all and sundry (other than those particular Magistrates) that young Mr Moriarty was a stranger to the truth.

Moriarty then progressed to becoming a well-known North London blagger who was not particularly well-liked, since it was thought – quite possibly with some justification – that he was a grass. In March 1965, he was walking along Highcroft Road, Holloway, having left The Favourite public house, Hornsey Rise, when a van pulled up alongside him and a man armed with a shotgun got out and let him have both barrels, sending Moriarty to the Whittington Hospital to be dealt with for suspected fractures of both legs and multiple lacerations. He accused one Francis Smith of being responsible.

Smith denied it, quite rightly, because on a remand appearance at Marylebone Magistrates' Court in June, Mr Nigel Robinson, the Magistrate stated, 'I have never heard a witness in whose evidence I could put less credence than Moriarty', after Moriarty confessed that he'd lied to police.

The Favourite featured again three years later when, following an altercation there during a wedding party at which he was best man, Moriarty was shot, once again, in the legs; additionally, he was charged with causing an affray, as was the bridegroom.

When police arrived to discuss the cause of Moriarty's wounded legs, he replied, 'I fell down the fucking stairs, didn't I?'

Once again, he was being less than candid, especially shortly afterwards when he went on to accuse a salesman of wounding and possessing a shotgun with intent to endanger life. That charge went the way of the previous one. Understandably, due to undesirables' penchant for discharging both barrels of sawn-off shotguns at him, Moriarty's nickname became 'The Target'.

Micky Cornwall was a friend of Moriarty who in 1975 mentioned that he was planning 'a big robbery, possibly in the Blackpool area'; and friend or not, that was probably a mistake, because shortly afterwards, the West Midland Crime Squad put him under surveillance. Not that that did Moriarty or the Crime Squad any good, because three weeks after Moriarty's last sighting of Cornwall, his body was found in woodland; he had been shot in the back of the head as a result of a gangland contract.

The years went by, and by now Moriarty had well and truly lost his bottle; he was terrified at the thought of going back to prison. It appeared he changed tactics, because in the late 1970s when the licensee of The Castle public house, Kentish Town, became the victim of 'the Corner Game' (so-called, because criminals would induce the victim, or mug, to part with cash for dodgy goods – usually spirits or cigarettes – which were awaiting collection, 'just around the corner'; then the mug discovered, too late, that the crates contained nothing but rubbish), he named John Moriarty as the perpetrator. Because Moriarty was a notorious C11 Main Index man, the detective sergeant at Kentish Town police station thought it would be good for Detective Constable Gordon Livingstone's reputation to investigate, and he now takes up the tale:

> I got as much info about him as I could and with a bit of trepidation (and with a few of my buddies) I went through his front door early one morning over on Holloway's section. He was a very imposing figure but he gave no trouble. He was nicked and charged at Kentish Town and committed for trial at the Inner London Crown Court. Some months later, on the morning of the trial, Moriarty arrived at the pre-fab courts at the Inner London Crown Court. He was handcuffed to two burly No. 9 Regional Crime Squad detectives (in their obligatory sheepskin coats, with a hint of permed curly hair). They led Moriarty into the police waiting room, where he sat down and was uncuffed. His whole persona had changed; he was like a rabbit caught in the headlights.
>
> The next thing was that Detective Inspector John Kemp arrived, introduced himself to me and said to Moriarty, 'This is the first favour we're doing you today. No evidence will be offered on DC Livingstone's case and the matter will be left on the file.' He then explained that Moriarty had become a resident informant. The Judge had obviously been briefed beforehand and justice was dispensed, without fuss. That was the last I saw of Big John Moriarty.

Moriarty became part of Operation Albany, which had been set up to investigate allegations of impropriety regarding Detective Chief Inspector Tony Lundy and his top informant, Roy Garner. The enquiry lasted a year, but all Moriarty was able to provide was hearsay evidence.

Gordon Livingstone (later to become a valuable member of the Flying Squad) told me, 'Later, I heard about his demise in Spain; taken out by a hitman.'

It may be that Moriarty's decease was not the result of an encounter with a professional assassin, although 'hit' did come into the equation. I did hear that in June 1990 he was dragged out of a bar in Benalmádena on the Costa del Sol and either fell or was pushed under the wheels of a passing 32-ton lorry. I suppose that Spanish lorry drivers can act quite recklessly, although various dodgy characters inhabit that part of Spain's north-east coastline – many of them ex-pats.

# Chapter Twenty-One

# Hitman

There was one offender who, it was thought, would become the supergrass of the decade. That was Maxwell Thomas Piggott, and on the face of it there was every reason to believe he would be.

In 1965, Piggott should have attended the Inner London Sessions to answer charges of housebreaking and false pretences. he failed to appear, and when he was arrested he sought to evade capture by squirting ammonia into the eyes of the arresting officers. Following his conviction on the housebreaking charges, when he asked for ninety-five other offences to be taken into consideration, on his first conviction he was sentenced to four years' imprisonment. Later the same year, Piggott pleaded guilty to throwing a corrosive fluid with intent and two cases of housebreaking, asked for fifty-eight other offences to be taken into consideration and received a 7-year sentence, concurrent to the four years. Three years later, he escaped from Wormwood Scrubs and in 1969 he was arrested for fraud while in possession of an automatic pistol, and was sentenced to six years' imprisonment.

In 1978, he was arrested for a series of armed robberies, and for using a firearm with intent to resist arrest he received a 10-year sentence. One year into that sentence, Piggott decided to turn supergrass and in seventy-four separate statements, he named 105 criminals who had been involved in armed robberies; but what he also offered was a jewel in the crown of supergrassing.

In 1970, David Knight – a member of a notorious family of scoundrels which included club owner Ronnie Knight, then married to the actress Barbara Windsor – was stabbed to death in the Latin Quarter nightclub, Leicester Square, by Alfredo 'Italian Tony' Zomparelli, who then fled. Six months later, he gave himself up, pleaded guilty to manslaughter and was sentenced to four years' imprisonment. Released from prison, Zomparelli was playing pinball in Soho's Golden Goose amusement arcade, when two men entered and he was shot dead. Ronnie Knight was the prime suspect but he was impressively alibied; and for the moment, there the matter rested.

Now Piggott dropped his very welcome bombshell. He stated that he and Nicky Gerrard Jr had been paid by Ronnie Knight – with what appeared to be the rather miserly sum of £1,325 – to shoot Zomparelli. On 17 January 1980 at the Old Bailey, Piggott pleaded guilty to the murder and also an arson, two armed robberies and shooting a man with intent to cause him grievous bodily harm, and asked for 107 offences to be taken into consideration. Sentenced to life imprisonment, Piggott was now able to give evidence against Ronnie Knight and his accomplice, Gerrard.

However, one must assume that Barbara Windsor – and by association, her husband Ronnie – was much loved by the jury, because they acquitted both men of murder; and now Piggott was viewed as an unreliable witness, and his desirability as a supergrass tempted his handlers no longer. He spent ten years in Wakefield Prison on Rule 43 – in prison parlance, 'behind the door' – and following his release, slipped quietly below the radar.

As a result, 105 possible felons went free, and Ronnie Knight went on to participate in the Security Express robbery, flee to Spain, dump Babs, remarry and later receive a 7-year sentence. He also admitted his involvement in the murder in his memoirs, until the double-jeopardy rule came in, when he swiftly denied it.

Of course, it was hardly Piggott's fault that the jury had acquitted two extremely guilty men.

★   ★   ★

Black informants were referred to as 'Black Gold', and that was a well-deserved epithet. I ran several black informants who provided me with impressive results. Other officers were not so diligent. Two Yardies recruited as informants promptly ran rings around their handlers; one of them carried out a series of armed robberies, dealt drugs, ran extortion rackets and a chain of prostitutes, whilst the other raped, then murdered a young woman. Those dopey handlers should have waved the big stick at their informants to tell them what was what; I always did.

The first black supergrass was Errol Walker. Arrested for a robbery in 1982, he decided to roll over and name names, and after admitting twenty-six other robberies he received the (almost) statutory 5-year sentence. It seems that Walker was released in double-quick time, because in December 1985 he murdered his sister-in-law and, in a siege situation, held her young daughter captive. He had tied the child to a chair with flex, slashed her arms and legs with a kitchen knife, severing several tendons, placed a plastic bag over her head and threatened to cut off her right hand. It was one of those doomed situations when negotiations simply don't work.

Screaming, 'She dies, she dies!' Walker plunged the knife into the little girl and was shot, twice. Mercifully, the child survived. Unhappily, so did Walker, who, one year later, his left arm and left leg paralysed, was sentenced to life imprisonment.

So by 1982, over a 5-year period, fifty offenders had become supergrasses. It had resulted in 451 people being charged, 262 convicted and eighty-five acquitted.

But by then, dark clouds had started to form over London with the advent of Operation Countryman.

# Chapter Twenty-Two

# Operation Countryman

In the summer of 1978, rumours emerged from a supergrass that huge sums of money were being paid to corrupt City of London police officers to water down evidence and arrange bail in serious cases of armed robbery (those where a murder had been committed), and then to offer no evidence at all. Then, as the rumours gathered momentum, it was suggested by a supergrass being run from Finchley that Flying Squad officers were also involved. The head of the Squad immediately informed the commissioner, and these concerns were forwarded to the Home Secretary. It was a matter that required a task force of seasoned, hard-bitten detectives from a major police force – Liverpool, Manchester or Birmingham – to tackle these immensely serious allegations head-on. Instead, the Home Secretary selected the sleepy Dorset police force to deal with the matter, and that force's Assistant Chief Constable to lead a team to spearhead the enquiry.

It was a calamitous decision which would later prompt the Home Secretary to say, 'I have always had slight doubts about it' – by which time the wheels had well and truly come off.

To start with, very few officers who staffed the enquiry were detectives at all. Many were traffic patrol officers who had their rank elevated and the title 'detective' plonked in front of it. That didn't fool the detectives they were trying to investigate, and it certainly didn't fool the supergrasses (or any other criminals) that they were interviewing. Next, informant-running was an art developed on a day-to-day basis, learnt over a period of years by Metropolitan Police detectives: how to differentiate the genuine snout from the 'tapper' – someone giving flimsy or bogus information for the price of a drink; how to run the informant and how to protect him – or her – from identification; how to develop the trust needed when speed was essential – when there was no time to procure a search warrant – to 'go in with one's head down'.

It was a skill seriously deficient in the Dorset team.

Last – and by no means least – those officers had just a flimsy outline of what evidence was required in criminal law to prosecute an offender to conviction. Therefore, if a person was found in possession of property that they believed was stolen, they had no idea that they had to prove (a) that the property was, in fact stolen and (b) if it was, then that person in possession of it had known or believed it to be stolen.

This was not a problem for career Metropolitan Police detectives; quite apart from practical experience, they had all attended the excellent 10-week Initial Course at the Detective Training School.

The supergrasses could hardly keep straight faces when they were interviewed by officers whom they regarded as simpletons. They simply told them whatever it was they wanted to hear and refused to make statements to authenticate their claims, so those officers made statements which repeated what they'd been told. It's known as hearsay evidence, not that they appeared to be aware of that. The Dorset officers had already been nicknamed 'The Swedey', in mocking parody of 'The Sweeney', and now they were making promises to the supergrasses that they could not possibly keep: telling them the length of sentence they would receive at court, or assuring them that there would be no sentence at all, because they would engineer free pardons to permit them to walk free.

One supergrass trial after another buckled after it appeared their evidence was hopelessly compromised, but still 'The Swedey' (they were also known as 'Malice in Blunderland') continued to commit one gaffe after another. Just as bad was when officers accused by Countryman were suspended from duty. They were regarded as 'tainted', and in any trials in which they were due to provide testimony – and because they were hard-working officers, there were usually a lot – they were obliged to offer no evidence. By the time those officers were acquitted, their suspensions lifted or in any other way completely exonerated, months, sometimes years, had gone by and the trials of men accused of very serious offences in which they had been due to give evidence had collapsed. It meant that scores, if not hundreds, of very guilty, dangerous criminals had simply walked free. It went further than that. Since the prosecutors had offered no evidence and since the officers who had supervised those cases had been branded as corrupt, those criminals felt aggrieved. They were clearly innocent – indeed, the courts had said so – so they sued for unlawful arrest and malicious prosecution, and won. Those settlements were tax-free; just like their ill-gotten gains from banks and other victims.

Allegations – sometimes most profoundly stupid ones – were made against 187 Metropolitan Police officers, from which emerged not one single criminal conviction.

After a 4-year enquiry that cost £4 million, eight Metropolitan Police officers who went on trial were acquitted, and the two City of London police officers who were at the centre of the enquiry from its commencement were convicted. That was due to the courage and expertise of the head of the City of London's CID – who had joined that force after spending most of his career with the Metropolitan Police's Flying Squad.

As one former detective superintendent at Scotland Yard told me, 'If I'd been sent down to Dorset to investigate cattle rustling, I'd have been out of my fucking depth, too.'

As a result of these ludicrous antics, it was only slightly amazing that the whole supergrass system wasn't abolished there and then. That would have suited the eminent barrister Michael Mansfield KC, who stated:

> Supergrasses are inherently dishonest witnesses who act out of self-interest knowing there is a reward in it for them. These people know about crime but in order to inveigle their way into their favour, they dress it up – they put people at the scene who were not there. They have axes to grind, they have vendettas to settle.

Some of those assertions might well be true; similarly, it could be said there are certain defence barristers who act in exactly the same way, defending people who they know to be guilty, screeching histrionically at witnesses who they know are speaking the truth, concocting defences and alibis for their clients and accepting their fees in cash, knowing it to be the proceeds of crime.

But despite Mr Mansfield's strictures, fortunately, supergrassing continued.

# Chapter Twenty-Three

# Don Barrett

We left Donald Walter Barrett in Chapter Four, languishing in prison, serving a 12-year sentence for the botched raid at Lloyds Bank in Bournemouth. It's now time to take a closer look at his antecedents.

Barrett already had two findings of guilt as a juvenile offender behind him for offences of storebreaking, theft and taking a vehicle without consent, for which he had been sent to approved school, when he appeared at Greenwich Magistrates' Court on 13 April 1954, aged seventeen, and a charge of receiving a stolen pedal cycle was dismissed.

'You are young and don't know enough about the ways of the world, perhaps', said the Magistrate, who was unaware of his record. 'But don't go buying things on street corners again, for this is the sort of thing that happens.'

Barrett was not so fortunate four months later, when he was committed to the London Sessions for breaking into a neighbour's house on 17 July 1954, rifling the gas meter and helping himself to some rings and cash. For a haul worth just £7, it hardly seemed worth his while, but it was sufficient for him to be sentenced to Borstal Training. Barrett was one of three youths who escaped from Borstal and broke into a shop in Kirton, Lincolnshire, stealing sweets and cash, and after an appearance at a special court at the Sessions House, Boston, on 25 October 1954, they were sent straight back.

By July 1958 Barrett had acquired four more convictions, and when he appeared at the Middlesex Sessions for two offences of breaking and entering an office and stealing a safe and its contents, valued at £135, he was sentenced to four months' imprisonment.

He was released on 2 September, but within five months, he and another man attacked the manager of The Golden Dragon public house, Brockley who was taking £148 to the bank. Barrett punched the manager, breaking his nose, but with considerable courage a passing waitress went to the victim's assistance, sloshing the two attackers with her handbag.

They escaped in a car, stolen from a car park at Catford that morning, and although Barrett provided a specious alibi he was found guilty, and in March 1959, the Common Serjeant at the Old

Bailey sentenced him to four years' imprisonment, saying: 'This form of violence cannot be encouraged at any time. I am taking into consideration your age and the sentence for this type of offence is a lenient one, in the circumstances.'

It was not lenient enough for Barrett who, as we know, enjoyed a short-lived escape from Wandsworth Prison on 6 February 1961 in company with one Micky Salmon.

Barrett was released from Lincoln Prison on 13 February 1963 – he must have been a recalcitrant prisoner, since he had served all but one month of his 4-year sentence – but his girlfriend, Sheila Saker, who swore she would wait for him, did just that, and within two hours of his release they were married at St Giles' Church, Lincoln. The *Retford, Worksop, Isle of Axholme and Gainsborough News* reported that as the newly-weds set off to a secret location to start a new, happier life together, 'they turned their backs on the past.'

Don't you believe it; one of them didn't.

★　★　★

Following Smalls 'doing the Royals' (it would soon become colloquially known as 'doing a Bertie'), Barrett had the finger of blame pointed at him while he was serving his 12-year sentence, which resulted in him appearing, together with others of 'The Wembley Mob', at the Old Bailey. There were a number of offences that Smalls accused Barrett of complicity in, but he was acquitted of some, and others were left on the file. However, in September 1974, he was convicted of his part in the Ilford Bank robbery in 1970 and for that, was sentenced to seventeen years' imprisonment, to run concurrently with his 12-year sentence for the raid on Lloyds Bank, Bournemouth. In March 1975, Barrett appealed against conviction and sentence. The conviction stood, but his sentence was reduced to one of twelve years' imprisonment.

Released from Maidstone prison, it took no time at all for Barrett to get back into the swing of things: acquiring associates, equipping himself with a variety of firearms, planning a raid on the KLM security depot at Heathrow to relieve them of their stock of gold and diamonds, carrying out two robberies which made him £80,000, another at a Safeway supermarket at Sydenham, attempting four robberies and shooting a man at Catford.

But he was caught, and this time, he decided to follow the current trend of supergrassing, because no matter how bad a criminal's record might be – and let's face it, Barrett's was pretty bad – a more or less unofficial tariff of five years' imprisonment for supergrasses had, as we know, become the norm.

Ken Grange was a detective sergeant on the Flying Squad and he describes what happened:

> When I spoke to Barrett, he named John Hilton as being a man with a long and serious criminal history. I really got into Hilton's head and he confessed to a robbery at Barclays Bank, Canning Town and a couple of very nasty country house robberies. After that, he got 'cold feet' stating that he couldn't cope in dealing with me as he would open up too much and he had been involved in one particular offence which was of national interest.

That was a curious thing to say, and it is worthwhile taking a closer look at Hilton, if only to describe the type of criminal that Barrett was associating with.

Hilton received a life sentence for murder, committed during the course of a robbery in 1963, and was freed on licence in February 1978. He met Barrett just by chance in Lewisham, in 1980; they knew each other from being incarcerated in Hull Prison together, and they agreed to go to work. Arrested as a result of the evidence provided by Barrett, in June 1981 Hilton pleaded guilty to five robberies, two attempted robberies and conspiracy to rob and was sentenced to fourteen years' imprisonment. He escaped from Kingston Prison on 6 October 1990 and within a month committed a £90,000 robbery at a jeweller's in Brighton. On 4 December 1990, he and an associate robbed Harvey & Gore Jewellers, Burlington Arcade, London of valuables worth £420,000 and shot and wounded one of his pursuers. Arrested, he astonished his interviewers by confessing that within a month of his release in 1978, he and an associate had murdered a jeweller and robbed him of diamonds worth £280,000; Hilton had also accidentally (but fatally) shot his confederate.

This was the secret he had kept for thirteen years; the secret over which he'd got 'cold feet' when speaking to Ken Grange.

On 9 December 1991, the Judge at the Old Bailey told Hilton, 'I shall recommend that you are a man who should never be allowed to be at liberty again.'

So Barrett grassed up everyone he'd worked with, and at the Old Bailey on 26 June 1981 he pleaded guilty to a total of sixteen offences. James Crespi QC put up a creditable line in mitigation, saying that his client's life would be in jeopardy for years to come, but while Mr Justice Mustill said that he took into account Barrett's full confession and his willingness to testify against fellow criminals, he regarded him as 'an exceptionally dangerous man' from whom the public had to be protected and weighed him off with fourteen years' imprisonment.

Well, that was a shock to the system and no mistake, and Barrett successfully appealed, getting his sentence slashed to one of seven years. Taking into account his time spent in custody, his good behaviour and perhaps a little string-pulling, Barrett served just three years and four months.

He was provided with a new identity and a job, but working as a £200 per week scaffolder came hard to someone like Barrett, who had thoroughly enjoyed living 'the good life' and was extremely reluctant to give it up.

So he didn't.

★　★　★

There were not too many seasoned villains who'd want to go to work with Barrett now that he had a reputation as a grass, not that they could be particularly blamed.

It was Ronnie Dark who suggested that Barrett should work with David Terrence Croke, which was odd because – on their first outing – it appeared that the unprepossessing-looking Croke was a non-starter when it came to armed robbery. Short, slim, wearing glasses and with a wispy moustache, Croke had not shown any particular expertise during his lifetime – save in one area. He had an aptitude for inventions. Croke – he also used the name Gray – had been forgotten about, until his name came up in conversation with Ronnie Dark and Don Barrett. So Barrett was persuaded to give Croke a try-out, and furthermore, he had a piece of work that was ideal for a two-man team.

A security van which made deliveries to municipal offices in Wansey Street, Southwark, always parked in Ethel Street at the rear of the premises at the bottom of a cul-de-sac. That was adjacent to Larcom Street, which abutted St John's Church. A low wall separated the churchyard from Larcom Street, and from behind it observation could easily be kept on the arrival of the security van and the custodians making the delivery. Barrett's plan was to attack the guards, grab the money, run into Larcom Street and vault over the wall into the churchyard where, secreted in some bushes, would be two stolen motorcycles. The cash would be inserted into rucksacks, they would ride to the entrance of the church, split up and get away to a predetermined rendezvous. There, the motorcycles would be ditched and a further getaway made in a nondescript-looking car.

Barrett had worked out the rendezvous point with Croke, the stolen motorcycles had been stashed in the shrubbery and now,

Barrett and Croke were in position to see the security van arrive – and that was it. This was purely a dress-rehearsal. Barrett was a consummate professional; but Croke was not, and on the way back to the motorcycles he grumbled that they could have carried out the robbery there and then. Barrett merely replied that now that Croke had familiarised himself with the plot, it could be easily done the following week.

Just as they reached the concealed motorcycles and Barrett started to pull his from the bushes, there came an enraged shout. 'So you're the ones to did it!' The furious, middle-aged verger advanced towards them, roaring, 'How *dare* you! Don't you know this is consecrated ground?'

Several thoughts flashed through Barrett's mind. First, the job was finished – all over and had to be abandoned, never to be resurrected; next, although the verger could have no conception that a robbery had been planned, it was essential not to let his face be seen, so he swiftly put on his motorcycle helmet; and lastly, it was crucial not to enrage the verger any further – he might mention it at the next parish meeting, but nothing should be said or done to inflame the situation which could lead to attracting the attention of the police.

With his natural inclination for survival, those thoughts took seconds to materialise, so now, with his face effectively masked by the helmet and as he swung his leg over the motorcycle, Barrett muttered, 'Sorry. Guv'nor. Didn't realise – stupid thing to do … won't happen again … we'll be off now. Sorry about that.'

Then he realised that Croke hadn't mounted his machine. Turning, he was astonished, as was the verger, because Croke had grabbed hold of him.

'You fucking slag!' shouted Croke. 'Fucking tell me what to do? I'll fucking stripe you, you – '

At that, Barrett grabbed hold of Croke, pulled him off the verger, pushed him towards his motorcycle and snapped, 'Get going!'

The two motorcycles roared away, keeping in convoy until Barrett spotted some deserted ground, sufficiently secluded and far enough away from the churchyard, and signalled to his companion to pull in there.

As Croke got off his motorcycle and took off his helmet, he said, 'Blimey, that fucking priest was well out of order – ' before he got Barrett's right hook in his eye.

'YOU CUNT!' roared Barrett, as Croke lay sprawled on the ground. Furious that a sweet little job had been ruined, Barrett was so angry that he found it difficult to find the right words. 'I must've been fucking mad, putting my lot in with a cunt like you! Crazy! You've got no more idea than … Right. Your bike – get rid of it. And you, you stupid bastard, I don't want to see or hear from you again – got it?'

And that might have been that, except that fate dictated that he should give Croke one more chance. After all, as previously stated, there were not too many top-class criminals ready to throw their lot in with a self-proclaimed supergrass.

There was one who took out his own private insurance policy. He told Barrett, 'I'll work with you but if you ever grass me, I'll kill you. I'll inject Paraquat into your milk bottle. Make no mistake, I'll kill you and your family.'

Paraquat is a life-threatening poison with no antidote. He'd obviously done his homework, and Barrett was in no doubt that he meant it. But, then again, Barrett couldn't afford to pass him up. Scheming, meticulous and ruthless, George Henry Ince was a top-class armed robber.

Detective Sergeant Dick Kirby.

Detective Constable Kevin Shapland.

Scenes of Crime Officer Paul Millen.

Flying Squad driver, PC 259 'CO' Tony Freeman.

The ambushed
security van on the
M1 Motorway ...

... and the robbers' van, used
to follow it.

Barrett's automatic pistol.

Croke's revolver.

Robbers' kit.

The prize on the M1 – value £283,500.

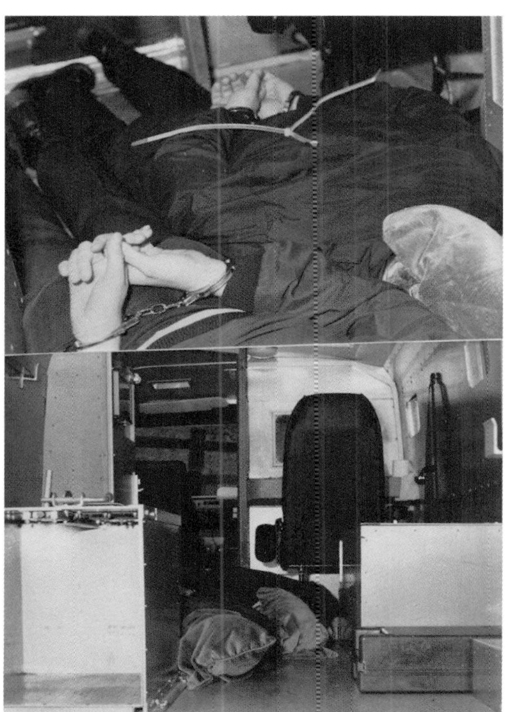

Two restrained custodians: one innocent, one not.

Croke's arrest.

'Emerald'.

The contents of Rita Croke's car.

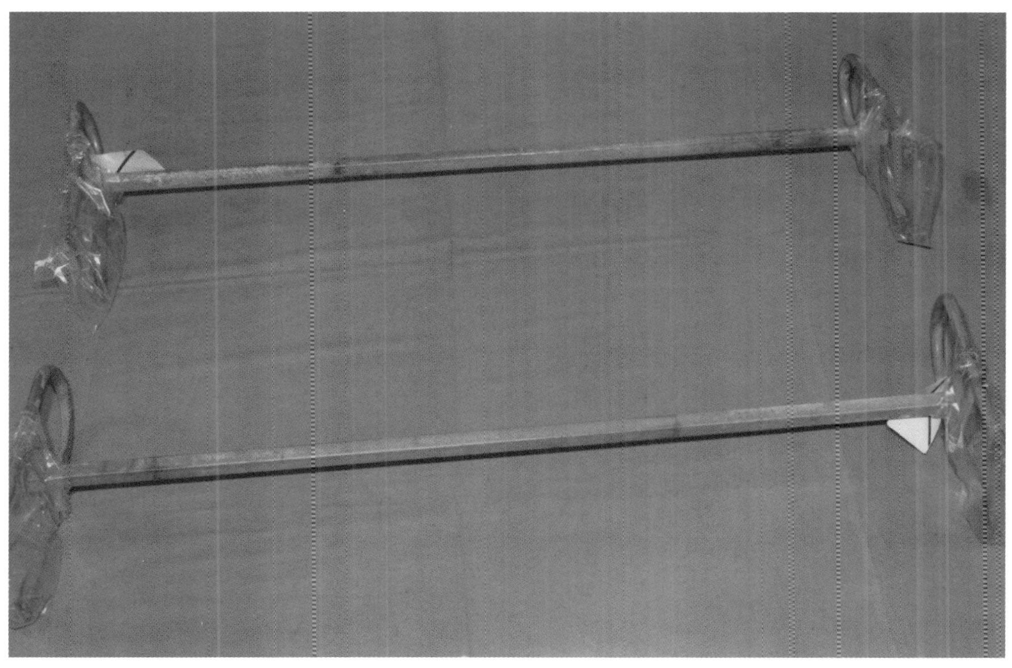

The roof rack from the Honda, used at Armaguard ...

... and all that remained of the Honda, left in France.

Croke's flat in Malta.

The DAF, purchased in France.

Croke's over-painted boat, in Malta …

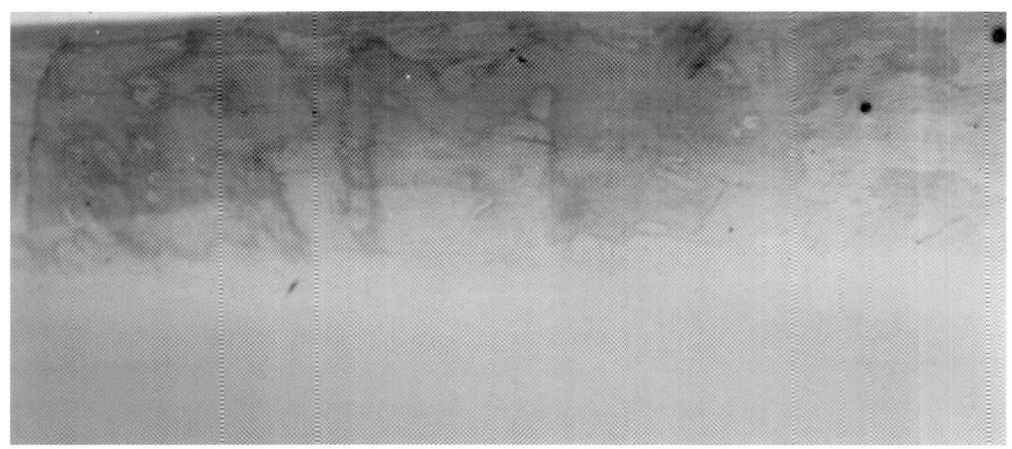

… but with 'ARMAG' revealed, under the paint.

Barrett's arrest: 'Hello, Phil; nice little tickle you've had here!'

# Chapter Twenty-Four

# George Ince

Born in Stratford, in London's East End, in 1938, Ince was a bit of a tearaway but probably no more or less than other youths in that area. His first brush with the law came at the age of seventeen, when he and another were seen by two aids to CID trying car door handles in Aberavon Road and Stratford Road, Bow on 18 February 1955.

Ince denied wrongdoing, saying, 'We never had nothing. I wouldn't mind if we had', and the untruthful manager of the Regal Billiards Hall (at that time owned by the Kray twins) turned up to alibi both men, although it transpired that at the time he told the Bench that he was chatting to them in the Billiards Hall, both Ince and his companion had been detained at Bow police station, some fifteen minutes earlier. Ince's companion, who had six previous convictions, was sentenced to three months' imprisonment; Ince, with a clean sheet, was placed on probation.

Ince spent just six months carrying out his National Service with the Royal Fusiliers before he was discharged; some said it was because he was too psychotic to be trusted with a gun, Ince's very protective family of five sisters and two brothers said it was on compassionate grounds.

He was next charged with a group of youths who attacked, kicked and punched an off-duty police officer; this time, he was sentenced to nine months' imprisonment.

On 17 October 1958, Ince was one of four young men who went into Ching's Restaurant in Pennyfields and loudly used bad language that was commented upon by a fellow diner, Albert Groves, who was there with his wife and a friend. Ince smashed a bottle of tomato sauce over the diner's head, causing a two-inch gash into which stitches had to be inserted. At the hearing at Thames Magistrates' Court, it was clear that Mr Groves had been got at, because he told the Magistrate, 'I thought it was Ince but now I'm not sure' and went on to say that whoever it was that had hit him, he did not wish to press charges. But the police constable who was called to the restaurant told the court that Groves had said in Ince's presence, 'This is the man who hit me.'

Furthermore, Ince had later told the officer, 'He came at me with a bottle. He's a big bastard. I wouldn't have stood a chance. I took it away from him and let him have it.'

This statement was definitely denied by Ince; nevertheless, he was convicted and sentenced to six months' imprisonment.

He was then arrested for breaking into Beverly Maintenance Service Ltd of Stoke Newington High Street on 1 January 1960 and stealing £9 12s 0d, and was bailed from North London Court to stand trial at London Sessions. But he failed to appear and was not arrested until October 1961; when he finally appeared at the London Sessions he was sentenced to two years' corrective training.

But by now, Ince had formed a relationship with Dolly Kray, the wife of Charlie, the third of the Kray brothers; understandably, a risky liaison. Accounts vary of how matters progressed during a confrontation between Charlie Kray and Ince, although the suggestion from members of Ince's family that matters were amicably discussed does tend to border on the ridiculous.

However, when the three Kray brothers were imprisoned in March 1969 (Charlie receiving ten years), it might appear to some that the path was clear for Ince and Dolly to continue their relationship – but not to those of us aware of the long arm that the Krays possessed, even when in prison. In November 1969, Ince was attacked by three men outside his Manor Park flat at 80 Hathaway Crescent. Hit over the head, he was then punched, kicked and had the fingers of both hands broken, before he was shot in the leg with a pistol. Interviewed by detectives in hospital, where steel splints were inserted into his damaged fingers, Ince refused to name his attackers. The following year, there was another attack. As Ince was walking home, a car pulled up, he was dragged inside, beaten unconscious, and a sawn-off was stuffed down the waistband of his trousers and fired. It missed the intended target but once more caused serious injuries to his leg. Dumped outside the Middlesex Hospital, Ince again declined to assist the police. Following his discharge from hospital, a shot from a passing car hit Ince's car. It appeared the Krays had neither forgiven nor forgotten.

Early in 1972, there was an incident at Bloom's Restaurant, then situated at 90 Whitechapel High Street. The police were called and were provided with the registration number of the car involved in the incident; the registered owner was George Ince. He was arrested and taken to Bethnal Green police station, and when a check was made at Criminal Records Office it revealed that Ince was 'flagged' to C11.

The reason for this was because Ince was already suspected of participating in armed robberies (especially one on 23 January 1971 in Portsmouth, where jewellery worth £7,000 was stolen) but there were no up-to-date photos of him; the last had been taken when he was sentenced to corrective training in 1961.

Therefore, when they discovered that Ince had been bailed for further enquiries to be made and were told the date he was to return to the police station, C11 operatives arrived and covertly photographed him while he was being interviewed. Those photographs were purely for their intelligence.

On 2 May 1972, a lorry containing 643 silver ingots valued at £393,758 was hijacked in Mountnessing, Essex by four men, one of whom was George Ince. They managed to unload ninety of the ingots, valued at £60,000, before escaping.

Ince went into hiding, but Essex police had 120 men working on the case and it was not too long before they identified those responsible.

Almost six months to the day after the robbery, there was an armed robbery on 5 November at the Barn Restaurant, Braintree, Essex. The proprietor was the slightly dodgy businessman Bob Patience, and during the attack, his wife Muriel was shot dead by one of the two gunmen, and his daughter, Beverley was seriously injured after being shot in the back. During the investigation, an informant told members of the Yard's Serious Crime Squad that one of the men responsible was George Ince.

Ince gave himself up and was identified by several people (including Beverley Patience) as the murderer. However, it was those covertly taken C11 photos which were shown to Beverley Patience to identify Ince. This was sharp practice and bad police work, which later brought much criticism of Essex Police.

Errol Flanighan, then a detective constable at Bethnal Green, was the officer who had arrested Ince for the incident at Bloom's Restaurant, and he told me:

Sometime later (I cannot remember when or by who) I was interviewed by a detective chief inspector regarding my dealings with Ince but particularly the secret taking of his photographs. I remember at the time I was initially evasive about remembering the incident, but the DCI produced a photograph of one taken of Ince and my left hand had been included. My unusual wedding ring was clearly visible. It was pretty obvious to me that they were only interested in the taking of the photos. I explained how and why they were taken. That was the end of the matter.

It was only some time later I became aware of the use of these photographs in the trial of Ince in the robbery and murder at 'the barn murder' in Essex.

Peter Moyes had joined the Essex Police as a constable in 1971, and in May 1973 he was instructed to attend Braintree Magistrates' Court for the five-day committal proceedings; he and another officer (who was armed) sat on either side of Ince in the dock. He recalled those times to me:

> At that time, Ince was (infamously) having an affair with Dolly Kray, the wife of Charles Kray. During the lunch breaks, she would collect a meal order from a smart local pub/restaurant and deliver it to the police station, where I took it to him. A couple of times he was quite chatty, but not about the case, of course. Two things stand out in my mind; the first was that he was a keen budgerigar breeder. The second was the story he told me about those who came for him in retribution for his affair with Dolly. He was seized by two men whilst a third shoved a sawn-off shotgun down his trousers in order to blow his nuts off as punishment. He struggled and the shotgun only succeeded in taking the muscle off the back of one of his legs.
>
> The case caused bad publicity for Essex Police, with several areas of bad practice, I'm sorry to say.

The first jury was unable to agree; following the re-trial (when Dolly Kray broke cover to provide Ince with an alibi on the night of the murder) Ince was found not guilty. This was just as well, because he was entirely innocent; three weeks later, the two real perpetrators were arrested and admitted the offences.

But now, Ince was to stand trial on 4 September 1973 at the Old Bailey for the Mountnessing silver bullion robbery, and part of his defence was that it would have been an impossibility for him to have run across fields for a distance of four miles, due to the injuries to his legs.

Nevertheless, Ince and three others were found guilty, and on 30 November Mr Justice Milmo told them:

> You and your co-defendants are dangerous criminals. This was armed robbery, planned and executed with military precision. You have played a major part in this extremely grave crime and you played for high stakes, so the penalty must be high. You will go to prison for fifteen years.

Six months went by, and Reg Kray (who utterly loathed Dolly Kray) was serving his life sentence at Parkhurst prison, where he got into conversation with Harry 'Hate 'em All' Johnson, who was serving a 17-year sentence and had seen the newspaper articles about Ince and Dolly.

Johnson took umbrage at their liaison and commented to Reg, 'If I come across that George Ince, I will cut him.'

Touched by this gratuitous gesture, Reg had charitably replied, 'I would rather you leave it out, Harry. The slag is not worth doing bird for.'

The reason for his benevolence, we must assume, was that following his discovery of Ince's relationship with Dolly, he had head-butted Ince outside the twins' Double R Club and obviously felt that that salutary gesture was sufficient.

Nevertheless, following a troublesome stay in the special security block at Parkhurst, Johnson was transferred to Long Lartin maximum-security prison where Ince was serving his sentence, having just arrived from Wandsworth. On his first day there, Johnson spotted Ince watching a football match (apparently, Johnson despised football as much as he did adulterous relationships) and slashed Ince's face with a razor blade, a wound that required eight stitches. Ince refused to identify his attacker, and Johnson stated, 'If I'd done it, he'd of needed eighty stitches, not eight', but the act was witnessed by prison officers, and at Warwick Crown Court on 26 June 1974, the easily manipulated 'Hate 'em All' Harry went down for three years for unlawful wounding, this sentence to commence at the expiration of his present one. Mr Justice Ashworth commented that he had unpleasant misgivings about the background to the case, but at least Reg Kray had sanctimoniously put himself in the clear.

Twelve months later, Ince appealed against his robbery conviction and sentence, both without success. He would deny involvement in the robbery for the rest of his life, but hunger strikes, writs, questions raised in Parliament and requests for enquiries would do nothing to nullify that conviction for prisoner No. 116079.

Dolly had long since divorced Charlie Kray and, in an attempt to distance herself from the Kray name, had changed hers by deed poll to Dolly Gray. On 7 July 1977, she and Ince were married at Hammersmith Registry Office but, denied a post-nuptial glass of champagne, it was back to Wormwood Scrubs for Ince, and he would not be granted parole until three years later, after which he and Dolly would remain devoted to each other for the rest of their lives.

However before that happened, in September 1978 Ince was transferred to Maidstone prison. It was there in 1979 that he met Don Barrett.

## Chapter Twenty-Five

# Barrett's Gang

Don Barrett was now almost fifty, but in many ways he was the antithesis of his former comrade, Bertie Smalls; Barrett was fit and hard, a man who seldom drank. Those attributes, plus experience, cunning and utter ruthlessness, placed him in the premier league of armed robbers. He gathered his team around him. Two were also top-class robbers. Another had also been a robber, albeit one practised in tying up elderly ladies. There was also a newcomer to robbery who possessed a creative streak. The inventor had two relatives, also newcomers but who plunged into criminality at the deep end. And there were one or two runners and riders, there to receive and convert the property that would be stolen. It was time to go to work, and that kicked off on 3 August 1984.

Three armed suspects entered Brooke Bond Oxo at Suez Road, Enfield, North London and tied up the staff, holding them hostage until the arrival of a Securicor van bringing the company's wages. The van duly came through the company's open gates, and the driver, 43-year-old William Graham, looked into the window of the wages office but could see nobody there.

'I got out of the van to see where the usual staff were', said Mr Graham. 'I walked round to the other side of the van, and the next thing, I was looking down the barrel of a pistol.'

One of the gunmen screamed at the guard to get down on the floor, and petrol was poured over his legs, while the other custodians in the van were told to get out, with the threat of their petrol-soaked companion being ignited if they demurred. Shots were fired, four of the custodians were pistol-whipped, and the robbers escaped in a small red van driven by a fourth man, taking with them £78,431.37p.

It was slickly done, over in minutes, and one of the robbers took time to inform the terrified Mr Graham how much they had on board, as well as which other clients they were going to deliver to.

A senior Flying Squad officer said at the time, 'Petrol seems to be the weapon in vogue. In the sixties, it was the pickaxe, in the seventies, firearms, and now, it's petrol.'

However, later, the gang would go one better.

But not yet. Slightly over three months later, the gang struck once more. As before, they were in possession of top-rate information, because on 26 November, as a Ford Sierra Estate was travelling from Hatton Garden to Johnson Matthey plc, 33 Jeffries Road, Brimsdown, Enfield, only 300 metres away from their previous robbery, the vehicle was forced to a halt. The driver, Roger Anthony Stowe, was threatened with a gun, and a second gang member smashed the vehicle's rear window, which had the effect of both disorientating the driver and gaining access to the haul inside: silver and gold bullion valued at £250,000. The thieves thrust the loot into their getaway car but not for long; they had known exactly where to stop because they drove only a few hundred yards before abandoning the stolen car by a railway bridge. They then raced across the bridge and down the other side, where a second getaway car was parked; and from there, they drove sedately away.

The following day, the precious metals were received and disposed of by Anthony Morteye Ocquaye and Brian Charles Wade. Three years later, they would be sentenced to three and four years' imprisonment, respectively, with Wade additionally being made criminally bankrupt to the tune of £219,000.

The members of the gang on that occasion were Barrett, Ince and a newcomer, John Kenneth Johnson.

Johnson's entry into crime commenced in 1952, a mixture of serious and not-so-serious offences (for example, a fine of £20 in 1961 for the theft of some electric fires), until he hit the big-time in June 1966 with the tie-up robbery of a 70-year-old lady in Manchester, where £300 was stolen, and Judge J.R.D. Crichton sentenced him to five years' imprisonment. However, just eleven days later, Johnson appeared at the Old Bailey after he had been identified on fingerprints for two more robberies, one at Clapham, where two sisters in the twilight of their years heroically fought back, and another tie-up robbery on an equally elderly lady at Wanstead, where jewels and furs to the value of £1,000 were stolen. Judge Edward Clarke QC was obviously of the opinion that Judge Crichton's sentence was one that bordered on the limp-wristed and sentenced Johnson to ten years' imprisonment, to run consecutively to his previous sentence, thus a total of fifteen years. Six months later, Johnson was one of several convicts to escape from Dartmoor Prison on Boxing Day. He was returned, four days later, freezing cold and sopping wet, just in time for Princetown's New Year's Eve festivities.

Now, aged forty-eight, he was a member of Barrett's band of brothers.

Precious metal appeared to be the current flavour of choice for the gang. On 17 December, a Vauxhall van was hijacked at Queen's Road, Bishopworth, en route between Bristol and Sheffield, by two armed men, namely Barrett and Croke, using a .32 revolver and an automatic pistol. The 40-year-old driver, Christopher Roger Feltham, was bound, gagged and blindfolded and taken to the Heston Service Station on the M4 motorway, where he was discovered, five hours later, minus his consignment of silver and gold bullion valued at £250,000.

This was a matter that was investigated by officers from the Avon and Somerset Police, but I remembered it because, when details of the offence were circulated, the bullion's value was shown as being £250,000. However, the following day a further teleprinter message was sent out amending the value to just £97,000. I thought at the time how odd that was – stolen property values usually ascended rather than descended – but it was not until much later that this made sense. The gold had been transported from a company known as Scadlynn Ltd. Three weeks previously, there had been the sensational robbery of gold valued at £26 million from the Brink's-Mat warehouse at Heathrow. The managing director of Scadlynn was Garth Chappell, and on 23 July 1986, he was convicted of conspiracy to handle the gold from the robbery, was sentenced to ten years' imprisonment and fined and ordered to pay costs totalling £275,000.

Therefore, when the Vauxhall van was hijacked, the value of the stolen gold was indeed £250,000; but as an afterthought, Chappell realised it would be injudicious to try to prove to his insurers the provenance of that amount of gold. Since it had come from the robbery at Brink's-Mat, £153,000 was quickly deleted from the total. Although Messrs Barrett and Croke were certainly guilty of armed robbery, they were conspicuously innocent of knowingly receiving stolen property!

Also arrested, on the same charges as Chappell, was Terrence Edward James Patch, and on the same day that his associate was convicted, Patch was acquitted.

Much later, in 1986, Detective Sergeant Rodney Briggs was one of several officers who assisted materially in the investigations that followed. He told me:

Towards the end of the year, I spent a lot of time in the Bristol area investigating the Scadlynn robbery which was the most interesting of the robberies, as Don and his associates had stolen gold from Scadlynn which had originally been stolen on the Brink's-Mat robbery. Later on in December, Tony Freeman drove me down to 'Bali-Hi', Bishopsworth, Bristol, the bungalow home of Terrence Patch, an associate of John 'Goldfinger' Palmer. Patch was a tough, shrewd man and despite a long interview and a visit to his commercial premises, he gave nothing away about his dealings at Scadlynn's.

So back to 1984, when, in the space of three weeks, the gang had become half a million better off; but two months later, they were at it again, this time in a jewellery robbery where Johnson felt much more at home with the modus operandi.

He and Barrett (armed, once more, with a .32 revolver) burst into Select-a-Property, an estate agent's at Penn Road, Beaconsfield on 24 February 1985 to confront former singer, 36-year-old Karen Young and a male assistant, who was coshed and kicked almost unconscious. Miss Young later stated, 'One of the gang had a gun and smashed me in the face with it', and a solitaire diamond ring valued at £125,000, plus another valued at £7,000, were torn from her fingers, while £800 in cash was stolen. Miss Young lost consciousness and she and her assistant were bound and gagged; suffering from spinal and facial injuries, she was later admitted to High Wycombe General Hospital, where she was detained for several days, declaring, 'I'm determined to see the gang behind bars. I'm willing to pay a £10,000 reward.' So that was property valued at £132,800 that had been stolen; except later, she told police that the property had been worth £500,000 and was most incensed when this sum was queried by detectives.

So was Barrett. 'Bollocks!' was his surprised and indignant response. 'I fucking wish they had of been!'

Whatever the sale of that stolen jewellery realised, it must be hoped that it kept Barrett and his team in the style to which they'd become accustomed, because over the next five months four more attacks would be carried out, all of which, although well-planned, would result in complete and utter failure.

The first came on 24 April 1985, when Barrett, Croke and Ince arrived at Enfield Crematorium, Great Cambridge Road at 7 c'clock in the morning, wearing plastic false moustaches, reflecting sunglasses and a ski mask. Armed with handguns and a sawn-off shotgun, they surprised the sixteen workers there, tied them up and made them lie down on the floor. Cleaner Lynn Mace and tea lady Pat Evans were afforded chivalrous treatment by a gang member, who provided them with armchairs to sit in when they were tied up.

'He even said he was very sorry', remarked Mrs Evans, magnanimously.

The gang waited for the PPR Security van to arrive – but, alas, in vain. They believed that the crematorium was the van's first port of call, but they were wrong by six hours, because the security company had switched delivery times; whereas the robbers were hoping to collect several thousand pounds, had they remained until lunchtime when the van made its last drop, the most they would have got would have been a measly £1,000.

So they left, empty-handed, in a Ford Escort van. Matters were not made any better for the trussed-up workers when the crematorium superintendent arrived; incredibly, he believed that the workers were making some kind of protest about the wages not being delivered in the morning as usual.

'So', he said, 'I decided to let them stew for a bit longer.'

It was debatable who was the more pissed-off: the raiders or their victims.

Nine days later, the gang struck again, a few miles to the north this time at Cross & Herbert, Charlton Mead Lane, Hoddesdon. Croke and Barrett took the staff hostage and waited for the PPR security van to arrive, and it did – but the crew were unhappy about the area being so unusually deserted, prudently decided against delivering their consignment, and left. So did the robbers, but now Croke made the first of several important mistakes. He left behind a viable remote-controlled explosive device, which had been intended to be fixed to one of the security van's custodians to control his movements. Instead, it was left for the police to find – which, upon their arrival, they did.

Several weeks passed. Then on 27 June, Barrett, Croke and Ince rushed into Amtico, a company based at the Trafalgar Trading Estate, Brimsdown, Enfield, tied up the staff and waited for the Group 4 Security vehicle to arrive, together with wages amounting to several thousand pounds – and promptly left, when it didn't.

The next offence took place on 18 July. The last three attempts had been carried out in the Enfield area of North London; now, Barrett, Croke and Ince switched to South London, to Mauritius Road, Greenwich, where, as a Security Express van was about to make a delivery, its tyres were punctured with high velocity bullets and its armoured window was fractured using a Hilti gun, a device used in the building industry for blasting nails into concrete. The alarm was sounded, and after the gang tried and failed to smash their way into the van, with police sirens getting closer and closer, they decamped in one of the getaway cars, leaving the other behind.

With such a succession of failures behind them, would the gang ever again achieve success? The answer was that in five weeks time, yes, they would, but the subsequent investigation would also herald the beginning of the end for Barrett and his gang.

★　★　★

Portland Road is a cul-de-sac off Green Road, Tottenham; beyond it lies the local technical college and the town hall. The gang's target, this time, was Imperial Cold Storage, a hops warehouse, and on

13 September 1985, three men armed with a pistol and shotgun burst in to take the gateman hostage.

A Security Express van then arrived, and when the custodian got out he was seized by the gang, and an explosive device – similar to the one left behind by Croke following the abortive robbery on 3 May – was strapped to his waist and he was marched to the van. Under the threat of the device being detonated, the other custodians quickly surrendered the cash. One of the staff saw what was going on, and as he tried to escape, a shot was fired, and he was pistol-whipped. The company's director arrived, refused to get out of his car, and another shot was fired. A lorry driver who had spent the night in his cab in the compound was ordered out and told to lie under his vehicle. The sound of the shots alerted four members of staff, including a young girl cleaner, who were tied up in the wages office. The bomb was unstrapped from the guard, and this time, the raiders took it away with them.

The members of the gang were Barrett, Croke and a newcomer: Glen Ronald Armsby, a no-account crook who was living with the daughter of Croke's wife Rita. They escaped, having relieved the custodian, James Stuart, of £98,702.52.

That was the robbery in a nutshell. A better, more detailed account later came from Don Barrett, which I wrote down at his dictation:

We saw the gateman arrive and, after about five or ten minutes, we went in. Dave went into the tearoom and laid out a mock-up bomb which he had made up. It consisted of a box with a strap and contained workings he'd bought from a model shop and a shotgun cartridge which had the shot removed and a cloth put in its place. Two guards came into the office, which took us by surprise as on all the occasions we'd watched it, there had only been one. We took them both into the tearoom, where Dave showed one of the guards how the device worked by remote control. He then placed the cartridge on it and strapped it on to the spine of the older guard. We made a cup of tea and told the guard to carry it back to the van. As Dave was coming out of the van, the manager arrived in a Vauxhall. I went over to him and told him to get out. He refused, so I fired a shot into the ground. Because of the noise, three people came out of the storage area. Glen went towards them, and meanwhile I took the manager into the toilets. While I was there, I heard another gun go off, which I later discovered from Glen was his shotgun going off because he'd had it cocked. I came back out and Dave told us to go. He had put the money into the back of the gateman's car as we'd taken the keys from him earlier. Glen got into that car with Dave and I took the manager's car so I could block the road if anyone came after us. We went to the garages where the Marina was and transferred the money. Dave drove off in the Marina, and Glen and I walked further down the road to where I'd left my car. We then met back at Dave's house and shared the money out. We got thirty thousand each and the bags containing the money were later burnt.

The robbery was reported to the police, and the enquiry was taken up by the Flying Squad.

# Chapter Twenty-Six

# An Inquisitive Boy

On 15 September 1985, I was posted to Rigg Approach, Leyton as a member of 9 Squad (the previous North-East office of the Flying Squad, based at Walthamstow police station, had become too small and crowded) and got stuck in to the never-ending investigations into armed robberies. Three squads worked out of Rigg, under the control of a detective chief inspector and three detective inspectors. Of the rest, there were sixteen detective sergeants and twenty-eight detective constables.

I arrived two weeks after Kevin Shapland who, having joined the Met in 1975, had served his CID career at Kentish Town, the 3 Area surveillance team and Enfield. There was no aspect of investigative work at which he faltered: informant running, submitting correspondence, making arrests and interviewing suspects. On one occasion I was present when Kevin interviewed a large, sullen, black robber, who until then had had little to say for himself. But quietly and persuasively, Kevin put every piece of evidence he had gathered to the suspect, who suddenly shouted, 'STOP! You know everything!'

Without doubt, he was the finest detective constable attached to the Flying Squad that I ever worked with. But not immediately. All of us had our own robberies to investigate, our informants to meet, observations to carry out, arrests to make and courts to attend – and an endless avalanche of paperwork to deal with.

But Kevin picked up the Imperial Cold Storage investigation, and when he heard of the proxy bomb being attached to the guard he linked it with the raid at Cross & Herbert, where a similar device had been left behind.

It was such an unusual modus operandi that Kevin took the details to the popular BBC television programme *Crimewatch UK*, who filmed a reconstruction. It was broadcast on 14 November 1985 showing the unopened explosive device from Cross & Herbert, and Kevin sat in the television studio eagerly awaiting a flood of responses; but probably as a result of the 'Miss World' contest being televised on ITV the same night, none materialised.

No matter how good a detective may be, he also needs a certain amount of good luck; and two days later, Kevin had the good fortune of encountering a 14-year-old boy from Broxbourne who had telephoned his local police station. His information was enlightening, and the local officer contacted Kevin at Rigg Approach to arrange a meeting. This is what the boy had to say.

Earlier that year, he and his friends had been playing in a Broxbourne street, when they saw some rubbish sacks piled up against the front wall of a bungalow. Inside the bags was an 'old man' face mask, false hair, glue, a radio receiver and a home-made electronic device. He took them home and put on the mask to frighten his mother – he succeeded, and she made him throw it away. But he kept the electronic apparatus, stripped it down and realised that it was a remote control device, similar to one he had once installed in a model racing car. Then he lost interest and threw that away as well.

The boy didn't see the *Crimewatch* programme on the night of its broadcast, but it had been recorded, and when he searched the video recorder for something else to watch he suddenly caught sight of the device shown on the programme – hence his call to the police station.

When Kevin questioned the boy, the device he had found had, of course, been disposed of months before, but on asking the youngster to draw it, Kevin realised that the remarkably accurate drawing of the four corner blocks was exactly like the device left at Cross & Herbert – the interior of which had never been displayed on the television programme. The youngster took Kevin to Riverside Avenue, Broxbourne and he pointed out the bungalow where he had found the items. The name of the property was 'Emerald', and it had recently changed hands. The previous occupier, who had moved into a much more prestigious property, was the managing director of an electronics factory in Highbury.

That man and his business premises became a subject of intense interest to Kevin who, when time permitted, would sit outside the factory to see if any suspicious characters arrived. He did not bother keeping watch on the present occupiers of 'Emerald'. They were just a nondescript couple – whose names were Dave and Rita Croke.

# Chapter Twenty-Seven

# Armaguard

'How long did you spend looking at the previous owner of "Emerald"?' I later asked Kevin.

'Too long!' he grinned.

It would be nice to think that, given an investigation, detectives could follow up every possible lead to a successful conclusion, to the exclusion of any other investigation; but this was never the case. The workload of every officer on the Squad was enormous, and when an operation was underway, all the officers were taken away from their current investigations and seconded to it. Operation Safari was one such massive, time-consuming Squad initiative, run by Detective Inspector Ken Grange and involving a highly dangerous gang of top-notch armed robbers. It swallowed up most of the office personnel (including Kevin and myself), and therefore, following up information at 'Emerald' was practically impossible. It would have been interesting to have discovered that, following the robbery at Brook Bond Oxo, and the two subsequent gold bullion robberies, there was more than enough in Croke's share for he and his wife to move out of the Edmonton council flat they had occupied for eight years and to purchase Emerald for £85,000 in cash, in Rita's name.

But with so much work being generated into and from the Squad office, police were unaware of it. Then, on 12 December, came Armaguard.

★   ★   ★

The gang were going to relieve Armaguard, a security company's depository, of all the cash contained in it. The raid had been meticulously planned over the preceding twelve months, and they had finally decided how the depository's doors were going to be opened for them; it would be with the unwilling assistance of one of the company's employees, Joe Symes. Unwilling, for two reasons: first, his wife and daughter would be left as hostages at the family address, handcuffed, the previous night; and second, because when he drove in his own car to the depository, Symes would be sitting on an explosive device. If he were to do anything to alert another member of staff, the device would be detonated by remote control, and the person receiving the warning would be shot dead.

Joe Symes was unaware that the gang's leader had previously used proxy bombs and discharged firearms during robberies, but he had no reason to disbelieve him. Two and a half years later, a Judge at the Old Bailey would describe this – and other offences – as being, 'one step away from terrorism'.

He wasn't far wrong.

★　★　★

Croke had noticed a cash-in-transit van, bearing the legend 'Armaguard', a company he had never heard of before. Out of curiosity, he had followed it back to the company's base at The Pinnacles, Harlow, Essex. It was quite a small depot, with few vans, and this raised the question of whether it could be attacked and relieved of all its cash. Well, why not? That's what had happened two years previously, at both the Security Express depot, Curtain Road, Shoreditch and the Brink's-Mat depository at Heathrow. Of course, both of those premises were quite large, with considerable staff, and therefore a large number of raiders were needed. But Armaguard? Could it be dealt with by, say, three determined men? Could be.

It was discussed, and later, Barrett drove an Austin Princess to The Pinnacles, got out, locked the car and left. Inside the car's boot was Croke, peering at the depot through unobtrusive holes bored in the car's bodywork, patiently screening the various employees to determine the most suitable subject for their plan. Joe Symes was not the first choice of victim. Initially, they had settled on Bill Warman who, like Joe, was one of the two keyholders required to open the premises – and the surveillance that the gang carried out on him was up to MI5 standards. They would wait for Bill to leave the depot for home, then follow his car until he reached a junction and turned off. They – the gang – would drive straight on. This would be repeated until they were satisfied that the turn-off at the junction was Bill's normal route home. Then they would park up at the junction and wait for Bill to come along; once he had turned into his usual route, they would follow him until the next time he turned off, left or right, and once more, they would drive straight on. This would be repeated along all of Bill's usual route, so that after a period of weeks, unsuspecting Bill had led them straight to his home address.

Next, the gang observed Bill's address on his days off. When he and his family went shopping, so did Croke and Barrett, unobtrusively walking behind, beside or just in front of them as they visited Tesco's or Sainsbury's, listening for snippets of information: the children's names, what they'd done at school, the name of the family's pet, where they were going on holiday. All of this information was stored so that when the time came, it could be used to control them. And this works. In a situation of fear on one side and aggression on the other, making people believe that their adversaries know everything about them strips them of their resolve and renders them defenceless.

And then Bill was shelved, for the simple reason that the gang realised you can't tie kids up in front of their parents – and not for any moral or ethical reason, either. But try doing such a thing, and it's perfectly possible that parents – especially a mother – will go berserk in defence of her children, and what should have been a sweet little job will go awry. So Bill and his young family were out, and the second keyholder – Joe, with a wife and grown-up daughter – was in.

At 6 o'clock on the evening of Wednesday, 11 December 1985, two armed, masked men rang the front doorbell of the Symes family home in Harlow. The door was opened by 65-year-old Mrs Rita Symes, and she and her 33-year-old daughter Edna were overpowered and handcuffed.

'We were having a cup of tea when the doorbell rang', said Edna later. 'Mum went to answer it and a man grabbed her round the neck and put his hand over her mouth. A second man came in and said to me, "You know what's going to happen, don't you?".'

The men were in possession of two-way radios, and at 7 o'clock, Mrs Symes heard a female voice on the radio say, 'He's on his way.' In addition, they had a pair of Realistic UHF radio scanners to listen in to police communications. Police frequencies had changed to 450MHz from the previous 88-100MHz, to prevent people listening on their ordinary radios; but these effective battery-powered multi-channelled devices could easily be programmed to intercept police transmissions, and since Harlow police station was less than a mile and a half away from the Symes' family home, no difficulties were expected, and none occurred.

The sight that confronted Joe Symes as he entered his home was of his wife and daughter handcuffed to the dining room table and two men, masked in balaclavas and dressed in 'NATO'-style pullovers with dark trousers and shoes. One held a sawn-off shotgun and had a handgun holstered at his waist, while the other held an automatic pistol.

One of them said, 'You know what we want.'

As Joe told me later, 'Of course I bloody well did – I was terrified!'

Not that he betrayed his fear.

As Barrett told me later, 'He just went on, pretending everything was normal. He just casually looked around the room at us, nodded, picked up his dinner and started to eat. All the time, he was looking round, just to see if he could get the jump on us. He had a lot of guts.'

This was very true. At the outbreak of the Second World War, Joe had escaped from the Nazis who had overrun his native Poland, arrived in England, anglicised his unpronounceable name to 'Symes', joined the British Army and survived being made a prisoner of war by the Japanese. In 1946, several Japanese soldiers convicted of war crimes were hanged at Changi Jail, Singapore. I was told that Joe was the executioner. True or false? Whatever the case, Joe was one tough cookie.

Joe was sat down and handcuffed. He and his family were threatened, and Joe was questioned about money available at the depot. Later that evening, a third man arrived at the house. This was Glen Armsby, fresh from his successful initiation at the Imperial Cold Storage robbery. He, too, was armed with a sawn-off shotgun and had a pistol holstered at his waist. The handcuffs were removed from Mrs Symes in order for her to make tea, and at 10.30pm she and her daughter were allowed to go to bed.

The raiders knew a great deal about the company's security procedures, but nevertheless, Joe was closely questioned about them; it appeared that they required confirmation regarding certain details. During all this time, different voices were heard coming from the two-way radios, and Joe Symes was convinced that the gang had the house surrounded. The detailed questioning went on throughout the night, and then one of the men reached into a holdall and produced a plastic box measuring eight inches long by four inches deep and wide. As well as batteries, there were wires attached to soft, pliable material, and a switch which, when clicked to 'on' caused a red light to glow. This, Joe was informed, meant that the explosive device was now armed. The box was bolted to a broad leather belt and this, Joe was told, would be strapped around his waist at 5.45am when they left to go to the depot. Any attempt to warn Bill Warman when they arrived would result in the bomb's immediate detonation by remote control and Warman being shot. Given all that had happened over the preceding twelve hours, it was not surprising that Joe Symes believed every word he heard.

At 6.15am, Joe and the gang arrived at Armaguard. The belt was removed from Joe's waist and placed under the driver's seat and, with the red light glowing, the grim warning was repeated. The minutes ticked by. At 6.30am, Warman arrived, the main gates were opened, the raiders appeared and Bill Warman and Joe were forced to open up. Another employee arrived, and he and Warman were bound with cable and taken inside.

The gang used large light-blue and orange holdalls, from which they took green canvas-type sacks about four feet high that might have once belonged to Security Express. In these they packed £480,000 in used notes of various denominations.

After twenty minutes, one of the gang called out, 'That's it, lads', and the three employees were bundled into a security cage and locked in. After another fifteen minutes, the raiders left, And the men managed to free themselves and raised the alarm. Mrs Symes and her daughter were found handcuffed and bound in a back bedroom at their home.

This was the biggest robbery in the history of the Essex Police, and an incident room was set up at Harlow police station, headed by a detective superintendent and a detective inspector. Joe said he believed that five people had been involved in the raid, detectives from all over the Essex area were called in and investigations got underway.

Several matters came to light. First, the device used on Joe Symes was disarmed by personnel from the Royal Army Ordnance Corps, who discovered it was not viable. The 'explosive material' had been 6oz of plasticine. Others used by the gang in the preceding twelve months had been viable, but this had been a dummy, albeit a totally convincing one. Next, a witness had noticed a vehicle parked outside the premises at 6.50am. It was described as a beige or bronze saloon of a 'wedge' shape – possibly an Austin Princess. One used by the raiders? Possibly; it was there when the raid was underway but not when the police arrived.

In the meantime, the cash had been loaded into a rather shabby, repainted Honda van, registration number PBM 263W. It was not built for speed and had been selected for its dullness, the sort of nondescript vehicle that might be used by a not very successful builder and certainly not the mode of transport utilised by a group of First Division armed robbers. So with daylight still an hour away, off went the Honda van, chugging away at a discreet 30mph on its nine-and-a-half mile journey west to Hoddesdon in Hertfordshire.

Oh, one more thing. Remember the Judge's comments about this offence being 'one step away from terrorism'? Think that statement was mere polemics? Well, consider this.

That confrontation so traumatised Mrs Rita Symes that she later went to her grave without uttering one word about her ordeal to police, her family, anybody. Joe, too, died shortly after his wife. Edna Symes told me that she was in no doubt that the incident had hastened her parents' deaths.

Nor was I.

So, with up to fifty Essex detectives working flat-out on this investigation, the question arose: could this robbery be linked to the other robberies Kevin was investigating? He was seconded to Essex Police for a week to see if there was a connection. The device at Cross & Herbert had been a viable one – the one attached to Joe Symes was not. Could this have been a copycat offence inspired by the *Crimewatch* programme? Quite possibly. Could it have been the work of the gang who made up Operation Safari? Again, that was possible; it was professional enough. But by the end of the week, Kevin returned to Rigg Approach far from convinced that there was a connection.

★  ★  ★

Christmas 1985 came and went; those of us able to take annual leave did so, because Operation Safari was about to go into overdrive. In January 1986 matters suddenly reached a conclusion when the gang leader realised that he was being kept under observation. He met up with his colleagues, advised them of this and stated he intended to draw a gun from their armoury and return to shoot the person on surveillance. Since shots had already been fired at an off-duty Flying Squad officer who had disturbed the gang when carrying out one of their robberies, this was no idle threat. Fortunately, this conversation was overheard, and before the dirty deed could be done, the whole gang were arrested. Since the officer on observation was me, this came as a profound relief.

So the mopping-up operation continued. Kevin became aware of the circumstances of the purchasers of 'Emerald' and switched his attention from the erstwhile occupier to the present owners. From time to time he would drive past the bungalow since, as it was in a cul-de-sac, it was very difficult to sit up there for any length of time. And then, two months after the Armaguard raid, on 4 February 1986, Kevin spotted three cars on the bungalow's driveway. One was an Audi GT – but Kevin was already aware that this was registered to Croke. There was a Porsche, for which no current keeper was shown, and also a Nissan Sunny Estate. The registered keeper was shown as Dolly Ince, wife of George, a top London robber.

It was sufficient for Kevin to request a surveillance operation from the Yard's C11 Department, but for several months little if anything seemed to happen. Croke seldom went out, and the Nissan Sunny never reappeared. And then, in July, a limited edition green Volkswagen Golf GTi arrived at Emerald. A tall, balding white man got out of it, and the C11 photographer snapped off pictures of an individual who called himself Steve Goodman.

However, his baptismal name was Donald Walter Barrett.

# Chapter Twenty-Eight

# Operation Standard

The officer in charge at Rigg Approach was Detective Chief Inspector Duncan MacRae, who had served in every rank of the Flying Squad with the exception of detective sergeant (first-class) – and nobody better could have been appointed to head what had become 'Operation Standard'. Now, with the knowledge that a man strongly suspected of manufacturing proxy bombs was keeping company with two of London's top-rated armed robbers, he swept into action. He ordered full-time surveillance to be set up on Emerald and, within a week, things started to happen. Barrett arrived in his Golf GTi, Croke got into the passenger seat and, with the C11 surveillance team following, they drove to the Battersea area of South London and then on to the large industrial estate at Nine Elms. As Barrett and Croke drove around the estate, the watchers noted that they slowed as they approached one particular premises. This was Unit 4, Havelock Terrace, occupied by a cash-in-transit company named Shield Transit Ltd.

The surveillance team split between watching Shield and Emerald. A few days later, an officer strolled past the depot and saw a black Volkswagen Golf parked on the forecourt. He noted the registration number, then suddenly realised that he had seen the same vehicle parked up on the driveway at Emerald. The registered owner of the car was Al John Turner, a man with no known criminal convictions, who lived in Clacton-on-Sea, Essex. It was clear that Shield – or what the building contained – was the gang's target.

This put MacRae in a quandary. Nobody at Shield could be approached, for someone in the company might be involved. If Turner was an inside man – and it looked very much as though he was – word could filter through. If there was another inside man he could warn the gang, and the police would have no idea of his identity. And yet, if the suspected robbery were to go ahead, innocent people could be hurt. If the premises were going to be hit – and it looked very much as though that would be the case – once Barrett and Croke were inside, at least they would be contained. But how would they get in? Would it be Turner who let them in – would he be a keyholder? Would there be another keyholder, and if so, would he be involved in the plot as well? The robbers who had hit Armaguard had used scanners to monitor the police frequencies; how, then, could the police communicate with each other, without being overheard? And once the robbers were inside, would other members of staff be already there – people who could be taken hostage, something this gang was quite used to. But if the operation were to be aborted, the gang could go on to attack another premises – or a cash-in-transit vehicle – or a custodian or some other innocent employee, and the police might have no idea where that might be or when it would happen. All ifs, ands and buts; a bit of a tricky one.

However, MacRae was up to the challenge and, following a series of consultations with senior officers at the Yard, it was decided to go ahead; despite the possibility of a hostage situation developing, every possible eventuality would have to be catered for.

On all Flying Squad ambushes, observation points (OPs) would be set up, to cover – whenever possible – the venue where it was anticipated the attack would take place. In many cases – a cash-in-transit vehicle arriving at a certain, static location, such as a bank or building society – this was relatively straightforward. The occupiers of adjacent shops and houses were usually quite willing for their premises to be occupied by police officers for a few hours at a time.

But here, at Nine Elms estate, where observation had to be kept on the front door of Shield Transit, the situation was rather more difficult, and it took days to find the most suitable premises. The depot backed on to a railway line, and the nearest OP was a pub several hundred yards away; that was number one. The entry to the estate was from Battersea Park Road, with one way in and one way out; fortunately, Nine Elms police station at 147 Battersea Park Road, closed in 1977 and now a disused police building for operational purposes, overlooked the junction and therefore would be able to monitor all vehicles going in and coming out – so it was number two. A caretaker at a nearby school, deserted during the school holidays, was taken into the officers' confidence, and now, despite the difficulties, the Squad had three OPs: Tom, Dick and Harry.

When would the raid take place? The Squad men and the surveillance teams, plus all the technical support at their disposal, knew it was imminent. Barrett and Croke were constantly in each other's company, and then, on Friday, 8 August 1986, Barrett and his family flew out to Faro, Portugal, on holiday. Had the raid been postponed? Not a bit of it. Barrett was merely establishing an alibi. He was spotted arriving back at Heathrow on Sunday, 10 August – and after the robbery, he'd hop on a plane back to Portugal, as though he'd never been away. Passports were not stamped going in or coming out, at either end. Therefore, if he were questioned about the robbery after his return, he could produce the counterfoils of the original return tickets for him and his family. With the intervening ticket counterfoils destroyed, to all intents and purposes he had been in Portugal the entire time. Simple. But now, from the airport, he was tailed all the way to Emerald.

With the pressure building up, the next part of Operation Standard would rely – a lot – on top-notch surveillance. Right at the centre of it was Colin Ellis. Let's pause to take a look at him; and what happened next.

★   ★   ★

Ellis joined the Met in 1968, and thirteen years later he transferred to the Fraud Squad Surveillance Unit; the training included lectures as well as instruction from Special Branch, MI5 and Military Intelligence. In 1985, he joined the C11 Surveillance Team at Scotland Yard and, having completed his training course, was posted to the East London team, on which there were two 'Rural' officers – trained to seamlessly assimilate themselves into the countryside and carry out surveillance wearing camouflage clothing. It required intensive training from both Military Intelligence at Ashford and the Special Air Service Regiment at Hereford. The two 'Rural' officers were John Fordham and Neil Murphy, and after Fordham was tragically killed by stolen gold receiver Kenneth Noye in 1985, Ellis was requested to take his place. He now takes up the tale:

> On Sunday, 10th August 1986 I attended Broxbourne police station at approximately midday for a briefing for our surveillance team to observe and follow a suspect, David Croke. Neil Murphy and myself, both rural officers, were tasked to get control of a house where Croke was living. The properties in the road signified a wealthy area where strangers would be easily spotted. We were able to obtain the use of a nearby driveway, with the owner of the house being very helpful. He supplied us with garden shears to cut his hedge so that we could legitimately keep Croke's house in view. Other C11 units were in the area to cover any movement of vehicles leaving the suspect's house.

After several hours, Barrett arrived, and during the early evening, he and Croke drove down to Clacton-on-Sea and spent some time in Turner's company, before returning to Emerald. Ellis continues the story:

> Both men entered the house and all lights went out around midnight. Weather conditions deteriorated during the night,

leaving it difficult to watch. To get closer to the premises I managed to get into a slipway opposite that led to the nearby River Lea. Concealing myself in a large group of bushes, a dog started barking and then its owner came out with a torch and looked around. He probably thought the dog was barking at a fox, and they returned to the house.

Ellis's description of the weather was an understatement. English weather turned bad from 20 July onwards that year, and by the night of 10 August it was exceptionally cold and a violent thunderstorm struck the area of Broxbourne; in conditions that could only be described as atrocious, the C11 surveillance team were utterly soaked, but were nevertheless able to advise the other officers that at 4.20am the lights at Emerald had come on.

The watchers saw Barrett and Croke, wearing suits and ties and carrying holdalls, get into Croke's car and then drive for several miles to a lock-up garage, from which they emerged in a blue Ford Escort 7cwt van, registration number JMM 556W. These plates were the correct ones, although the vehicle was registered to someone other than the driver on this occasion. It was the perfect vehicle for the job: nondescript but not so tatty that it would attract the attention of a Traffic Patrol officer. And as it drove away in the direction of Battersea, so the C11 Vehicles began their unobtrusive follow … Meanwhile, Kevin was in the main observation point in Battersea, overlooking the junction. Duncan MacRae was away; his place had been taken by Detective Superintendent Peter Gwynn, a highly experienced (and like MacRae, completely unflappable) Squad officer who had previously served on the Flying Squad. In addition, at the highly detailed briefing were members of the Met's elite Firearms Team – PT17 – who formed part of the eighty officers on this operation.

Another Squad officer and I were in the back of a lorry containing PT17 members. When the crunch came, the back doors would burst open, the Firearms unit would contain the situation and we would make the arrests. At least, that was the idea.

At exactly 5.45am, Al Turner drove his black VW Golf into the estate and stood chatting to some colleagues, after which he paced up and down, smoking nervously. Then, seventeen minutes later, a man who turned out to be the company's keyholder arrived in a Vauxhall; Croke and Barrett drove the blue Escort in after him. And then, as we tensed ourselves in readiness for the attack, something odd happened. The Escort van drove by, out of the estate, and parked in a nearby street.

Turner, meanwhile, had entered Shield and emerged a few moments later carrying something about the size of a shoebox, although it appeared to be quite heavy, and this he put into a white Volkswagen security van. Three minutes later, at 6.13am, Turner and another man got into the van and drove off, out of the estate. They were followed by the blue van and, in turn, by the surveillance team. Well, I thought, as W.S. Gilbert put it, 'Here's a how-de-do!' and no mistake.

'Right', said Peter Gwynn. 'They may be going to pick something up and return to the depot, and Barrett and Croke will attack them then, and clear out the whole firm. On the other hand, they may be intending to attack the van in the near future. Therefore, half of the team will stay at the estate, the other half will join in the follow.'

Well, that was me left behind, but would I see a little action if the raiders returned? As the convoy reached Hyde Park Corner, turned north into the Edgware Road and eventually onto the M1 motorway, that seemed less and less likely. Meanwhile, with the surveillance team shadowing the two vans, followed in turn by Ken Grange, Kevin Shapland, other Squad officers and members of the Firearms team, the police helicopter 'India One-one' was scrambled at the Battersea heliport. Keeping about two miles from the convoy, they received updates from the followers which, in turn, they passed on to Scotland Yard's Central Communications Complex – this had replaced the old Information Room two years previously. From there, the constabularies that the convoy passed through could be apprised that armed Metropolitan Police officers, in plain clothes, driving nondescript vehicles, were coming through their area, and no, thank you very much, they didn't require any assistance.

On and on they went and then, at 7.45am, the white van signalled that it was going to pull off the motorway into the Newport Pagnell service station; the blue van followed, and both vehicles parked up. The police vehicles that were following parked up stealthily on the motorway's hard shoulder and waited; meanwhile, officers from the surveillance team approached on foot, keeping the rest of the team informed via their covert body sets.

Ken Grange now takes up the tale:

I had put the SO11 foot units down on the service station pump area and asked for a full description of the area and presence of the public. Danger to the public was of paramount importance as I did not want to deploy armed officers into an area blind to the environment.

The feedback was such that, to me, there were too many members of the public there to safely deploy armed units into that environment.

I decided to let them leave with the vehicle and take them out as they rejoined the M1 northbound. I knew that at least one of the security guards was involved and this was what I acted upon.

Colin Ellis now describes what happened:

The security van stopped in the middle of the lorry car park with no other vehicles nearby. The Escort van was parked in the car parking area. The bullion driver got out and walked to the services to get coffee/tea and was followed by myself. While standing in the queue he was in conversation with, I think, Barrett, and it was clear that they were known to each other. Meanwhile, Neil, dressed as a service area worker, borrowed a broom from another worker who was sweeping up in the lorry area. Neil now had complete control of the bullion van and saw the guard coming back with the drinks. He then saw one of the suspects approach the van and appear to put a weapon to the head of the guard; as he did so, the Blue Escort van drove towards the bullion van and stopped. Both guards were tied up in the back of the bullion van, which moved off.

Events then moved very quickly. As the white van drove off, onto the slip road for the northbound M1, it could be seen that Croke was driving. The blue Escort followed, driven by Barrett, and now the order was given: 'Attack! Attack! Attack!'

The Squad cars raced down the motorway, and Tony Freeman, driving Ken Grange in a Rover 3500, forced the white van to a halt. Croke decided to make a fight of it, but Squad officers do not resemble indignant church vergers in a graveyard, as in Croke's previous confrontation with authority. He reached for his fully-loaded .32 revolver but he had no chance to use it, nor the flick-knife, nor even the CS gas canister that he had in his possession. He was grabbed by Ken Grange, an encounter in which he sustained a little physical damage ('I gave him one on the nose'), was overpowered and handcuffed.

Detective Sergeant Paul Lowden was in a Flying Squad car driven by Police Constable Micky Sutherland, who was gay, very popular with the Squad officers and adored by their wives and children. Had an outsider commented derogatively on Micky's sexuality, his face would have been punched inside-out. We Squad officers were a clannish lot. Hurt one of us and you hurt us all. It doesn't happen nowadays – but then again, neither would Operation Standard.

Be that as it may, back to the M1 motorway, where Paul gave an interesting account to me of what happened:

We were parked up on the hard shoulder and Mick said to me, 'Paul, every morning at six o'clock, I have to have a shit and now, it's nearly eight.'

I said, 'Well, you'll have to hang on because I think it's just about to go off.' We got the 'Attack' and I was tasked to arrest Barrett, who was driving a small blue van. We took off after him and at speeds of 65–70mph we drew alongside. I pointed my gun out of the window and shouted at Barrett to stop, and he did – but Mick kept on going! When he stopped, I had to run back but I'd previously loosened my trousers for comfort and now, I was running down the motorway with a gun in one hand and holding my trousers up with the other! Barrett wasn't any trouble, the helicopter was circling overhead and I took a gun out of his pocket. The next thing I know, Mick was reversing down the motorway to get to the service station to have a crap!

Barrett was in possession of a loaded 7.65 automatic and CS gas canisters, and both men had radio scanners; also gold bullion, valued at £283,500, which they'd just stolen. Ken Grange recalls that the first comment from Barrett was, 'Hello Ken, what are you doing here?' and that he probably replied, 'Never mind that, Don, I think that's a question for you to answer.'

Al Turner and the other custodian, Peter John Alsemgeest, were in the back of the security van hooded and bound, Turner with plastic ties, Alsemgeest with handcuffs, and they, together with Croke and Barrett, were taken to Milton Keynes police station.

It was soon established that Mr Alsemgeest was an entirely innocent party – unlike his fellow custodian. Al Turner's baptismal name was Al Capon, but he was mercilessly teased at school, his classmates telling him it was reminiscent of the American gangster 'Al Capone', so he changed it to 'Turner'. Then again, he could have changed it to 'Croke' – after all, he was Rita's son.

The prisoners were held incommunicado; there were others to arrest, and premises to be searched before any incriminating evidence could be destroyed.

Detective Constable Mark Bryant (later Colonel Bryant MBE) arrived at Emerald just as Rita Croke was getting into her Honda Civic. She was stopped, the car was searched and two sacks were found.

'What's this?' asked Bryant, pointing to the sacks.

'Rubbish!' retorted Rita, but when the sacks were searched they were found to contain a Reck .65 self-loading gas pistol, twenty-eight gas cartridges, shotgun cartridges, spectacles, a holster, hats, clothing and adhesive; also a quantity of correspondence. A great deal more incriminating evidence was found inside Emerald, and Rita was soon on her way to Milton Keynes police station.

Meanwhile, I was told to arrest George Ince and I lost no time in getting over to the vicinity of his address at Fairfield Road, Bow. He wasn't at home – as I later found out, he was waiting at some strategic point to collect the gold bullion – but after a while I saw Dolly's Nissan Sunny Estate arrive and Ince park it around a corner, get out and make his way to the house. I crossed the road towards him, broke into a sprint and, with a couple of yards to go, launched myself at him, fully expecting that the contact would bring us crashing down to the pavement, with me on top. But he didn't go down. He just stood there, as solid as an oak tree, with my arms wrapped round him and my little legs kicking up and down, and d'you know what he quietly said? 'Leave off. You know I've got a bad leg!'

So I climbed down to the ground and arrested him. It was all a bit of an anti-climax – I did feel silly!

So George joined the others at Milton Keynes, and that was the end of round one of Operation Standard.

I assure you, that was the easy part.

# Part IV

# Double Supergrass

# Chapter Twenty-Nine

# 'You Simply Can't Do That!'

This was the situation at Milton Keynes police station on 11 August 1986. Barrett admitted his part in the robbery – he could hardly do anything else! Croke could have done, but he had feigned illness and had been taken to hospital. Turner admitted his part, once the evidence of the observations had been put to him. Rita wasn't saying much, and George Ince said nothing at all. As far the others involved in the gang were concerned, we had no idea of their identities.

★   ★   ★

There were 559 beds available at Milton Keynes University Hospital, but Dave Croke had a private room all to himself, plus two attendant police officers. They had attempted friendly conversation, but Croke was having none of it. He lay on his bed, his mind in turmoil, and it's easy to imagine his thought processes.

How the hell had all this come about when everything was going so well? The police had been waiting for us when we arrived at the service station – they hadn't been there by chance. How did they know? Of course, they were tipped off, but by who? It was only me, Don and Al. Could it have been Al – had he lost his bottle? No. George. George knew. He was waiting to take possession of the gold. Yes. It must have been George. So what do I do now? Tell them nothing, that's what. Stay completely buttoned up. If I say anything, it'll be that I want a brief. I'll need one. What's George told them? How much? He's got enough on us to sink us. Even if I just go down for this one, what'll I get? Five years? Ten? What'll they find at Emerald? They won't get anything out of Rita, she won't give them the time of day. I won't think about that now. I'll just stay schtum. They won't get anything out of me. Not a word.

★   ★   ★

Croke wasn't the only one who was thinking furiously Barrett sat in his cell, his mind going into overdrive. What could he do to minimise his predicament? He'd been caught bang to rights for this offence, and there was no way out of that. He had committed a number of offences since his release. Could we link him to them? What did we know? Even if we knew nothing – not very likely! – a conviction for this offence alone, even with a guilty plea, could still result in a substantial lump of porridge. Being in possession of a loaded automatic didn't help, either. So what could he be looking at? Well, with his form, practically all for robbery, a twenty, certainly. In front of the wrong Judge, life imprisonment. Christ, he thought bitterly, that would just about see me out; they might just as well throw away the key. Then there was another thought; how could he do any normal bird, with all the chaps he'd grassed up? He'd be dead in a week or two; a month, top whack. The alternative would be to go behind the door with all the sex cases, the nonces. What a thought! And here's another thought. What happens if Dave Croke rolls over? He'd spoken to me often enough about the time when I was a supergrass. He's got enough on me to hang me. Dave's a good bloke, but he's never been inside before, never been nicked before, never, for Christ's sake, even been questioned by the filth before! Once those cunning Squad bastards get to work on him … now, wait a moment. Calm down, Donald. What was it that George Ince said, just before they went out to do a bit of work, knowing as he did that he'd been a Supergrass? What were his words?

'I'm working with you, Don', he'd said, 'because you're the best. Also, because you've been a Supergrass, you can never be one again. Mind you, if you ever grass me, I'll find you and kill you.'

He'd meant it, too. 'Because I can never be a Supergrass again.' Who says not? Because it's never happened, it doesn't mean to say it can't be done. And why isn't Crokey answering me? I've been calling out to him for bloody ages. Where is he? Upstairs? Spilling his guts? Cutting a deal? Time for me to make my play!

And with that, Barrett got to his feet, took two quick paces across his cell, stuck his thumb on the bell-push and kept it there.

'A Supergrass, twice?' said Kevin. 'Never heard of that before, Don. Don't think it's ever been done.'

The three of us were seated round a table in the interview room.

'Doesn't mean it can't though, does it?' replied Barrett.

He said it casually enough, but I noticed that the pulse in his neck was beating strongly.

'The thing is, Don,' I said, 'do we really need you? We can link you to Armaguard, Cross and Herberts, Enfield Crematorium and the rest.'

'You don't know how many I've done,' replied Barrett calmly, 'and you need someone like me to bring in the rest and point the finger at them and convict 'em. But if you reckon you can get me down for things that I'm not even admitting, fine. I'll just wipe my mouth and walk away.'

'So what are we talking about then, Don?' asked Kevin.

'Right,' replied Barrett. 'Including today's job, I can tell you about eleven robberies, attempted robberies and conspiracies. I can give you about the same number of top-class robbers. I can tell you where the guns are, I can tell you what happened to the money, which comes to a couple of million, and how to get it back, and I can tell you where to look for corroboration.'

He sat back, having laid down an impressive hand of cards, and watched us intently. There was a bit of a silence. Of course, Barrett had left the best bit to last. He knew full well that independent corroboration was essential in any Supergrass trial.

'First of all,' I said, 'if we're going to do anything, the Director of Public Prosecutions has got to agree.'

Barrett nodded. This was nothing new to him.

'So what I'll need,' I continued, 'is something in writing, to show him.'

Barrett threw back his head and guffawed.

'Leave off!' he laughed, although there was very little humour in his laughter.

'What I want to do,' I continued, 'is take a "without prejudice" statement. We'll put something like, "I, Donald Walter Barrett, make the following statement on the understanding that if I am not accepted by the Director of Public Prosecutions as a Resident Informant, nothing in this statement can be used in evidence against me." Then, what we'll do is just put down what you've said to us, as briefly as that.'

Barrett smoked and thought.

Eventually, he said, 'All right, we'll do it.'

And we did.

As he signed the statement he grinned wryly.

'Well, that's it,' he said. 'I'm bollocksed now, aren't I?

I picked up the statement and put it in my briefcase.

'Whatever way it goes, Don,' I said, 'we're playing this one straight down the line.'

'You simply can't take a statement like this!' screamed the pimply representative of the Crown Prosecution Service.

This worthless organisation had just got underway, and this little twerp was flexing his muscles.

I gave him a look and said, 'Shut up! It's done.'

He flounced away, and I settled down for a long wait. To tell the truth, I didn't know if I had done the right thing, never having done anything like this before, but it seemed to me to be the fairest thing that I could do, for everybody concerned, in the circumstances.

Peter Gwynn agreed: 'This was a unique occasion to get a man to be a supergrass again.'

The following day, Peter Gwynne emerged from the Director's office.

'Right, we've got the go-ahead', he said. 'Mind you,' he added with a grin, 'the Director did wince when he saw your statement!'

⋆   ⋆   ⋆

Before civilian Scenes of Crime officers (SOCOs) were introduced in the late 1960s, inspection at the scene of a crime was a task carried out by detectives. When they were called – for instance – to a burglary, they would take a little wooden box with them which contained various tools to collect clues: a brush to dust for fingerprints (if they found any, a photographer had to be sent for from the Yard's C3 Department for the photographic result to be compared with any in the Fingerprint branch), tweezers to pick up minute objects, and so on. Success usually depended on whether the detective was fired with sufficient enthusiasm. I thought the same lack of keenness applied to the majority of SOCOs with whom I'd had dealings. Apart from the fact that I thought they were a pretty useless bunch at solving anything, I didn't believe they had the commitment for the job. Each Flying Squad office had its own SOCO. I'd been instrumental in getting rid of the previous SOCO at Rigg Approach; Christ, what a nightmare he was.

And then along came his replacement, Paul Frederick Millen, short, balding, his eyes blinking owlishly behind his spectacles.

I glared at him.

'You the new SOCO?' I said, abruptly.

Paul nodded.

'Hope you're better than the last one,' I said, shortly, 'because if you're not, out you fucking well go!'

Paul said nothing, just blinked at me once or twice, turned round and got on with his job. Paul's career in forensic science started in 1978, when he became an assistant scientific officer at the Metropolitan Police forensic science laboratory, and I learnt very quickly that he was the absolute Billy Bollocks. He was a keen and tireless worker, and if Paul said something couldn't be done, it meant that he'd exhausted every possible solution. In fact, although he was a civilian worker, Paul was a far better detective than many I knew who held that rank.

So Paul was with us on the case from the word go – he had been at Battersea listening to the radio as events progressed and, following the attack, he made his way to Milton Keynes. There, he met four local fellow SOCOs. He introduced himself and described the type of help he needed; three were immediately enthusiastic and did a tremendous job. The fourth displayed no interest whatsoever, so he was out of the team. The vehicles were brought in for minute examination, and the prisoners needed to be examined and samples taken – Paul divided up the work.

Paul was present when Barrett was to be examined by the police surgeon, and when the doctor asked what samples were required, it was Barrett who casually replied, 'Oh, the usual, blood, urine, saliva, hair samples'.

Paul couldn't understand why the doctor hadn't addressed his question to Kevin, but then he got it. Barrett was still dressed in his immaculate Savile Row suit and Kevin, looking fairly dishevelled like the rest of us, was in a T-shirt and jeans. The doctor had mistaken robber for detective. But amusing though that was, Barrett, true to form, was just trying it on. Arrested and in custody in a police station, he was alert and still most formidable.

★　★　★

Barrett, the two Crokes and Turner were all charged and, with the exception of Barrett, they were remanded in custody. There was nothing to connect George Ince with at that time, and he was released. Barrett was moved into a suite of cells at Woodford Green police station (it has since moved), which had been especially adapted for Resident Informants; in fact, that had been Barrett's home the first time round as a supergrass. Entry to the suite was gained through a series of electronically controlled doors, each having to be closed before the next could be opened. Barrett later told me he'd found a way of overcoming those security procedures. Again, he was just trying it on; he hadn't. This, the feeding facilities and the searching of permitted visitors were administered by armed uniformed officers who worked a three-shift system in the claustrophobic atmosphere of what Kevin christened 'The Bunker'. It was here that the first six months of this intensive enquiry took place, with Kevin and myself as Barrett's handlers.

Police Sergeant 116 'YE' Stephen Stocker was one of the uniformed officers, tasked to guard Barrett; he recalled several occasions when Kevin and I were not dealing with Barrett and, being in a good mood and wanting to chat, the prisoner would regale the staff with stories of his criminal life. Stocker was in no doubt that many of these stories were embellished but, like the newspaper editor in John Ford's *The Man who Shot Liberty Valance*, he thought it unnecessary to let the facts get in the way of a good story. He also felt that Barrett was trying to put a positive spin on being a grass. In any case, these are the stories which Sergeant Stocker related to me:

Don said he sometimes used mopeds or motorcycles as they didn't tend to attract attention. Early one morning, he was on a motorbike going to do a job when he got into an altercation with a car full of young men who had been out for the night. He directed them to a side street, so that they could have it out. As they got out of their car, he pulled a sawn-off shotgun from a side pannier and threatened them with it. They looked shocked, stopped in their tracks, then ran back to their car and made off at speed.

He described why he became a supergrass the first time: someone he was going to do a job with got into an argument with a neighbour and started waving a gun around. This was just before he was due to meet up with Don. He failed to tell Don about this. When they both returned to his address after carrying out a robbery, police were waiting for him and raided the address. They found them both with the money from the robbery and guns. He explained that he became a grass because he felt hard done by, because it was the stupidity of another person that had resulted in his arrest. This wasn't a very convincing argument, particularly as he grassed up other criminals who had nothing to do with his arrest.

His neighbours thought he was a businessman, and he explained that becoming a supergrass for the second time was partly linked to the fact that his wife was younger than him and he felt she wouldn't wait around for him to come out. And he wasn't getting any younger.

He talked about bent coppers but said he would only talk about those that had retired (that was an uncomfortable conversation).

In relation to getting round the security procedures in place, I can remember Don saying that he could have got his solicitor to stay in the cell and pretend to have been overpowered. Don went on to explain that he would then have pretended to be the solicitor. He didn't try this because he didn't feel it was in his best interests to do so. Don didn't always leave his living space, so if officers who were unfamiliar with him were on duty, this might have been possible. The officers dealing with him were updated about this conversation.

The second time he became a supergrass related to the gold bullion van job. A relative was working for a security van company and told him how lax the security was. He told us he was trying to go straight, but the job was too easy to let it pass. He had radio scanning equipment in his car. As he drove off in his car on route to the job his scanner picked up that 'the target was on the move'. He was confident it didn't relate to him and just thought someone else was unlucky to have a team on them. As he was following the gold bullion van up the motorway, he noticed a car that stayed in the nearside lane a couple of cars back. He said that because it was a woman, he ignored the car and just thought, a typical woman driver; he realised she was a police officer when he later saw her at the police station!

As we now know, there was no way in which Barrett was endeavouring to go straight at the time of the gold bullion job, since this was his twelfth robbery, attempted robbery or conspiracy to rob in succession since his release from prison after being a supergrass the first time; but to a professional armed robber, caught bang to rights, self-justification is a necessary weapon in the armoury!

Ken Grange had the overall charge of this small squad of nine, which included a typist, a woman police constable for indexing and filing and my driver, Tony Freeman, to drive the Squad car in furtherance of any of the investigations.

*   *   *

The Flying Squad commander, Jerry Plowman, arrived to give Barrett a pep talk. The girlfriend of a previous supergrass had apparently conceived whilst her paramour was in police custody, and during the cross-examination in court which followed this revelation there was an awful lot of media speculation. It might, or might not have been true, but that, plus Jack Slipper being alleged to have been supergrass Billy Williams' best man, fuelled the media frenzy, and Jerry, a rather crusty old character, was having none of it. He laid down the strictures on conjugal visits in no uncertain terms, but Barrett was up for that one.

'I hope you don't think I'd treat my wife like an animal, having it off with her on the floor of my cell, Commander?' he said, frostily.

I made sure I didn't smile until Jerry had left the area; he could be a funny old bugger!

# Chapter Thirty

# Investigations at Home and Abroad

Now it was time to go to work, but there was a problem. I'd never handled a supergrass before. However, all my working life as a detective had been spent with informants, and I had my own set of rules governing them. With very few exceptions, informants were criminals themselves; therefore, we were on separate sides of the fence. It didn't mean that I should adopt a condescending attitude to them; better to be friendly, have a drink with them but still let them know who was boss. If I found out they were using me as a cloak for their own criminal activities, not only did I drop them, I nicked them myself. That only happened on a couple of occasions. What I would not do would be to socialise with them, and every penny that I got from the informants fund or insurance company went straight to the informant concerned. That may sound all very moralistic, but it worked. I looked after them in other ways. Sometimes their enthusiasm ran away with them to such an extent that, if I acted on their information, it would become abundantly clear to the perpetrator who the informant was. In that eventuality, steps were taken to bring the matter to a successful conclusion, details of which need not be recounted here!

However … it was one thing to meet a snout in a pub, a café or a car to have them mutter pieces of information to you, then go your separate ways; but quite another to be practically banged up with a full-time informant and take down in writing everything he's telling you. I knew that those people could be difficult and trying; that, I could accept. But what I would not stand for was being manipulated and having conditions laid down, which was what Jimmy Humphreys, the Soho pornographer, did when he was being debriefed by an Assistant Commissioner (Crime) who had spent all of his previous service in uniform. So I made a pact with myself. I decided that the first time Barrett did that, I'd tell him he was going straight back into the prison system, then tell a senior officer what I'd done; and if he didn't back me (and in all honesty, I didn't suppose he would), I would demand to be taken off that duty (no doubt he would agree to that). However, that eventuality never arose.

I took a statement for each offence, rather than one long, rambling statement to encompass everything. It was a lot easier that way, and if further evidence came to light, or if Barrett wanted to add something that had previously slipped his memory, it was a simple matter to take a further short statement and attach it to the first one.

Barrett went into great detail; in fact, he had a phenomenal memory for detail: what cars and guns were used, what clothing and disguises he and the team were wearing. It was suggested that Barrett should tell us where forensic evidence for the offences might be found, but Paul Millen was unhappy about that approach. He felt that it was important to corroborate as much of his evidence as possible, no matter how trivial, by studying not only Barrett's statements but also all the other witness statements; this, Paul felt, would ensure that Barrett's accounts were completely accurate. Corroboration was something we badly needed; not one incriminating fingerprint had been found at the scene of any of the robberies.

The witness statements from all of the robberies were brought back to us, as were the exhibits, and there was only one that was not properly packaged and labelled, which made it useless for further comparison.

The examination of Emerald was paramount. Besides the bungalow, there was a large garden and a garage. Therefore, it was made a crime scene, was photographed and, after each examination, everything was left as much as possible as before. Police were in control of the premises for weeks.

Hundreds of items were seized, packaged and labelled. Now, Paul called in the senior investigator of each robbery, his deputy and the exhibits officer, and every item was evaluated. It was an enormous task; but it paid off.

Remember the explosive device which had been so thoughtlessly left behind at the Cross & Herbert raid? A piece of cloth was found stuffed inside a shotgun cartridge inserted into the bomb device. It had been packaged at the time and sealed. Fifteen months later, Paul searched Croke's address and discovered an identical piece of cloth, complete with stitching.

Regarding the Security Express van that was attacked in Mauritius Road, Greenwich, Barrett disclosed the whereabouts of the Hilti gun that was used to shatter the van's window; forensic tests revealed that glass jammed inside the mechanism of the gun matched exactly the laminated glass from the van. Then a piece of cloth found inside one of the getaway cars, complete with a seam and stitching, matched the cloth found at Cross & Herbert, as well as at Emerald; they had all originated from the same garment. Barrett stated that in connection with this raid, Croke had been experimenting with armour-piercing bullets and had accidentally discharged one in his garage. A search at

Emerald revealed the damage as well as a steel-tipped, home-made bullet, together with home-made silencers.

A dustcoat found at Emerald was examined for firearms residue; none was found, but fragments of bullion-quality gold were found in the pockets; this linked the coat to the gold bullion robbery at Bristol.

But it was the Armaguard raid that yielded the most evidence. Following the robbery, the share-out came to £140,000 each. Barrett had told me that the Crokes had an account with the Bank of Ireland, Seven Sisters Road, Holloway in the name of T & R Moore. Shortly after the robbery, £140,000 was deposited in the account. During – or perhaps, prior to – the robbery, a perimeter chain link fence at the Armaguard depot was cut. Wire cutters were found at Emerald, and microscopic examination revealed that they were the ones that had been used. Adhesive used in the manufacture of the explosive device found in Joe Symes' car was also found at Emerald. Several items were left behind following the robbery: a battery cover plate was found at the scene – the radio device, minus the cover plate was also found at Emerald. A balaclava, too, was left, and fibres were discovered inside it. They matched fibres found on the wig worn by Croke at the time of his arrest. Croke was later picked out on an identity parade by Joe Symes and his daughter.

Remember the shabby Honda that was used to transport the money? A point was raised that needed clearing up. Barrett had told us that the van had been repainted yellow. Checking through the enormous bundle of witness statements taken by Essex Police at the time of the robbery, it was found that a couple of witnesses had said that they had seen a Honda van leave the vicinity of Armaguard at the relevant time. However, both categorically stated that the van was white.

Could Barrett have made a mistake? No, he couldn't, he replied irritably, and then, when he was pushed on the subject, he finally lost his temper. He knew what was yellow and what was white, and that van had been painted yellow. He didn't care what the witnesses had seen. If they said the van was white, either they were wrong or they'd seen a different van; one that was white, right? Not fucking yellow! In fact, nobody had got it wrong; everybody was right.

Paul Millen solved the conundrum. When the van had first rolled off the assembly line, it had originally been painted white. However, it had indeed been repainted yellow, and Barrett mentioned that it had met with a slight accident when it struck the garage door in the lock-up. Paul went to the premises and found a flake of yellow paint on the door of the lock-up; this appeared to match yellow paint fragments found on a roof rack, left behind on the garage floor, which had been set to the exact dimensions for a Honda van of that model.

Barrett had not mentioned the roof rack; in fact, he was probably unaware of its existence. Paul covered the grips of the roof rack with small plastic bags to protect and preserve it, then sent it to the Forensic Science Laboratory at Huntingdon (who had received all the other exhibits by the Essex Police from the Armaguard offence), where a detailed microscopic examination was carried out on the grip ends of the bars. It was established that the layer structure of the paint – primer, undercoat and topcoat – were those of a Honda van of that period. But the final coat was yellow – and this was not the manufacturer's original finish. It had been re-sprayed – so Barrett was right. Therefore, the witnesses must be wrong – or were they?

The two witnesses who had seen the van on the morning of the robbery were re-interviewed, in exactly the same spot that they had seen the van. This solved the puzzle. They had seen the van before dawn and because it had been seen under sodium street lighting, it appeared to be white.

This was carefully explained to a very sulky Barrett, still annoyed that his word had been doubted.

'Told you so!' was his only response.

But where was the van? Barrett knew. Following the raid, it had been driven by Croke, together with Rita and Glen Armsby, across France to a town (now a city) named Chalon-sur-Saône, fairly close to the Swiss border. There, it had conked out, and Croke had purchased another cheap vehicle, a DAF. From there, they had made their way to Malta, where David and Rita had a flat, and whilst they relaxed in the sun, Croke purchased a boat. As Barrett told me, a man named 'Victor' looked after both the flat and the boat. Now, there are two things that are considered bad luck by sailors; first, don't kill an albatross, and second, never rename a boat. I can only assume that Croke had never heard of the latter superstition; it certainly seemed the height of stupidity to paint the name 'ARMAG' on the side of the boat, in commemoration of his latest piece of work.

Armed with a *Commission Rogatoire* – an absolute necessity before conducting enquiries in Europe – issued by the Director of Public Prosecutions, the Competent Judicial Authorities of the Republic of France were requested to permit me to make enquiries to trace the Honda van, believed to have been used in the commission of robberies and sold in France; furthermore, to obtain samples of the paintwork and to ascertain what, if any, property was left in the van and any other evidence that the van was used in the robberies. I needed to get details of the accommodation used by Armsby and the Crokes while in France, and evidence of any transactions made by them, in particular any large cash transfers. I wanted to get details of a DAF vehicle believed to have been bought by Croke in France, and to search the customs records with a view to establishing the destination of the Crokes and Armsby. Oh, and any other enquiries which might be necessary. Phew!

I went to the Ministère de l'Intèrieur, Paris, where my enquiries were sanctioned by Mme Geneviève Liotard, *Premier Juge d'Instuction*, and thence to Dijon, from where, accompanied by *Inspecteur Principal* Alain Cassabois and *Inspecteur* Michel Lefort, I made my way south, to Chalon-sur-Saône and discovered the fate of the Honda at 81 Avenue de Paris, 71100. The proprietor of the garage Automarche de Chalon-sur-Saône, Jean Jack Bied, informed *Sergent-Détective* Kirby (with considerable interpreting assistance from the two *Inspecteurs*) that the Honda, PBM 263W, had indeed arrived at his garage on 13 March 1986 and the owner, Monsieur David Terrence Croke, had signed a certificate of abandonment (his signature was illegible) and purchased a 1976 DAF 66 super luxe, bearing the registration plates 5201 SG 71 and with 35,599 kilometres on the clock, for 3,000 francs. The Honda had been scrapped and cut up; the top part was used as a chicken coop and the rest as a dog kennel. With a small razor blade (supplied by Paul Millen) I took careful scrapings which were found to be part and parcel of the paint left on the roof racks, found in the garage 536 miles away. All that remained of the original vehicle was the chassis plate, so I took that too. Nobody wanted it. It's in front of me, together with an impressive-looking French evidential red wax seal, as I write.

My enquiries took me on to Lyon, and then my friendly French colleagues provided me with a first-class ticket to return to Paris, as well as the necessary but temporary rank of Superintendent, to permit such luxurious travel. I tried not to let this sudden, unexpected promotion go to my head when I shared a compartment with a middle-aged lady on board the Lyon to Paris express and during the two-hour journey she explained that she earned a supplement to her housekeeping by soliciting prostitution on the train. Although I had no hesitation in diplomatically rejecting her blandishments, she told me that this was a rather good wheeze used by many bored Lyon housewives for a little *argent de poche* – pocket money, to you and me. So the journey passed, with the lady grandly informing me of her visits to milliners along the Rue de la Paix and sumptuous lunches at the Tour d'Argent. I bade her farewell at the Gare de Lyon, hoping that on the return journey from the City of Lights she would encounter a willing, panting customer to reimburse her for her '*charmant, leedle 'at, non?*'

Comparisons could be drawn with Dumas' 1844 novel, in which D'Artagnan, transformed from a rather bolshie Gascon farm-boy to a King's Musketeer, meets up with the executioner of

Lille; while I was converted from being a humble detective sergeant to a splendid – if temporary – superintendent who met the hooker from Lyon.

We Flying Squad officers led *such* interesting lives!

Kevin and Ken Grange went to Malta, which proved to be quite a productive trip. At St Paul's Bay, they searched No. 2 Maria Bambina flats, the expensively furnished holiday home of Mr and Mrs Croke. Amongst other items, they found a KLM luggage ticket bearing Glen Armsby's name and address and a receipt for the DAF vehicle. In a nearby garage, they found the said vehicle and a boat with an outboard motor, although there was no sign of the boat's name. The boat had been painted, but when an area of the bow had been scraped and subjected to ultraviolet light, the resultant photograph revealed the name 'ARMAG'. Kevin, the complete detective, knew what evidence was required to prove criminal offences; he was also aware of crafty defence tactics used to negate such evidence. Ever the perfectionist, he obtained a statement from a suitably competent person to confirm that 'ARMAG' was not a word in the Maltese language.

# Chapter Thirty-One

# Arrests

On Monday, 23 February 1987, Barrett appeared, under armed guard, at the Old Bailey, where he admitted a total of twenty-three offences. Sentence was deferred, but now, as a witness, he was able to give evidence against his past associates.

Barrett never stopped blaming Croke for his current situation.

'It's all his fault,' he'd say. 'If he hadn't left that stuff in the sack outside his house for the kid to find, we wouldn't be in the mess we're in today. Well, fuck 'im!'

In fairness, Barrett did have a point. All of the scientific forensic evidence gathered in the investigation pointed to Croke – none to Barrett, who had been very careful to cover his tracks.

Thirteen others were pulled in, and I was allocated George Ince to arrest.

'You'd better watch him', said Barrett to me. 'He usually carries a knife, stuffed down the front of his underpants.'

Early in the morning, I arrived at 37 Fairfield Road, Bow, and George, just wearing his underpants, answered my knock.

'Excuse the informality, George', I said, and pulled down the front of his underpants which revealed nothing more threatening than his male organ of generation.

'No offence', I said.

'None taken', replied George.

I searched the place – I was looking in particular for bank statements – but if they were there, they were in a place that I couldn't find. Dolly Ince was present, courteous and slightly aloof. I took George into Bow police station and gave him a preliminary interview, during which he gave nothing away, and he was charged with the robberies in which Barrett had implicated him. As with all of the prisoners, Barrett confronted him, was asked to identify both himself and the prisoner and then to state what offences he had committed. After that, the prisoner would be cautioned and asked if he wished to respond to the allegation.

Most said nothing, but George Ince snapped, 'Yes – tell the fucking truth!'

I was involved with other arrests and interviews. I'd arrived at the Magistrates' Court with one of the prisoners – it was his first appearance at court and he was going to have a lay-down. To ensure that this was the case, I approached the representative from the Crown Prosecution Service and told her that I, not she, would make the application for the remand in custody. This, I should mention, was in the early days of the CPS, when their untrained representatives could be treated rather like naughty children in a kindergarten – although in fairness I never dealt with them in any other way.

Just then, I was approached by a tall, smartly dressed chap with an extremely pleasant manner, who introduced himself as the prisoner's barrister. With him was a small, rodent-like individual, who turned out to be the instructing solicitor. The barrister courteously introduced me to the solicitor as well, but I ignored the little runt; I'd met him once before when he'd made a cheeky remark to me and he'd been extremely lucky to walk away unmolested from the encounter.

'Will you be applying for a remand in custody, Sergeant Kirby?' asked the barrister.

I conceded that I would.

'I see,' he said, nodding solemnly. 'Would you mind telling me what your objections will be?'

'Certainly,' I replied. 'Firstly, due to the gravity of the offence, I believe that if granted bail he will abscond, and secondly, I believe that he will commit further offences.'

The barrister nodded again, and now the solicitor, unable to contain himself any longer, launched into the attack; just as I anticipated he would.

'On what do you base your assumption that my client will abscond?' he snapped. 'And what's more, I should very much like to know how you have come to the conclusion that he will commit further offences. My client can provide substantial sureties and I should like to know what possible grounds —'

And now, I'd just run out of patience.

'Stop,' I interrupted, and laid a steadying hand on his shoulder.

The solicitor stopped in mid-sentence and gaped at me.

'Now, let's get something straight, shall we?' I said. 'First of all, I am under no obligation to speak to you outside of court at all, let alone give you reasons as to why I'm objecting to bail. I did so on this occasion, because this gentleman' – I indicated the barrister – 'has far better manners than you'll ever have and because he was courteous to me. Next, never presume to cross-examine me or any other police officer out of court. I for one won't stand for it, and furthermore, it's a wasted exercise, because you're not very good at it – got it?'

With that, I turned to walk away and then stopped, turned back and looking at the area just below his waistband, added, 'And please cover yourself up – you're making a bit of a spectacle of yourself!'

The solicitor gasped and clutched at the family jewels with both hands, before realising his fly buttons were quite secure. He hardly had time to start spluttering with indignation, when suddenly I heard my name called. I turned and, rushing towards me was a woman with the sort of voluptuous figure that would have brought Rubens out in a muck sweat.

'Dick Kirby!' she cried again, and crushed me to her ample bosom. 'I haven't seen you in fifteen years – what a lovely surprise!'

I emerged, inhaling deeply, from this asphyxiating encounter and greeted the Clerk of the Court.

'Janice!' I gasped. 'You look ravishing – are you in this court today?'

'Yes, of course,' she replied. 'Oh, let me look at you – now, what're you doing here?'

'Just a remand in custody,' I admitted, carelessly.

'That'll take all of two minutes,' she scoffed and, putting her arm around my waist, she led me away. 'Now, what about a drink afterwards?'

As we strolled away, out of earshot of the defence team, I made a slightly salacious remark which caused her to throw her head back and shriek with laughter.

A colleague later told me that, as we sauntered away, the barrister leant towards the small solicitor, who was still seething with rage, and murmured, 'I think we'll give the bail application a miss this week!'

★ ★ ★

John Kenneth Johnson admitted to being part of the gang who had attacked the Ford Sierra in Brimsdown, Enfield and also to attacking the staff at Select-a-Property. Glen Armsby, too, came in and admitted his part in the Imperial Cold Storage raid (which was later left on the file at court) and the Armaguard robbery. Two other men were charged with receiving the gold stolen in the Brimsdown robbery.

There was one infuriating matter that arose from an arrest. Barrett had named the man who he said had received a piece of jewellery following a robbery. This man was arrested and questioned regarding the jewellery which, following a search, was found at his address.

He persistently denied receiving it but eventually, to the officers' astonishment, he told them, 'I didn't receive it – I stole it during the robbery!'

He was immediately cautioned, that he need not say anything, etc. – the usual well-tried formula – and he made a full written statement admitting being one of the robbers.

Back to Barrett, who was told of the man's admission to being one of the robbers.

'I didn't know that', he replied. 'I was late getting on the plot and the rest of the team were already masked-up. It was only later on that I saw him with that bit of tom [Cockney rhyming slang: tom = tomfoolery = jewellery] and he didn't look like a blagger, so I assumed he'd received it.'

I said this case was infuriating, and this is why. That ridiculous piece of the legislation, the Police and Criminal Evidence Act 1984, had just come on to the statute books, putting time limits on how long suspects could be held in custody.

'That'll stop them CIDs going off to the pub', muttered one ill-informed uniform chief superintendent who advised on the legislation, but that was not all.

The Act also introduced a whole host of pettifogging rules for working cops – just the type of thing that Chief Constable Fred Wensley had got rid of, sixty-five years previously, when he formed the Flying Squad. The man pleaded not guilty at the Old Bailey, and although Barrett gave accurate evidence against him, the man's written admission to the offence was ruled inadmissible – and why? Because when he admitted the offence, although he was correctly cautioned, to comply with these newly introduced ludicrous rules and regulations, the officer should also have said, 'I'm arresting you for robbery.'

It was a situation very much like 'O'Grady says', the game for 5–10-year-olds in which the leader says, for instance, 'O'Grady says, touch your toes' and the children who comply stay in the game. But if the leader just says, 'Touch your toes' those children who obey without the magic words 'O'Grady says' being uttered are eliminated. That was how ludicrous the legislation had become. The robber was acquitted and walked from court a free man. Personally, I think he should have thanked his lucky stars, but he pushed his luck too far when he tried to sue us for return of 'his' piece of jewellery under The Police Property Act 1897 and got very short shrift from the Magistrate before whom he appeared. He got even less satisfaction when the insurance company sued him.

The months passed in the bunker – the case correspondence in each offence was drawn, scrutinised and re-investigated. I was seconded to work with the details of the Armaguard case with the Essex detectives. What a good bunch they were; there was absolutely no resentment at our presence, and they worked just as hard as we did to clear the matter up. Barrett came out in the Squad car and pointed out the robbery sites, where vehicles were parked and where lock-ups were situated. Keep-fit equipment was placed in his cell – a heavy punch bag and weights – and although they were seldom used at first, later they were, in order to sharpen up his mind for the trials. His moods went up and down; sometimes, thinking about his predicament and the possible outcome, he would be morose, because the question on his lips all the time was, what sort of sentence was he going to get. It was a question to which nobody could supply the answer, and Kevin and I would pull his leg to cheer him up. One day, when he was in a pensive mood, Barrett's leg was pulled so seriously that it was in danger of coming out of its socket.

'You know,' he said, 'it's a pity you couldn't have got Croke to have rolled over. He knows a lot – more than me, I reckon.'

I think Barrett wanted Kevin and myself to rush to his defence, crying, 'Oh, no Don – there's no one like you!'

If so, he was to be sorely disappointed.

'Be a change from listening to a boring fucker like you,' said Kevin, winking at me.

'That's right,' I replied, joining in, 'and what's more, Croke's got no form, either; he's got more cred than you! Come on, Don, get your kit together – we're fucking you off to Brixton this afternoon!'

In the end, Don had to laugh with us – but it took a bit of time!

On another occasion, Barrett and I were talking about Ronnie Dark, that very high-ranking armed robber, whom he knew very well.

'He really screwed his loaf, Don,' I said. 'He got nicked for a half-million-pound VAT scam involving krugerrands and copped just twelve months. All that dough and nothing like the same amount of bird you'd get for a blagging – didn't you ever fancy something like that?'

Barrett smiled and his eyes were far away, reminding me of T.E. Lawrence's 'men who dream with their eyes open'. The answer he gave provided another insight of the committed armed robber's psyche.

'You can't understand it, Dick,' he said, 'because you've never been across the pavement.'

He shook his head.

'There's no other feeling like it,' he added, quietly.

But Barrett would often be in an amusing mood, and we'd all have a laugh over things that had happened. On one occasion, he mentioned the name of a thief who was a prolific robber.

'Yes,' I laughed. 'Big fat fucker!'

Barrett frowned.

'Why'd you say that?' he asked.

'Well,' I replied, 'anybody who's 5′ 8″ tall and weighs over 20 stone has earned the right to be called a big fat fucker!'

Barrett shook his head.

'The bloke I'm talking about is 5′ 8″ all right,' he replied, 'but the last time I saw him was in Albany and he weighed about 11 stone and he was as hard as a lump of concrete. I wouldn't have gone up against him!'

We were talking about the same man; inside, he'd work out as though there was no tomorrow and actually built himself an assault course in one prison; outside of prison, he simply ballooned. In fact, he'd recently been arrested by the Squad during an ambush, and when I interviewed one of the small fry, he said he'd been told that the flabby robber had been a member of the SAS, perhaps to keep him in line. I don't know if he was; I do know that he'd been in Africa, because when he was chatting to the Squad officers, he proudly told them, 'I can speak Swahili.' This statement was met with derision by the Squad officers, but the robber insisted that he could.

'Go on, then,' said one of the officers. 'Say something in Swahili.'

'*Mimi nataka pesa*!' snapped the robber.

'Blimey!' replied one of the round-eyed Squadmen, impressed at the fluency and authority in his voice. 'What's that mean?'

The robber grinned.

'It means, "Give me the money"!' he replied.

It did, too – he had got two years' hard labour in Nairobi to prove it.

Another thing which amused me greatly was when Barrett told me of seeing a well-known armed robber and an eminent Queen's Counsel busily dividing up a stack of stolen jewellery between them. Much later, I was being cross-examined in a case at the Old Bailey by that same QC, and he suggested that during my testimony I had told a pack of lies.

'I would no more be untruthful under oath, sir, than you would receive stolen jewellery', was what I would have *liked* to have replied; but I'm afraid my nerve failed me!

I was pretty sure that during his long criminal career Barrett had had illicit dealings with some rather dodgy cops, but when I jokingly put this to him, his whole demeanour changed and he shut up like a clam. Odd, that.

But he soon cheered up again and told me of a very amusing incident when he was giving evidence during his first supergrass trial. It was suggested to him in cross-examination that the only reason he had accused the barrister's client of robbery was because on a previous occasion, Barrett and the prisoner had had a homosexual relationship, and when the prisoner had decided that enough was enough, Barrett had decided to take his revenge by accusing him of these trumped-up charges. Barrett – who was resolutely heterosexual – was furious at these clearly ridiculous accusations and said so, very forcefully. But the barrister continued to insist they were true, until Barrett, incensed beyond belief, demanded that a doctor carry out a rectal examination, right there in the witness box, telling the Judge and jury, 'That'll prove my arsehole's not been punched!' The barrister wisely backed down, and Barrett left the witness box with both his masculine reputation and his rectum intact!

Barrett, as previously mentioned, confronted the people he was accusing, giving them the opportunity to confirm or deny his accusations. Croke just sat there hunched up in a corner, saying nothing, but his eyes never left Barrett's face. With his perpetually downcast expression, his droopy moustache and his spectacles, he gave the appearance of being one of life's losers. But he didn't fool us for one moment, nor Barrett, either.

'It's when he looks like that,' Barrett told me once, 'that he's at his most dangerous.'

Not only did Croke have nothing to say on that occasion, he had little to say on any other occasion either. It was only when my questioning became a little too persistent that he uttered his only words of the interview: 'I want my solicitor to be here.'

On one occasion his solicitor was present, as was Paul Millen, when we wanted to take hair samples from him; under the recently introduced legislation, we were permitted to do so, but Croke refused.

'Look, mate,' I said. 'Just be a bit sensible. If you refuse, we can take the samples by force.'

Still he refused, sitting in a corner of the interview room and glaring at me, but by now I'd just about run out of patience with him.

Pulling off my jacket, I said, 'Right, Paul – get that comb out!'

'Oh, Sergeant Kirby!' cried the solicitor, as I moved towards Croke. 'Just a moment – let me speak to my client!'

There was a hurried conference, permission was given and Croke's hair was added to the growing mound of evidence against him. Every time Croke had carried out a successful robbery, whatever his share was would appear the following day in the T & R Moore bank account in the Seven Sisters Road. A finance expert drew up graphs: a blue column revealed Barrett's findings as to how much Croke had taken as his share for each robbery; next to it, a red column showed how much had actually been deposited in the T & R Moore bank account. The amounts were remarkably similar.

★ ★ ★

I have never stopped criticising the Police and Criminal Evidence Act 1984, or the Crown Prosecution Service, both of which were foisted on the police at the same time, slowing down criminal justice for the police, the public and defendants to a snail's pace. I hope I never will.

A typical example of the ineptitude of the CPS occurred during this case. One morning, I was in the office when I received a frenzied telephone call: 'Get up to the Royal Courts of Justice straight away!'

Why, I knew not – but I told Tony Freeman to put his foot down, and in no time at all, brake drums smoking, the big Rover 3500 came to a halt in the Strand and I rushed into the court, where I was ushered into the room of a Judge who, minus his wig, was sitting 'in chambers'; also present was a defence barrister.

'Ah – now, are we all here?' asked the Judge.

'Excuse me, my Lord', I said. 'May I say something?'

'Yes, of course you may, Sergeant Kirby', replied the Judge courteously. 'What is it?'

'It's just that I haven't the foggiest notion as to why I'm here', I said. 'I was simply told to get up here as soon as possible.'

'This is a Judge in Chambers application for bail in respect of my client, Al Turner', said the defence barrister.

'That's the first I've heard of it', I replied, realising that the Crown Prosecution Service had been told of the application the previous day and had failed to instruct counsel to oppose the application, or to inform us.

'Dear me', said the Judge. 'This is most unfortunate. Would you wish for an adjournment so that the police can be represented?'

I'd realised at an early stage that the CPS were an organisation who were unable to differentiate their arses from their elbows, and since I'd been opposing bail applications since time immemorial, I replied, 'I'll deal with it, if I may, my Lord.'

It wasn't too long before I was back in the Squad Rover.

'Back to the office, Tone', I said, Al Turner having been refused bail in double-quick time.

★  ★  ★

Despite our best endeavours, we could find no corroborative evidence to support the charge of robbery, three attempted robberies, three charges of conspiracy to rob and four charges of unlawfully possessing firearms against George Ince, and on 20 November 1986, those matters were discharged at Lambeth Magistrates' Court. I couldn't let George off that lightly, so I charged him with dishonestly handling a quantity of road fund licences, stolen between 19 February and

11 August 1986, that I'd found when I arrested him, and he was bailed to Waltham Forest Magistrates' Court on 11 December.

'Nice one, Sargie!' beamed Tony Freeman.

'That was out of order, Mr Kirby', remarked George frostily as he and Dolly strolled arm-in-arm out of court.

Not that it did any good. The CPS were furious that I'd dared to charge George without consulting them, and at Waltham Forest court one of their representatives snootily declared that there was insufficient evidence and that anyway, an attempt to prosecute would be a waste of public funds. That, I knew, was consummate bollocks; being an experienced detective, and knowing far more about the criminal law than that bunch of mealy-mouthed tossers, I was not in the habit of charging someone when I believed there was insufficient evidence.

## Chapter Thirty-Two

# Weighed Off – and Reflections

Rita Croke and the two men accused of dishonestly handling stolen gold bullion were committed for trial to the Old Bailey, on bail totalling £170,000 – everybody else was sent for trial in custody.

Barrett gave evidence against Brian Wade and Anthony Ocquaye, who had received the stolen gold taken from Scadlynn's. Found guilty, Ocquaye was sentenced to three years' imprisonment, and Wade received four years and was made criminally bankrupt in the sum of £219,000.

One amusing incident when Barrett was in the witness box at the Old Bailey was recalled by Ken Grange:

> He was being cross-examined by one of the defence counsel and it was suggested that his evidence was a pack of lies from beginning to end and he was only doing this to gain a reduced sentence.
>
> Don's response was as follows and along this line: 'Of course you will accuse me of this, because almost everyone who comes here is innocent. That's their plea, so the police are deliberately arresting innocent people and the prisons are full of innocent people. The police are conspiring to convict innocent people and make sure the guilty are outside.'
>
> I felt the jury found this both amusing and true!

Rita Croke was initially charged with conspiracy to rob, perverting the course of public justice and receiving sums of £5,000, £5,500, £42,000 and £43,000, plus a car, knowing or believing the money and the vehicle to be stolen. All of which, like the spirits in Shakespeare's *The Tempest* 'were melted into air, into thin air ...'

After stating that she was offering only £50,000 from the £150,000 sale of Emerald to repay the losers in the case, Judge Michael Coombe told her:

> I have given you an opportunity to show what restitution you were willing to make because you know everything you possess is the result of these series of serious crimes, although claimants

might have difficulty in tracing assets. I am sorry you have not offered to sacrifice more. I have no power to make compensation orders; that must now be left to the civil courts.

In mitigation, her barrister mentioned that her marriage had brought her no happiness, that she had undergone plastic surgery following an attack by her husband, 'a man of extreme violence', and that the couple were now getting divorced.

Describing Dave Croke as 'the worst type of vicious professional robber, who was part of as dangerous a gang of robbers as ever existed', the Judge sentenced Rita, who pleaded guilty to one charge of possession of a prohibited weapon, to three months' imprisonment, suspended for one year, and fined her £5,000. It was a sentence of remarkable leniency.

John Kenneth Johnson, with a long string of criminal convictions including a 15-year sentence for three robberies, pleaded guilty to two armed robberies and was somewhat surprisingly sentenced to concurrent terms of thirty months' imprisonment. With the time he'd spent on remand, it seemed hardly worthwhile returning him to prison.

Despite his full and frank written admissions at the time of his arrest, Al Turner pleaded not guilty to the Milton Keynes robbery. In giving evidence, Barrett stated that Turner had been promised £6–7,000 for his willing participation in the gold bullion robbery, but Turner stated that he had been coerced into doing so. Telling the jury that he had refused to take part in the suggested robbery, he said he had walked out of Emerald, but Barrett had followed him outside.

> He opened the door to his car, leaned down and took a pistol from underneath the driver's seat. He pushed me into the car and stuck it in the back of my leg, behind my kneecap. I thought he was crazy. I was terrified. He said if I didn't play ball with them, not only would I get hurt, but my family could get hurt. I told him the destination of the gold delivery – Buxton – because he asked; because I was dead scared of him. He said if I said anything to anybody, my family would get hurt.

It appeared that Turner was between a rock and a hard place; part of his stepfather's defence was going to suggest that Turner (plus the entirely innocent security guard) were all in the plot together, and in that event, there was no robbery because nobody would have been threatened; it would have been a simple case of theft.

But Croke never put forward that – or any other – defence, as we shall see. Turner, found guilty, was sentenced, on his first offence, to seven years' imprisonment, with a 3-year concurrent sentence for possession of a firearm.

Glen Armsby initially pleaded not guilty to the Imperial Cold Storage and Armaguard robberies, but on the second day of his trial, before Barrett could give evidence, he pleaded guilty to the robbery at Armaguard, imprisoning the Symes family against their will and possession of firearms.

The other offence was permitted to lie on the file, and telling him, 'This was about the worst type of organised crime one can imagine', His Honour Judge Michael Coombe QC sentenced him to a total of fifteen years' imprisonment and ordered him to pay £100,000 compensation to Armaguard.

The prosecution team had stated that the trial would last four months, but the night before it was due to commence, we were told that Croke was going to plead guilty – guilty, that is, to the offences that we could strictly prove. The hijacking of the gold from Scadlynn's, the robberies at the Imperial Cold Storage and at Armaguard, as well as imprisoning the Symes family, plus the robbery at Newport Pagnall plus all the associate firearms offences resulted in a total of twenty-three years' imprisonment; he was also made criminally bankrupt to the tune of £528,352, with the Judge telling him:

An unpleasant aspect was that your evil influence brought your stepson and the man with whom your daughter was living into your criminal schemes. The home-made bomb device, strapped to victims to force them to comply was a diabolical feature. You are a ruthless criminal with no feeling for the suffering and terror of others.

Turning to Barrett, the Judge said:

I think it would be reasonable to recognise the assistance you have given to the public in revealing so much to the police by giving a discount which also takes into account the difficulties you are going to have in your lengthy prison sentence. What credit can I give you for the enormous assistance you have given police? In my judgement, rather less than last time. I am giving you a 25 per cent discount. Nobody could be permitted for a second time the leniency you were given.

He then sentenced Barrett to a total of sixteen years' imprisonment and made him criminally bankrupt in the sum of £840,519. Barrett, in his 500-guinea suit with his fedora clasped to his chest, bowed gravely to the Judge before being led away. His evidence had put eight criminals away for a total of seventy-one years.

To the prosecuting counsel, Mr Julian Bevan QC, the Judge said:

> It is quite obvious the team of officers dealing with very dangerous criminals in the case of both Croke and Barrett have done splendidly.
>
> I bear in mind the evidence I heard about Newport Pagnell, for example, when they were dealing with armed robbers and chasing them and arresting them, but the whole investigation must have required hundreds of hours of devoted and dedicated work and with one possible exception, where the evidence was not admissible, they seem to have been remarkably successful in bringing a team to justice where, as I have said already, the robberies seem to me to be far more serious even than the type of armed robbery that we have to deal with so often in these courts.
>
> I want to congratulate them and commend them. The officers really concerned are Detective Chief Inspector Grange, Detective Sergeant Lowden, Detective Sergeant Kirby, Detective Constable Bennett, Detective Constable Cuthbertson, Detective Constable Shapland, Detective Constable Murphy and Detective Constable Ellis. Some of those I have certainly seen myself in the course of their giving evidence.
>
> Would you be good enough to pass to the commissioner my commendation and I am sure I can add not only my thanks but also thanks of the public for what they have done.

These were sentiments echoed by the Director of Public Prosecutions, the head of the City of London CID ('a proud day indeed for the Flying Squad'), the Chief Constable of Essex ('the officers showed considerable professionalism when conducting the operation') and the commissioner, who commended Ken Grange, Kevin Shapland and myself for 'outstanding detective ability and diligence', with Deputy Assistant Commissioner's commendations to the two C11 operatives, Neil Murphy and Colin Ellis and to that superlative SOCO, Paul Millen.

But to my mind, if only one commendation could have been bestowed, it should have gone to Kevin Shapland. It was always his job, nobody else's.

*   *   *

To use that repulsive phrase beloved of senior police officers (and other politicians), could 'lessons be learnt' as a result of this case?

I suppose those armchair detectives (who've never confronted anything more threatening than an Income Tax return) would say that since both Don Barrett and George Ince were top-notch armed robbers, why wasn't a watch kept on them as a matter of course?

Leaving aside the matter of resources, there has to be a reason for mounting surveillance, such as a whisper from a reliable informant. But with both those individuals, there was nothing. Even after Kevin Shapland spotted the Nissan Sunny registered to Ince's wife on the driveway of Emerald, the surveillance was very limited The C11 surveillance team was very much in demand, not only by the whole of the Flying Squad, but by other pro-active units as well, and it was only after Barrett was seen arriving at that venue that observation was stepped up.

Why, then – those armchair detectives might ask – was an intercept not put on Croke's telephone? The explanation is simple: it is enormously difficult to gain permission for a telephone intercept from the Home Secretary; only a certain number of requests for warrants are granted each year and then, only when tremendously complex criteria are met; and even then, the intercept can be kept on only for a very limited amount of time. If nothing productive is forthcoming during that period, off comes the intercept.

However ... once Barrett came into the frame, as well as George Ince, two renowned armed robbers, plus the home of a suspected bomb–maker, now thoroughly suspected of a string of armed robberies which could have resulted in loss of life, plus the difficulties experienced in keeping the premises in a cul-de-sac under observation, matters did indeed change – and of the 573 warrants issued by the Home Secretary for the whole of the United Kingdom in 1986 to intercept telephones, one was allotted to Emerald.

Thus it was known that when Barrett and his family flew out to Portugal, just one member of that family would be returning prematurely to take part in a robbery, in what was described as 'double-bubble' – a large consignment of a valuable commodity.

It begs the question, had it not been for the intervention of the 14-year-old boy who just happened to spot a vital clue on a recorded programme, would the gang have been caught? In my opinion, in respect of those offences already committed, no, probably not. Had they gone on to commit further offences – and I have no doubt that they would have – then yes, it's possible; but only if a first-class informant had propped them up or if police had just happened to chance upon a robbery being carried out.

This highly dangerous gang was brought to justice because of the boy, Kevin Shapland's determination to push ahead, Don Barrett's 'rolling over' and Paul Millen's brilliant, painstaking forensic examinations.

It was *Crimewatch UK* who kicked off the whole investigation; on 10 August 1988 they broadcast *Crimewatch File: Double Supergrass*, a reconstruction of all the cases that were uncovered. It featured some of the investigating team – the programme was narrated by Sue Cook and Kevin Shapland – and included actual police video footage and photographs; brave-as-buggery Joe Symes made a very impressive appearance, and actors played the parts of Barrett and Croke.

Both were amazing lookalikes; when I saw the actor playing Croke, I exclaimed, 'Fuck me, Dave – you made parole pretty quick!'

The actor stayed in character and simply scowled at me.

The *Today* newspaper managed an interview, with the involvement of Kevin Shapland, with the 14-year-old boy, after stressing that 'Contacting him was like arranging a secret meeting with a top spy'. The lad said:

> I found one of the devices the gang was using and I wanted to go to the police but my mum was afraid the gang would get me. I insisted we tell the cops. After I convinced my mum, the police came round. As I'd thrown the device away, I had to draw it for them. Since then, I've virtually lived in secret. During the court case I was known as Witness 'A'. Even now, I get scared someone will try to get me. But I don't regret what I did. These people have to be brought to justice.

The rest of the press reaction to Martin O'Collins' programme was mixed. Most were supportive, the *Evening Standard* saying:

> Television in this case was a citizens' vigilante force, mobilising the public to cooperate with the police. Be sure your sins will find you out. There may be arguments against such power and its potential misuse, but it was certainly reassuring to see that crime doesn't always pay.

However, there was a decidedly unpleasant review in, of all newspapers, the *Daily Telegraph*, which read in part:

> I confess that ever since overdosing on 'Dixon of Dock Green' as a child, police investigations on television leave me cold. Moreover, living in a part of London where the detection rate for crime is said to be extremely low, I viewed this complicated

success story with a certain sourness. A boy ... recognised that the explosive device featured in the reconstruction of a robbery was the same as one he had fished out of a dustbin outside a nasty Essex [*sic*] bungalow called 'Emerald'. lair of a villain named Croke. No doubt dustbin-scavenging will now become a number-one hobby for glamour-starved teenagers, throughout the land.

But what made up for that was a letter to *Crimewatch* from a viewer and his family in Kidlington, Oxford, penned minutes after the programme's ending, that was duly passed on to me. It read:

Dear Sir,

Please convey our thanks to the Flying Squad officers and their colleagues for all their incredible work in helping to rid our society of the villains who threaten the safety of our lives. We are sure that all the decent citizens in our country are most appreciative of the work and expertise they show in ridding our streets of these evil people. Keep it up.

Yours sincerely

It was a nice pat on the back which brought the *Crimewatch* proceedings to a close.

## Chapter Thirty-Three

# The Good Guys and the Bad Guys

So that was that. What happened next? The good guys first.

Peter Gwynne and Tony Freeman both died – far too young. Duncan MacRae was promoted to Detective Superintendent and solved a number of murder cases while working on an Area Major Investigating Team, before retiring in 1997. Ken Grange finished his career in 1998 as a Detective Superintendent (Higher Grade) with the Home Office.

As for the C11 surveillance team, although Neil Murphy did a magnificent job at Newport Pagnell on Operation Standard he had suffered badly from the trauma he experienced following the killing of John Fordham, and he was not looked after by the Met as well as one might have hoped. He later left the Met, got married and moved out of London. His partner on Operation Standard, Colin Ellis, spent fourteen years of his service with C11 and during the last ten years was an instructor on the annual C11 course. He retired in 1999.

Paul Millen had his findings published in the *Journal of the Forensic Science Society*, resumed Flying Squad duties and, in another complex and demanding case, was commended by the commissioner for 'determination and ability resulting in the apprehension and conviction for two men for armed robbery'. He was later promoted and later still went to Surrey Police as a Crime Scene Manager. He went on to conduct forensic examinations both at home and abroad and was appointed Vice-President of the Forensic Science Society. His memoir, *Crime Scene Investigator*, was published by Constable & Robinson in 2008.

Following a fascinating career in the police, Kevin Shapland retired in 2001, moved out of London and in 2004 founded Media Outcomes & CJS Event Solutions, crafting tailor-made events for private and public sector organisations. At the time of writing, he assists Lord Timpson in finding employment for – and the general rehabilitation of – offenders.

I was always under the impression that Kevin had an informant working for him on Operation Standard, a belief I held for almost forty years; and what was more, I thought I knew the informant's name. At lunch recently, I mentioned this to Kevin, who shook his head.

'No', he replied. 'It was only the boy.'

Only Kevin knew the true identity of the 14-year-old known as Witness 'A', whose information led to the arrests in Operation Standard. Police recovered almost £500,000, and consequently the boy should have received a 10 per cent reward of £50,000. However, by 1989 he had received just £1,700 and was threatening to sue the insurers of the security companies.

A spokesman for Security Express said, 'The losses are covered by a conglomerate of underwriters. We will be contacting them to put this situation right.'

It was Jeff Edwards, chief crime reporter for the Mirror Group, aided and abetted by Kevin Shapland, who put things right. Edwards told me:

> I remember this well. It was Kevin who drew it to my attention, so I did contact the security company and their insurers and pointed out how bad they would look if they continued this cheating behaviour, were it to get into the public domain and – on the reverse side – how good they would look and feel if they did the right thing, so they topped up the reward to the proper level.

The young man joined the Royal Air Force but was tragically killed in a motorcycle accident at the age of just twenty-one.

After retirement, Bernie Craven kept in contact with some of his Flying Squad colleagues but otherwise led a very private life. His health continued to suffer as a result of his injuries.

That leaves me. From time to time, while being driven through London in a Flying Squad car, I'd see Joe Symes, still working for Armaguard, and we'd stop and chat. Several years later, I was invited over to Harlow police station, where the team who'd investigated the Armaguard robbery presented me with an Essex Police shield, inscribed:

DICK KIRBY
BEST WISHES FROM ALL
YOUR FRIENDS PAST & PRESENT
'G' DIVISION

Also present was Edna Symes. She'd lived with her parents until they both died and then went on to form a happy relationship; she also had some nice things to say about me.

Following a car crash, then a troublesome eighteen months in Northern Ireland, I was medically discharged from the Met with an injury pension in 1993. In 2000, my family and I moved out of London and settled in a small village in Suffolk. I then commenced my literary career, details of which you see before you.

*  *  *

Now for the not-so-good guys.

I first have to mention Michael John Paul Green – Micky Green – who took part in several of the robberies mentioned by Bertie Smalls, including the 1970 Ilford Bank robbery. Divorced in March 1973, he was released on parole from his 18-year sentence on 26 March 1979, with the condition that he reside at 2 Rosslyn Crescent, Harrow, Middlesex.

But he didn't. Instead, in 1983 he masterminded a £6 million gold smuggling VAT racket. He escaped unscathed, leaving others, including his old associate Ronnie Dark (see below), to take the blame and the porridge.

He moved into the drugs trade, big-time, and became a thorn in the side of the authorities in Britain (where he was wanted in connection with a £250 million cocaine seizure) and also in Poland, Morocco, Holland and Ireland. The French sentenced him to seventeen years' imprisonment in his absence – as did the Dutch, for twenty years – and he was said to have been involved in the gangland murders of Gilbert Wynter and Solly Nahome. Involved in running cocaine from Colombia, he was arrested by FBI agents whilst sunning himself at the pool of his Beverley Hills mansion, formerly owned by Rod Stewart – but was later released without trial. The same thing happened when he was implicated in a £150 million cocaine-trafficking ring in Spain. Arrested at the Ritz Hotel in Barcelona, he spent several months on remand before being released. Wanted by the authorities in the Republic of Ireland, his assets were seized, but he escaped to his villa on the Costa del Sol where, having sunbathed once too often, he died of skin cancer aged seventy-seven on 13 July 2020. The man said to have inspired Jonathan Glazer's 2000 film *Sexy Beast* starring Ray Winstone was believed to have amassed a fortune of between £75 and £100 million.

Next, Ronnie Dark, also involved in the Ilford Bank robbery, who was paroled in 1979. He had his fingers in a number of lucrative pies and became involved in a VAT tax fraud with a gang of gold swindlers which in less than three months made them £6 million. Customs and Excise finally caught up with them, but when it came to sentencing, an adjournment was requested so that it might be determined what had happened to the proceeds. Some money was recovered, but £2 million had mysteriously disappeared from a branch of Switzerland's

Credit Suisse bank. Dark pleaded guilty at the Old Bailey in 1983, was sentenced to twelve months' imprisonment and fined £3,000 with six months to pay. Thereafter, the man who had lived in Preston Road, Wembley, moved – it was thought – to Spain.

It's now time to reunite the reader with John Short, who absented himself from Torremolinos in 1972, at the same time that Bryan Turner moved away, nine miles north-east, along Spain's coastline to Malagá. Precisely where Short immediately went is unclear; it was known that he travelled to Canada and North Africa using aliases and false passports, and he was also in England at the times when major robberies were committed. But on Friday, 21 January 1977, Short – and sixteen others (including two women) – was arrested in London as a result of a combined Flying Squad and Regional Crime Squad operation. A search revealed two sawn-off shotguns, an automatic pistol and £7,000 cash. One of the matters that Short was questioned about was the Ilford Bank Robbery in 1970; another was the ambush of a Securicor van on the A2, near Dartford, Kent, on 27 March 1976. During the raid in which three of the five raiders carried two sawn-off shotguns and an automatic pistol, fourteen sacks containing a total of £102,929 were stolen and a 38-year-old security guard was shot dead; two others were wounded.

Perhaps the temptation of a £15,000 reward had brought about those arrests; but six days after his arrest, Short was one of several prisoners who appeared at West London Magistrates' Court accused of robbing banks and a security van of almost £400,000, and possession of firearms. Upon his appearance at the Old Bailey on 29 April 1978, the Ilford bank robbery charge was allowed to remain on the file; in respect of other matters, Short was sentenced to a total of twenty-one years' imprisonment.

Robert Alles King took an Open University degree whilst serving ten years of his sentence and became a reformed character. Apparently, having seen Bertie Smalls in Crouch Hill following his release, King attributed his refraining from effecting Bertie's immediate demise to his newfound education. That, in part, was substantiated by the *Guardian* newspaper, when King died aged fifty-nine in 2000, describing him as 'a former criminal and consultant'.

The murderer, John Hilton, who the Judge had said should never be released, was – naturally – released. At the time of writing, he's aged ninety-six and living, so he says, on the Isle of Sheppey.

John Henry Segars, one of the two supergrasses involved in Operation Ohio, had an oddly gentle side for a violent armed robber. He was a keen coarse fisherman, a naturalist and a talented painter of wildlife; he presented a painting of a goshawk to his handler, Dave Driscoll; it can be seen in the plates section of this book. This begs the question: would a profession as a wildlife painter have brought Segars more money than a career as a full-time blagger? Maybe, maybe not; but it would have saved him a lot of jail time.

From time to time, George Ince's name would crop up in connection with participation in armed robberies, but as far as I know, wily George always managed to slip out of the law's clutches. He was always affable to me, although I doubt if that would have been the case had I encountered him going across the pavement; he was one tough hombre, both physically and mentally. He and Dolly remained resident at 37 Fairfield Road, Bow until his death, aged eighty-six, on 16 April 2023.

Concerning the two receivers of the stolen bullion, I know nothing of what happened to them thereafter, and the same applies to John Kenneth Johnson, who at the time of his conviction was close to (if not actually past) his sell-by date.

Al Turner, I thought, had been a very foolish young man, having entered the world of serious criminality and received a 7-year sentence for a venture which earned him only the loss of his liberty. As to what happened to him after his prison sentence, I have no idea; I only hope he managed to put his past behind him and was able to build a new future for himself and his family.

The BBC *Crimewatch* programme which showed a full reconstruction of the crimes and the arrests was seen by Glen Armsby, and seven months after his incarceration, he wrote to Joe Symes from his cell in the top security prison at Albany, apologising for his actions.

Dated Tuesday, 25 August 1988, the letter reads:

Dear Mr & Mrs & Miss Symes,

Please excuse me Mr Symes as there seems to be no appropriate way to start this letter. I hope it's not too late (some say it's never too late) to offer my regrets and apologies, but I would surely understand in this case if you were to not even contemplate finishing reading this note.

I meant to correspond with you so many times before, as I, and I'm sure as you, have never forgotten the incident to which I was a party took place in your home on the evening of the robbery.

It just seems more appropriate now, as I'm sure your [*sic*] aware that the documentary of the crime was shown on TV which I was able to see from a recording.

So I guess if I don't write now I never will.

I can't be so ignorant as to not think of the fright you & your family must have felt, but at the time [I] was only thinking of my ends obviously, but where there was never <u>any</u> intention on our part to harm yourself or your family. I never really put my self in your shoes to think how you felt at the time but now seeing it on the TV and sort of reliving it again, its made more of an impression on me now.

I guess you would like too (or will) tear this up and think good riddance to you all, well Mr Symes I can only offer you my sincerest apologies I wish there was something more constructive I could do to repay you, maybe one day, somehow, an opportunity may present itself. I guess you would prefer never to set eyes on me again (by the way, I am, as I believe your daughter describes in one of her statements as the younger one). Really I don't think there is much more I can write now, other than to once again offer you my deepest apologies and I sincerely hope that the incident has not left any serious or lasting effects on your good self or that of your wife and daughter.

Yours humbly,

G. Armsby

Was it a sincere apology or a bargaining move to downgrade his security status and pave the way for an early parole? Joe had no doubt.

'Look at zhat!' he exclaimed in his thick, Polish accent, shoving the letter at me. 'Vhat a load of bollix!'

**Chapter Thirty-Four**

# Croke – The Aftermath

At the Royal Courts of Justice in August 1988, before Mr Registrar Pimm, a bankruptcy order was made against Dave Croke on the application of the Official Petitioner. In April 1990, Croke appealed against his 23-year sentence and it was cut, albeit to just twenty-one years' imprisonment. He made several unsuccessful attempts to escape and was released in May 1999, but while inside, he had acquired a serious drugs habit. Part of his sentence had been served in the maximum security Long Lartin prison with Robert Knapp, and they had stayed at Latchmere House, a Category 'D' Prison which had a good reputation for those about to be released into the outside world, although less success regarding drugs abuse.

Two months later, he and Knapp went to the Sutton, Surrey home of businessman Mohammed Raja. When Raja answered the door he was stabbed five times, shot in the face with a shotgun which was then reloaded and used to shoot him once more. As to who had actually carried out the murder, nobody knew. Neither the knife nor the shotgun was ever recovered.

Croke was now in a pitiful state; penniless, as thin as a rake, his possessions amounting to a bag of clothes, a few letters and photos, he initially went to live with his estranged wife Rita, but left her soon afterwards and went to stay with his sister Rosie at her maisonette in Moulsecoomb, Brighton. He became almost a recluse, sleeping on a couch in the lounge, watching television, reading the newspapers. When he did work, it was as a delivery driver; otherwise, he claimed Social Security.

We now fast-forward to 2001, when Croke was arrested in Bury St Edmunds, Suffolk on a charge of possessing drugs. A saliva sample proved a DNA match for a blood smear left at the murder scene in Sutton, and since it was a one in a billion chance it could have come from somebody else, two years after the murder, on 27 February 2001, Croke was arrested and charged in Brighton. At the time when Croke was arrested, Knapp was in Ireland; he returned two months later and was arrested in Bexleyheath, Kent.

Detective Inspector Andrew Sladen, who carried out Croke's arrest, told me:

When he was arrested, he was told it was for murder; Croke said, 'I've never been to Sutton!' but that was before Sutton was ever mentioned, which was rather telling! They'd turned their mobiles off for the job but put them back on afterwards, and we were able to track them right round the M25. Very shortly after the murder, we found that one of their credit cards had been used in South-East London. I knew Knapp had a girlfriend in that area, I saw her and she told me that at that time of the credit card transaction, 'Bob had come round with a bloke named Dave.' Croke never said anything during his interviews but I don't think he was worried. Nothing was going to worry him. He knew he was going down.

Croke's defence team suggested that the blood found on Mr Raja's front door frame might have come from Croke when he made a delivery there; it was also said that on the day of the murder, Croke had been painting his son's house in Enfield.

All to no avail; the prosecution's case was that this had been a contract murder, at the behest of the deeply unpleasant property developer, Nicholas van Hoogstraten, who had initially been arrested but released on bail. Andrew Sladen takes up the tale:

Hoogstraten answered bail between the others being arrested and came up from Brighton by cab to Bexleyheath police station. He told the cabbie to wait for him and keep the meter running while he answered his bail, but was then charged and bail refused. Yet another debt which Hoogstraten failed to pay, but a bit of an extreme way to avoid payment!

The men had used a white Transit van when carrying out the murder, with yellow wheels and 'Thunderbird II' on the windscreen, and a witness identified Croke as driving it as they left the scene of the murder. They were also seen when they doused it in petrol and set fire to it; but compost in the back of the van matched that found at Knapp's mother's home on van Hoogstraten's estate near Uckfield, East Sussex. The distinctive van had also been seen at the Orchard Caravan Park, Clacton-on-Sea, where Croke's mother had a mobile home.

Van Hoogstraten was jailed for ten years for manslaughter; however, the conviction was later overturned on the grounds of a misdirection by the trial judge. In the case of Croke and Knapp, the jury deliberated for six days before unanimously finding both men guilty in July 2002 of Raja's murder.

Passing sentence at the Old Bailey, Mr Justice Newman said:

You are both very dangerous men with no motive to kill, save greed. What brings men to take a sawn-off shotgun and a knife to an elderly man, and having stabbed him fatally, to shoot him in the head at a range of six to twelve inches? You showed no remorse between the stabbing and the shooting, simply delay sufficient to reload the shotgun. No holding back in the face of the presence in the house of the grandsons, no appearance of concern for the horrors they had to witness. Neither did you show remorse in court. Those who conduct themselves in this way do not just turn their back on society, they deliberately withdraw from it. The jury have now heard the appalling records of these two men. Someone, at some stage may have occasion to consider whether they should ever be released from the life sentence I impose on each of them.

Both were sentenced to life imprisonment, with the recommendation that they each serve twenty years before being considered for parole.

Croke lasted for five years before being found hanged in his cell at the Category 'A' prison for the most dangerous offenders at Whitemoor, Cambridgeshire at 9.23pm on 20 November 2007. He was on self-harm watch and had told a prison chaplain that he was suicidal.

And that was the end of Dave Croke, an enigma if ever there was one. It also begs the question: what was he doing in the area that I'd moved to, just a few months previously? Retribution? If that was intended, it seems a pretty odd revenge against someone to whom, when he'd spoken at all, he had just said, 'I want my solicitor to be here' – but then in his drugs-scrambled mind, who knows?

I purchased a Royal Crown Derby porcelain piece. It's a golden frog, to commemorate all the bullion that was stolen during Operation Standard. It sits on my windowsill as I type – I'm almost sure I can hear it 'croak'.

## Chapter Thirty-Five

# Barrett – The Aftermath

And that leaves us with Don Barrett.

He appealed against his 16-year sentence and had it reduced to twelve years' imprisonment, and I last saw him in the supergrass wing at Reading Prison. Over the next few years, he was moved around; it appears he was not well liked.

Supergrasses inevitably have bounties placed on their heads by the underworld: Smalls' was said to be £30,000 (later reduced to £10,000), in O'Mahoney's case it was £60,000, with differing sums for others of their ilk. Barrett's was said to be a whopping £250,000, but even if that was the case, nobody ever claimed it.

★　★　★

With his experience of informant-running from his Flying Squad days, Detective Constable Mick Geraghty was ideally placed to be a member of SO10 Department at the Yard, dealing with the Criminal Justice Protection Unit. This unit was set up in 1978, not only to provide new identities for supergrasses when they left the prison system, but also to secure documents covering educational qualifications, insurance, employment and medical histories, pension rights, bank accounts, mortgages and social security benefits.

Mick was dealing with another supergrass at Stafford, a Category 'C' Prison (in 2014 it would become a sex-offenders only prison) in 1996, and Barrett was in a cell in the secure block. Mick knew Barrett would be coming up for parole after serving eight years, so he introduced himself and they shook hands. In doing so, Barrett tried to crush Mick's hand, a typical trick to show how tough he was. The supergrass that Mick was dealing with thoroughly disliked Barrett, saying he thought he was a bully.

Barrett was moved to Woodhill Prison, Milton Keynes, a brand new secure unit for supergrasses, and although he was of the opinion that he would not be granted parole, he was, and Mick Geraghty, who became his case officer, now takes up the tale:

When he was released, he obviously thought he'd be driven away in a top of the range car. To impress the other inmates, he emerged wearing a long black coat, a hat and smoking the biggest lardie (rhyming slang: lardie = la-di-da = cigar) you've ever seen in your life. He was aghast when the transport I'd provided was the station van from Milton Keynes nick. We returned the van and used a car to take him to a pub in Kent for a meal and then on to a safe house in Dartford. At 5.30 the following morning, I was woken up by a phone call from Barrett – 'I've cleaned the house – what do you want me to do now?' This, as I found out, was typical of him, controlling the situation.

I took him back to the council house in Ilford where he'd lived with his wife before he was nicked. I remember we were all sitting round a big, shining dining room table, and Barrett said, 'Shall I show you how I used to shock the punters when we were carrying out a raid?' He leant forward, his jaw dropped open and then he let out the most terrifying scream – it frightened the life out of me and had his sons come running into the room to find out what was going on!

He asked me about my service. When I told him I'd been on the Flying Squad, he asked who I'd worked with. When I mentioned your name, his face lit up. 'Dick Kirby – what a diamond!' He obviously had respect for you, because of the way you'd treated him.

Detective Sergeant Dave Chappell had a background with the Anti-Terrorist Squad, so when he came to SO10's Criminal Justice Protection Unit he knew how to deal with characters who could be difficult, like Don Barrett. But as he told me:

DB never gave me any grief. He respected us for looking after him and his family. I was out with him one day when he suddenly pulled me into a shop doorway. 'I've just seen someone who knows me', he said.

But he didn't have an honest bone in his body. He couldn't exist without a big wedge in his back pocket. I knew that sooner or later he'd have to go across the pavement.

Barrett told Chappell that he'd never assaulted the police, never shot anyone and, in fact, never fired a shot – but that was just an example of Barrett self-justification; at different times of his long criminal career he'd done all of those things!

Jeff Edwards, then chief crime reporter for the Mirror Group, recalls meeting Don Barrett. He told me:

It was in The George public house at Wanstead, round about 1995/1996. I was introduced to him by Kevin Shapland, and Barrett produced a draft of his autobiography, a typewritten sheaf of A4, written in prison with no spacing between the lines and no punctuation; just a wall of words. I didn't take up his offer to become his ghost writer. I didn't fancy being closeted for weeks with him, trying to decipher his view of the world. Not my cup of tea, and I never had any subsequent contact with him. But I do remember one direct quote from Kevin later that evening, after Barrett had left. He said, 'On the face of it, he seems like a nice, reasonable chap, doesn't he? But you just know, deep down, if you were to cross him, he'd tear your face off with his bare hands.'

Mick Geraghty now resumes his narrative:

There was an attempt at a reconciliation with his wife but it didn't work.

Barrett wanted a car to get around in – I got him an old Skoda, and he was furious! I told him I thought that suited a 58-year-old man wearing a hat, and it didn't make things any better when the Skoda broke down, 'on a fucking roundabout!' as he informed me. I hired a car for him; he told me it was nicked from outside a pub in Wanstead High Street. It was found a year later in a lock-up garage in Barking; it hadn't been driven during that time.

I got a flat for him in Edmonton and took him to the DSS there. When he came out he was furious. I was driving a Rover 827 at the time, and Barrett was so angry he banged on the roof with his fist. The reason was that this was Dave Croke's neighbourhood.

Barrett's ex-wife lived in Australia with their daughter, and he heard that the daughter had been killed in a car collision and wanted to go to pay his respects. I got it arranged with the Australian authorities, and he stayed for a month. I arranged a flight with Cathay Pacific. Not a happy flight for him – he was a chain-smoker and was booked on a non-smoking flight.

I always knew that sooner or later he'd go across the pavement again, because he knew nothing else. I put him up to NCIS (The National Criminal Intelligence Service) as a target and I believe he got nicked, as part of a four-man team, hitting a cash-in-transit van in Nottingham. I did hear that he tried to become a supergrass for the third time, but no one wanted to know. He may have got 8–10 years – I'm not sure.

I retired from the Met in 2004 and I last saw him about ten years later, in a coffee shop in Loughton. He was very friendly and told me he'd just come out of jail in Jersey for, I believe, drugs offences; I think he said he'd done two or three years – but what happened to him after that, I've no idea.

★　★　★

A few years ago, I attended a police social function. I was approached by a former detective chief inspector I'd known for years, ever since my days as an aid. Surreptitiously, he showed me a piece of paper with writing on it.

'Mean anything to you?' he asked.

I shrugged my shoulders and grunted, which could have meant anything.

'The word is', he said softly, 'that he's snouting for Customs and Excise.'

I raised my eyebrows in a half-interested way, nodded and walked away.

The name on the piece of paper was 'Donald Walter Barrett'. True – or not? Who knows?

★　★　★

Many police officers formed the opinion that if Barrett had applied himself to an honest enterprise, with his ingenuity he could have made a success of it. But of course, he didn't. He was in the business of terrorising ordinary, decent people, and in the course of being a Flying Squad officer I met some of his victims, plus a lot of other victims besides. Some took weeks, even months to recover; others never did. I took great pleasure in arresting the attacker of a middle-aged lady, who had been a customer in a building society when a robbery took place.

'I thought I'd never see my grandchildren again', she whispered.

Neither the shocked look on her face, nor her words have ever left me.

No, Barrett was of the same vintage as his former chum, Bertie Smalls, who once famously said:

The nervous tension I used to feel before a job didn't stay with me all the time, only till I got started. Once I start, I feel completely calm, one hundred per cent, everything comes brilliant to me. I might be fucked-up a minute or two before but the minute it's on, it's like the sun coming out from behind a cloud.

It was that type of sangfroid that Barrett exhibited on 11 August 1986 on the windswept M1 motorway. He had been arrested for a high-value robbery in possession of a loaded firearm, and the future must have looked very bleak indeed for him. At forty-nine years of age, with his appalling criminal record, he realised that the shortest sentence he could expect from the most benign judge would be twenty years; with a hard-line judge, a lot more.

Handcuffed, and dressed in a 500-guinea suit, he casually looked round at the assembled police officers and spotted Detective Sergeant Phil Burrows, whom he knew from his previous supergrassing days.

'Hello, Phil', he said casually. 'Nice little tickle you've had, here!'

# Bibliography

Ball, John, Lewis Chester, Roy Perrott, *Cops and Robbers*, André Deutsch, 1978

Beveridge, Peter, *Inside the CID*, Evans Bros. 1957

Brown, Ian, *From the Krays to Drug Busts in the Caribbean*, Pen & Sword, 2017

Davis, Dr R.J. (ed.), *Journal of the Forensic Science Society, Volume 29, No. 3*, The Forensic Science Society, May/June 1989

Fielder, Michael and Peter Steele, *Alibi at Midnight*, Everest Books, 1974

Flynn, Errol, *My Wicked, Wicked Ways*, Pan Books, 1972

Gilliard, Michael and Laurie Flynn, *Untouchables*, Cutting Edge, 2004

Graham, Winston, *Great Cases of Scotland Yard Volume Two*, Reader's Digest, 1978

Hilton, John, *Armed and Dangerous*, Gadfly Press, 2023

Jennings, Andrew, Paul Lashmar, Vyv Simson, *Scotland Yard's Cocaine Connection*, Arrow Books, 1991

Kelland, Gilbert, *Crime in London*, Harper Collins, 1993

Kirby, Dick, *The Real Sweeney*, Robinson, 2005

Kirby, Dick, *You're Nicked!*, Robinson, 2007

Kirby, Dick, *Villains*, Robinson, 2008

Kirby, Dick, *The Guv'nors: Ten of Scotland Yard's Greatest Detectives*, Pen & Sword, 2010

Kirby, Dick, *The Sweeney: The First Sixty Years of Scotland Yard's Crimebusting Flying Squad 1919–1978*, Pen & Sword, 2011

Kirby, Dick, *The Brave Blue Line: 100 Years of Metropolitan Police Gallantry*, Pen & Sword, 2011

Kirby, Dick, *Scotland Yard's Ghost Squad: The Secret Weapon Against Post-War Crime*, Pen & Sword, 2011

Kirby, Dick, *Operation Countryman: The Flawed Enquiry into London Police Corruption*, Pen & Sword, 2018

Kirby, Dick, *Scotland Yard's Gangbuster: Wickstead's most Celebrated Cases Bert*, Pen & Sword, 2018

Kirby, Dick, *Scotland Yard's Flying Squad: 100 Years of Crime Fighting*, Pen & Sword, 2019

Kray, Reg, *Born Fighter*, Century, 1990

Millen, Paul, *Crime Scene Investigator*, Robinson, 2008

Mills, Liz, *Crimewatch*, Penguin, 1994

Morton, James, *Supergrasses & Informants*, Warner, 1996

Nesbitt, Michael, *Britain's Gangland: Vol 2*, Britain's Gangland, 2019

Read, Piers Paul, *The Train Robbers*, W H Allen, 1978

Short, Martin, *Lundy: The Destruction of Scotland Yard's Greatest Detective*, Grafton, 1991
Slipper, Jack, *Slipper of the Yard*, Sidgwick & Jackson, 1981
Swain, John, *Being Informed*, Janus Publishing, 1995
Thomas, Donald, *Villains' Paradise*, John Murray, 2005

# Index